THE CRUISE OF THE MARY ROSE

OR, HERE AND THERE IN THE PACIFIC

I0557626

W. H. G. KINGSTON

1st WORLD LIBRARY
Literary Society

The Cruise of the Mary Rose

W. H. G. Kingston

© 1st World Library, 2007
PO Box 2211
Fairfield, IA 52556
www.1stworldlibrary.com
First Edition

LCCN: 2007930914

Softcover ISBN: 978-1-4218-4871-6
Hardcover ISBN: 978-1-4218-4774-0
eBook ISBN: 978-1-4218-4968-3

Purchase *"The Cruise of the Mary Rose"*
as a traditional bound book at:
www.1stWorldLibrary.com/purchase.asp?ISBN=978-1-4218-4871-6

1st World Library is a literary, educational organization
dedicated to:

- Creating a free internet library of downloadable ebooks

- Hosting writing competitions and offering book publishing
scholarships.

Interested in more 1st World Library books? contact:
literacy@1stworldlibrary.com
Check us out at: www.1stworldlibrary.com

1ˢᵗ World Library Literary Society

Giving Back to the World

"If you want to work on the core problem, it's early school literacy."

- James Barksdale, former CEO of Netscape

"No skill is more crucial to the future of a child, or to a democratic and prosperous society, than literacy."

- Los Angeles Times

"Literacy... means far more than learning how to read and write... The aim is to transmit... knowledge and promote social participation."

- UNESCO

"Literacy is not a luxury, it is a right and a responsibility. If our world is to meet the challenges of the twenty-first century we must harness the energy and creativity of all our citizens."

- President Bill Clinton

"Parents should be encouraged to read to their children, and teachers should be equipped with all available techniques for teaching literacy, so the varying needs and capacities of individual kids can be taken into account."

- Hugh Mackay

CHAPTER ONE

UNCLE JOHN'S JOURNAL

My family had for centuries owned the same estate, handed down from father to son undiminished in size, and much increased in value. I believe there had been among them in past generations those who feared the Lord. I know that my father was a man of true piety. "Casting all your care upon Him, for He careth for you," was his favourite motto. What a world of doubt and anxiety, of plotting, and contriving, and scheming, does this trust in God save those who possess it. On this blessed assurance my father took his stand in all the difficulties of life. It never failed him, and so we his sons had a good training and a godly example.

The younger members of each generation followed various honourable professions, but they failed to rise to high rank in them, owing, I fancy, to a want of worldly ambition—the general characteristic of our race. Altogether, however, I believe them to have been a simple-minded, upright, clear sighted set of people, who did whatever their hands found to do honestly and with all their might. Such people ought to rise, it may be said. So they do,—but not to what the world calls the summit. They generally rise to a position of independence, where they may enjoy fair scope for the exercise of their mental and spiritual faculties. There they are content to remain, for a time. This world is not their rest. Another world opens to their view. In that they see the goal at which they aim. There is the golden crown. Why then be distracted by the glittering baubles which are held up to draw their attention from the real jewel—the gem without price? I am happy in the belief that such was the reason that my ancestors did not become men of much worldly note.

The occupant of the family estate had always attended to its cultivation, and was properly called a gentleman farmer. Unostentatious and frugal, he never lacked means, in spite of bad harvests or unexpected losses, to assist the younger members of the family in starting in life, or to help forward any good cause which required aid.

My father, Paul Harvey, was a perfect type of the family—so was my elder brother, his namesake. John came next; a daughter followed; I was his fourth child. He kept up a good old custom—never broken through from any excuse. An hour before bed-time his children and the whole household assembled in the sitting-room, when he read and explained a chapter in the Bible. A hymn was sung, and prayers full of fervour were offered up to the throne of grace. After this a simple supper was placed on the table, and we were encouraged to speak on the events of the day, or on what we had read or thought of. That hour was generally the pleasantest of the twenty-four. Our father guided, if he did not lead the conversation, and generally managed to infuse his spirit into it. Although many of the subjects discussed even now rise up to my memory, I will mention but one, which had a powerful influence on the career of some of those present. I had been reading an account of the Crusades, and my enthusiasm had been unusually stirred up on the subject. "I wish that I could have lived in those days!" I exclaimed (I was but a lad it must be remembered.) "What a glorious work those warriors of old undertook, who with sword and lance, under the banner of the cross, they went forth to conquer infidels, to establish the true faith, to recover the blessed land, hallowed by the Redeemer's footsteps, from the power of the cruel followers of the false prophet of Mecca. How degenerate are we Christians of the present generation! Who among us dreams of expelling the Turks from Syria? On the contrary, our statesmen devote their energies to keep them there. I really believe that were Peter the Hermit to rise from his grave, he would not find a dozen true men to follow him."

"Possibly not," said my father, quietly; "though he might find two dozen fully as wise, and as honest, too, as those he led to destruction. But has it not struck you, David, that there are other conquests to be achieved in the present age more important than winning Palestine from the Moslem; that there is more real fighting to be done than all the true soldiers of the cross, even were they to be united in one firm phalanx, could accomplish? Sword and spear surely are not the weapons our loving Saviour desires His followers to employ when striving to bring fresh subjects under His kingdom. That they were to be used was indeed the idea of our ignorant ancestors, when the teaching of a corrupt Church had thrown a dark veil over their understandings. Christians only in name, the truth was so disfigured and transformed among them, that it exercised no influence over their hearts; and though they believed the Bible to be of value, they regarded it rather in the light of a mystic charm than the word of God. Thus all the great truths of our most holy faith were so travestied and changed as to produce alone a degrading superstition. They believed that the Bible had the power of exorcising spirits of evil. So it has; but it is not the closed Bible, which they in their ignorance employed—not the mere printed paper bound into a volume—unread, or if read, misunderstood, at which the devil and his angels tremble. No; it is the open Bible—the Bible in many tongues—read and understood through God's gracious teaching, sought for by prayer earnestly. It is the blessed gospel of peace which alone can put to flight debasing superstition, gross customs, murderous propensities, cruel dispositions, barbarism in its varied forms, and all the works of darkness instigated by Satan and his angels. Again, I say that the Bible, and the Bible alone, is the true crusader's weapon; armed with that sword of the Spirit, with the shield of faith on his arm, and under the guidance (never to be withdrawn while he seeks it) of God's Holy Spirit, he may go boldly forth conquering and to conquer the numberless hosts of heathenism arrayed for battle against the truth. These weapons are dreaded by the spirit of evil more than all those iron implements of warfare on which man in his folly and blindness relies. The victories won by the Bible are lasting in this world, and not only in this world, but through eternity.

"To drop metaphor, what is, and what long has been the condition of those lands the crusaders vainly boasted they had won from the followers of Mohammed? In what state do we find those vast territories of the New World conquered by Spain? both gained by sword and spear, under a banner falsely called the `banner of the cross.' Compare these and similar conquests over heathenism with those victories won in pagan lands by the Bible—the sword of the Spirit. How great the contrast!"

Our father spoke with far more animation than was his wont. I listened respectfully, though I confess that at first I did not comprehend the full meaning of his remarks. Still, they considerably dimmed the bright halo with which my imagination had surrounded the crusades. My second brother, John, however, fixing his eyes attentively on our father, drank in every word he uttered. "Yes, glorious indeed are the victories gained by the gospel of peace in heathen lands, and happy are those permitted to fight them," he whispered, with

W. H. G. Kingston

a sigh, after a few minutes' silence. John was less robust in health than were most of us, and it was intended that he should devote himself to mercantile pursuits, for which I had long suspected that he had no great taste; still, at the call, as he believed, of duty, he had begun the task of acquiring the necessary knowledge.

"I suppose, father, that you are alluding to the labours of missionaries in foreign lands?" I observed. "But I have heard it said, that in spite of all the money expended, their preaching produces but meagre results. In India, for instance, the Company will not admit them. In Africa, the climate destroys them. The fanatical Turks and other Mohammedan nations will not listen to their message; and it would be but time lost and energies wasted were they to attempt to preach to the cannibals of New Zealand and the other islands of the Pacific, or to the almost baboons of Australia and New Guinea."

"You have not, I see, given much thought to the subject, David," observed my father, mildly; "God's grace is sufficient for all men. The gospel is to be preached to all men, without distinction of race, or colour, or nation, or rank. What says the Bible? 'Go ye into all the world, and preach the gospel to every creature.' Who is to decide then from what depths of moral degradation the power of God's grace will fail to lift up a human being? Certainly, we mortals, fallible, helpless, sinful, as we must feel ourselves, are not capable of judging. All we have to do is to receive the plain command, and obey it. Oh, there is scope, believe me, for the exertions, not of one missionary only, but of hundreds and thousands of the soldiers of the cross in those very regions of which you have spoken. How can we dare to doubt how the gospel will in the end be received? 'Blessed are ye which sow beside all waters,' 'Cast thy bread upon the waters: for thou shalt find it after many days.' 'In the morning sow thy seed, and in the evening withhold not thine hand, for thou knowest not which shall prosper, either this or that, or whether they both shall be alike good.' Our duty as disciples of Christ is plain. We are to sow. 'God giveth the increase.' That is not to be our care. We are to 'preach the gospel to every creature.' Some will hear; some will turn away from the truth. With that we have nothing to do, except to pray and work on, awaiting God's time. You have none of you seen more than the outside of my Uncle John's journal. Indeed, I had not myself till lately looked into it. He was, as you may have heard, a seaman, and he made more than one voyage to the Pacific. Possessing more education than most officers in the merchant service in those days, he seems to have carefully noted the observations he made as he sailed from place to place. His descriptions are graphic, and he was of an acute and inquiring mind; his remarks, too, are of value. I think, therefore, that we may glean from it both amusement and instruction."

We of course all expressed a wish to hear the contents of our relative's journal, and it was agreed that the next few evenings should be devoted to its perusal. I should observe that our father's interest in the subject of missions to the heathen in foreign lands had lately been awakened by the visit of an old friend, one of that band of great and good men who were then endeavouring against contumely, ridicule, and every opposition which the prince of this world could raise, to send the glad tidings of salvation to the perishing millions scattered thickly on the surface of the globe, over which midnight—the midnight of heathen darkness—reigned.

I believe that the thought of our dear father's heart at that time was—"I have many sons given me by God; surely not one of them have I a right to withhold from His service; all, all, every one of them should be freely, joyfully given if it be

His will to accept their services." I do not mean to say that he uttered these words, but that such was the language of his heart spoken to heaven, I am certain, from conversations and circumstances which subsequently occurred. Of all the family our brother, John, appeared to be the most deeply impressed with the remarks which had dropped from our father's lips, and as I watched his expressive countenance, I observed the changes passing over it, and am now certain that feelings were then working within his bosom too deep for utterance, and which afterwards exerted a powerful influence on his career.

The following evening, the word of God having been read and our frugal supper discussed, the looked-for journal, a dogskin-covered, somewhat worn folio, was produced. John, by a unanimous vote, was chosen to read it, and I am bound to say that the honest seaman's descriptions gained considerably by the spirit which our brother's animated voice threw into them.

CHAPTER TWO

Supped at the "Three Crowns" with Phineas Golding our supercargo, and so aboard, my leave being up, and work enough and over to get the ship ready for sea. A long voyage before us of four, or it may be of five years. Meeting our supercargo at the owner's, I had deemed him a quiet, well-behaved young man; I now find him a slashing blade, ever ready with his fist, or his sword, as with his pen,—hot in dispute, and always eager to bring a quarrel to the arbitration of one of the former. How differently do men appear when in presence of those they serve and when out of their sight! There exists One out of whose sight we cannot escape. How comes it that we do not always bear that truth in mind? Are we more afraid of a fellow-creature than of the Maker and Judge of all the world? I said thus much to Phineas Golding. He replied with an oath, which caused me to feel that I had been casting pearls before swine. And yet I was right, surely; for by speaking the truth boldly on fitting occasions, I do hold that the truth will in the end prevail, and may be conquer the unbeliever's heart. On one thing, therefore, I am resolved, to go on as I have begun, and speak the truth always with earnestness of purpose.

Of my other shipmates I will speak a word. The master Simon Fuller, is grave man, the snows of nearly sixty winters settling on his head. He has made many voyages, and seems

W. H. G. Kingston

a fit man to command men. The first mate, too, James Festing, is every inch a seaman, but somewhat handy with his fist, a rope's end, or a marline spike, or, truth to say, whatever lies nearest, and withal not over choice in his words when angered, or desirous of getting work done smartly. Of myself, as second mate, it becometh me not to speak. I have been five years at sea, am a fair navigator, and an average seaman. I fear God, and strive to do my duty, though not always succeeding. Our ship's company muster thirty-five good men, I hope, all told fore and aft. The ship, as is requisite, is well armed, with six guns with swivels on the quarters, and muskets, pikes, axes, and cutlasses for all hands. We have to visit many strange places and strange people, and we must expect often and again to fight for our lives with the savages. Phineas Golding rejoices in adventure, and says such chiefly induced him to leave home. He has never before been at sea, and dreams not of the troubles in store for him.

June.—We have taken our departure from the land, which is even now sinking astern, a strong breeze blowing from the north-east.

July.—We have touched at Madeira, belonging to the Portingalls, as the old voyagers call them. They are a suspicious people, though civil when not angered. I witnessed some public exhibitions, which I was told were religious. I cannot suppose that such performances are acceptable to our Lord and Master, or He would surely have ordered such. But it becomes not me, after so slight acquaintance with a people, to pass much censure on their customs, though I see not how to approve them.

Crossing the Line, we had a usual Father Neptune and his Tritons on board. Tony Hinks, our boatswain, was Neptune. He and his mates severely handled some of the men who had shown ill manners or bad tempers, tarring their faces, and shaving their chins with rusty hoops. Phineas vowed that he would not be so treated, but had to succumb, escaping with a thorough sousing from a dozen buckets. Phineas vows vengeance on the boatswain; but I warn him that Tony Hinks followed but the custom of the sea, and is not a man over whom it would be easy to get an advantage, for he boasts that he always sleeps with one eye open.

We have touched at Rio, the chief town in the Brazils. From what I saw, I should take the people to be heathens, such as I have read of in Roman and Grecian history; but they say that they are Christians. One thing is certain, that if they desire to keep the sabbath holy, they have a curious way of so doing. Still I say, it would be easy to sail from place to place and to condemn all we visit unheard. One thought occurs to me: "Look to it that we fall not into like errors."

Proceeding south before rounding Cape Horn, we again made the land, and standing in, anchored the ship in a sheltered cove. It was the southern part of that region known as Patagonia. The captain, with Phineas Golding and I, with a crew of eight men, well armed, took the long boat and went ashore. The aspect of the country was not pleasant; rocks, and trees, and marshes, but no signs of cultivation. Suddenly from among the rocks some creatures appeared watching us. "Are they men or are they baboons?" asked Phineas, levelling his musket; but the master held back his arm. They approaching slowly and with hesitation, we discovered that they were human beings, though marvellously ill-favoured in aspect. Their skin, which seemed of a dark brown, was covered with dirt, and their faces, which were flat with high cheek-bones, were besmeared with red and yellow ochre. Their long black coarse hair hanging down straight over their shoulders, their small twinkling bleared eyes peeping out between it, like two hot coals. They had spears in their hands

W. H. G. Kingston

and short clubs. They were nearly naked, their chief garment consisting in a piece of sealskin, which they wore on the side whence the wind blew. Again Phineas was about to shoot in very wantonness.

"What's the harm?" he asked. "We have no chance of trading with such people; and if we were to kill a few, what would it matter?"

"They have souls, Master Golding," said I, for I could not keep silence; "and souls, I have learned, are precious things."

A scornful laugh was his reply, and he still kept his musket ready, as if to fire. The savages, however, seemed in no way afraid, but lifted up their hands, and made as if they too had muskets; and when we laughed they laughed, and when we shook our fists they shook theirs; and so we discovered that, though hideous, they were a harmless race, and great mimics. They readily accepted beads, and knives, and coloured handkerchiefs, and such like things.

These people, we learn from Tony Hinks, who has before been on the coast (indeed where has he not been?) are different from the tribes of Patagonians who inhabit the country to the north as far as the Spanish settlements. These latter are a fierce race, often of large stature, though not giants, as some suppose, and dress in skins and ride on horseback. Again, there are other tribes whose dwellings are among the marshes and inlets of the sea up the Straits of Magellan. They move about only in their canoes, living on shell-fish, seals' flesh, and fish, their habits being more filthy and disgusting even than are those of our present friends. Phineas laughs at the notion of their being our fellow-creatures, and says that they must have sprung from apes; but Tony, who has seen many strange people, says that he would not give a fig for the supercargo's opinion, for that he has known white men become almost as brutish in their appearance, and much more brutish in their manners, just from living a few years among born savages, cut off from all communication with their fellow whites. A little practical experience often shows the folly of these would-be philosophers.

On the Pacific coast of this end of America are found the unsubdued tribes of the Araucanians in vast numbers, so that in this one small portion of the continent are many hundred thousand savages, all lying in the midnight of heathen darkness.

Phineas observes that it is a pity they cannot be swept away, and civilised men, with whom it would be an advantage to trade, introduced in their stead. He esteems men in proportion as they are able to exchange gold dust, ivory, spices or precious stones, not knowing their value, for glass beads and Brummagem knives and needles. I cannot help thinking that all those savages have immortal souls, and regretting that they should be allowed to pass away from this life without having the light of gospel truth set before them. Year after year passes by, thousands are swept away, and still darkness dense as ever broods over the land.

Once more we are under weigh. With a fair breeze gliding over a long heavy swell, we pass Cape Horn, which stands out boldly into the blue waters, and enter the mighty Pacific. Tony Hinks tells us that, though peaceable enough at times, he has seen here as fierce gales and heavy seas as ever sent tall ships to the bottom. Grant that we do not encounter the loss and disaster met with by Lord Anson, whose voyage I have been reading. Hitherto a kind Providence has favoured us, and we are standing up along the coast of Chili, the lofty Andes rising blue and distinct against the sky in the distance.

CHAPTER THREE

TAHITI IN HEATHEN DAYS

Anchored in the Bay of Conception to obtain meat and vegetables, and to refresh our ship's company. The town whence we obtained supplies is Talcaguana, the old town of Conception having been destroyed by an earthquake, and the new town standing some way inland. It is a wealthy place—no lack of silver and gold utensils in the houses, and flocks and herds outside, but the inhabitants lead uneasy lives, for not far off beyond the mountains are found tribes of fierce Araucanians, who, riding fleet horses, now and again pounce down on the town, and never fail to carry off a rich booty. They care not for the Spanish artillery and musketry, they keep out of range of them; but might not the power of gospel truth spoken in season change their savage natures? Could some Christian men find their way among them, they might tell them of happier employments than killing each other, and robbing their neighbours. Yet I dream. Such seems to be the chief occupation, not only of savages, but of civilised people all over the world. What power can assuage such a flood of iniquity? There is one and one alone, the bright light of gospel truth, and the living power of Divine grace.

Having shipped our stores, the boat was leaving the shore for the last time, when a brown man, dressed as a seaman, with strange marks on his face and hands, came down begging to be taken on board. His name he said was Taro, and that he was a native of an island far to the west, also that he had long been on board an English ship, the master of which had left him here sick. Captain Fuller believing his tale, and well pleased to obtain the services of one who might prove useful as an interpreter, consented to receive him among the crew. Our ship's company gave him at first the name of Tar, and hence he soon became known among them as Tom Tar. He proves an amusing, and seemingly a good-natured fellow till he is angered, and then he will cast off his clothes, and seizing a billet of wood or whatever comes to hand, will flourish it, threatening the lives of all near him, exhibiting his body covered with strange devices, appearing, as he is still, the fierce, vindictive savage. He comes from an island called New Zealand, where the inhabitants are terribly fierce, and undoubted cannibals. I asked Taro whether he had ever eaten any of his fellow-creatures. He nodded, laughing, and I doubt not, from the expression of his countenance, that he had often done so, and would not hesitate in again indulging in such a practice. Though living so long among men professing to be Christians, he is still a heathen in all his thoughts and ways. I asked him one day how this was. His answer was simple: "They say and do just what heathen man say and do. They no pray to their God; they no care for their God; they no love their God. Why should I?"

Taro spoke the truth; I felt abashed. How can we expect the heathen to become Christians, when those who call themselves so show so little regard to the religion of Christ? I see the same sad shortcoming on shore. Christians do not strive to bring honour to the name of Christ.

For three weeks and more we traverse the Pacific, keeping bright look-out by night and day for rocks and reefs.

W. H. G. Kingston

"Land on the starboard bow," is the cry. We haul up for it. As the ship rises and falls on the long, slow swell, now the trees appear partly out of the water, now they disappear looking thus at a distance like a fleet at anchor. There are cocoa-nut palms, pandanus trees, and many shrubs, growing on a low island, fifteen feet at most above the level of the sea, some twelve miles long, and not a quarter of a mile wide, with a deep blue lagoon inside. This is one of those wonderful coral islands of which I have read, formed by minute insects working upwards from rocky foundations amid the ocean, and ceasing their work when they have reached the surface. The waves have torn off masses and thrown them up so as to form an elevation above the water; then birds have come, dropped seeds, and formed their nests, and dwelt there; and timber and plants floating about have been cast on shore, and their vitality not yet destroyed, have taken root; and more coral and shells have been heaved up and ground fine by the toiling waves to form a beach; and thus a fit dwelling-place for man has been formed. Nearing the sandy beach we heave-to for soundings, but finding none, the ship stands off, while Phineas and I, with Tom Tar and our boat's crew, well armed, pull in with the intention of landing. This the surf will not let us do; and as we are lying off on our oars, presently, from out of the bushes, rush a herd of savages with spears and clubs, which they flourish furiously, making signs to us to be gone. We pull on, however, and find an opening in the reef, through which we get close to the beach. The natives shout and gesticulate more vehemently than ever. They declare (so Taro interprets) that we come for no good purpose, and that they want no strangers. Phineas hopes that they may possess pearls with which to trade, so we row in, he standing up in the bows of the boat, holding up a looking-glass and a string of glass beads in one hand, while he keeps his musket ready in the other. He is bold, and leaping on shore, approaches the natives. At first the savages retire; then one advances, stops, gazes at the supercargo, and with a loud shout, flourishing his club, rushes towards him. Phineas, flinging down the looking-glass and the beads, springs back, firing his musket in the air. The savage is upon him. In another moment that huge club will have dashed out his brains. I see his danger. I have no thought but to save him—no feeling that I am about to slay a fellow-creature. I raise my musket to my shoulder and fire, taking good aim. The savage falls. Phineas, shouting to us to give the Indians a volley, is hauled in. The men obey as the Indians, with terrific howls, rush towards us. Five more fall, some in the water, which is tinged with their blood, others on the land. Our passions are up. Golding urges us to load and fire again. Having thus done, we pull away. Says Golding, "They'll not meddle another time with strangers who peaceably visit their shores to trade." We leave ten or twelve poor heathens dead or wounded on their native strand. My thoughts are sad. The face of that hapless savage as he turned his eye on me when falling is still in my sight. True, I fired to save the life of a shipmate. Yet it is an awful thing to shed the blood of a fellow-being, let it be in warfare or in any other way which men justify as from stern necessity.

Are such, too, the blessings which we Christian and civilised men distribute in our course round the globe? The loud laugh of my companion sounds in my ear. "Come, rouse thee, John Harvey," he says. "Art down-hearted, lad, because we have not been more successful in our traffic? Not a good beginning, but the Pacific is wide, and there will be no lack of customers."

Standing on for three days we sight several islands. On the nearest is a grove of fine cocoa-nut trees. We require a supply of nuts. Two boats with crews well armed leave the ship. An opening appears in the reef—we pull through it and land easily. Our men climb the tall trees and shake down the

W. H. G. Kingston

nuts in heavy showers. While we are collecting the nuts, the men in the trees shout that they see a fleet of large canoes crossing from another island. We deem that it will be prudent to regain the boats. The Indians, seeing the broken nuts strewing the ground, and the heap we are carrying away, shriek, and shout, and shake their clubs and spears, and then furiously rush towards us. Golding, as before, cries out to the men to fire, but I order them to shove off, that we may escape without killing any, for which I see no necessity. We have stolen the savages' provisions, and they have right on their side. The men obey me, and we strive to get the boat afloat. No time to lose. The Indians draw their bows, and the arrows fall thick around us; some come on with stones, and others plunge into the water with clubs and spears to do battle for their rights. Our lives are in jeopardy, and one of our men is fearfully wounded. The savages throng around the boat and try to drag her to the shore. We keep back the savages with the stretchers, and I hope to escape without bloodshed. Again Golding shouts out, "Fire, lads! fire! Why keep back the men from firing? We shall all be murdered." Urged by his example, the men fire a volley among the surrounding savages. With fearful howls those grasping the boat let go; others fall back killed; the mass rush in terror up the beach. We escape into deep water, two or three arrows sticking in the arms of our men and in the sides of the boat. Golding cries out for vengeance; and the men fire till every savage has disappeared.

We return on board. It strikes me that we cannot appear very well favoured in the sight of these poor savages. I say as much that day at dinner to the captain. He is a man of few words.

"You are right, John; the next comers will suffer," he remarks.

"That matters nought to us," says Phineas Golding. "We shall not come here again."

"Scant kindness to the next comers; as scant as that we have showed the natives," I observe.

"We must all look out for ourselves in these seas," says the captain. "It will be our own fault if we are at any time caught unawares. Remember that, Master Harvey."

I make no answer, for the captain does not bear contradiction. The first mate, Golding, and the doctor, keep always well with him. So do I, for this reason: I heard him once say, "That John Harvey needs keeping under." On that, I resolved, as far as it should lie in my power, to keep myself under—to do my duty, and give him no occasion to find fault. Thus far I have succeeded—but not always with ease; for Simon Fuller has had uncontrolled power as a sea captain for many a long year, often over rogues and vagabonds, whom fear alone will keep in order, so he fancies. I have heard say that the rule of kindness will work wonders. I have never seen it tried as I could desire, but I find that the worst of our ship's company obey me more readily than they do James Festing, and yet the first mate is an older, and, I truly believe, a better seaman than I am. I speak quietly to the lads, eschew oaths, and never handle a rope's end in wrath. He swears loudly, and uses both.

I was called forward to see Tom Collis, the poor fellow who was wounded in the boat. The surgeon can do nothing for him, he says, and I see that the man's countenance is marked by death's hand. Around us, as I sit by him, we hear laughter, and oaths, and gross talking. Collis is suffering great agony. "Mercy! mercy!" he shrieks out. "To die thus—no time for repentance, with hideous crimes weighing down my soul!" Sometimes he raves, and says things which make my blood

W. H. G. Kingston

run cold; but I talk quietly to him, and he grows calmer. I tell him in few words of that simple plan God in His gracious mercy arranged before the world began, by which sinners even great as he might be saved. He drinks in every word. I tell him how the loving Jesus came on earth to live as a man a life of suffering, that men might understand that He knows how they suffer; that He was tempted, that they might feel assured He pities, and will help them when they are tempted; that He was crucified,—made a sacrifice, that He might take their sins on His shoulders; that His blood was shed that it might wash away the sins of all who trust in it, and look to Him; that He was buried, and rose again, that He might conquer death, and show that all who follow Him must conquer too; and that He ascended up on high, that He might present all who place their faith in Him washed from their sins pure and undefiled before the throne of God.

"But all that could not be done for such a wretch as me," says Collis. "If God would let me live, I might repent, and lead a different sort of life, and do all sorts of things to please Him; and then perchance He might think me more fit for heaven."

"Oh, my dear shipmate," I say, "don't think of such folly. You could never do anything to make you more fit for heaven than you now are, vile, sinful, guilty wretch as you may be."

I then read to him how the Israelites, bit by the fiery serpents in the wilderness, were saved from death and cured by looking at the brazen serpent held up by Moses. And then I read about the thief on the cross, and then I say:

"Just look to Jesus in that way. Feel that you are bitten by sin, helpless, and dying, and deserving of death; and He says to you, as He said to the thief on the cross, `To-day shalt thou be with Me in paradise.'—`Thy sins are forgiven thee.'"

"What, sir!" exclaims Collis, "you don't mean to say that the Son of the great God who made heaven and earth, and all those thousands of stars we see up there, did all that for me, and such as me,—that He says all that to me, and such as me?"

"Shipmate," I answer, solemnly, "He did do all that for you, and such as you,—and He says all that to you. Take hold of but the hem of His garment, so to speak, by faith, and you are saved. As to satisfaction to Divine justice, it is done. You have nothing to do with that, you have but to feel that you are sinful and guilty. You have to repent, which, may God the Holy Spirit help you to do. You have to look to Jesus as the only cure, as the only Saviour,—to His blood as the only means by which you can be cleansed; and the holy word of God says it, 'Thy faith hath saved thee,'—'By faith ye are saved,'—'His blood cleanseth from all sin.' He doesn't say from little sins, or slight sins, but from all sin. He doesn't say He will receive you by-and-by, perhaps, when you have done something to please Him; but He does invite you, He does receive you. No power of earth or hell can prevent Him from presenting you faultless before the throne of grace. Shipmate, if you only feel your guiltiness, it is you He invites, with all your sins upon you, to come to Him,—it is you He will present faultless and fearless before God's judgment throne, welcomed as a son of God,—not crying out, as numbers will be doing, for the mountains to cover them, for the rocks to fall on them."

"This is news indeed,—glorious news!" says the poor fellow, in a cheerful, happy tone, very different from what he had before spoken in. "I wish that I had known it before. But I know it now, and that's enough. Jesus died for me, and I trust in Jesus."

I have soon to leave him to attend to my duty on deck.

Captain Fuller would not hold it as an excuse that I was attending to a dying man. After some time, my watch on deck being almost out, Tony Hinks comes to me and tells me that Collis is dead; but says he, "It was strange to hear him saying over and over, again and again, `Jesus died for me, and I trust in Jesus.' What does that mean, Mr Harvey?"

I tell him. He goes forward, muttering, "Strange! I never heard the like."

I see Collis once more before he is sewn up in his hammock. There is a smile on his features, such as I had never before seen there.

Six days more, and we sight the high land of King George the Third Island, called by the natives Otaheite, or Taheite. As we draw near it, the prospect becomes truly pleasing to the sight. Lofty hills, covered with beautiful flowering shrubs, and fringed by pandanus, cocoa-nut, and various other trees which we see in these tropical regions, rise up into the clear blue sky, with green valleys between them, and sparkling waterfalls rushing down their sides. A line of white breakers intervene, however, foaming over a coral reef, with a belt of deep blue water between it and the white glittering beach and the feathery fringe of vegetation which springs up close to the strand, the trees overshadowing it with their branches. Never have I seen a more lovely picture; and Tony Hinks, who has been here before, tells us there is no country, to his mind, more pleasant to dwell in. "A man may live here," says he, "with nothing to do, abundance to eat, and plenty of people to tend on him." He gives the first mate and me a hint to keep a sharp look-out on the ship's company, or some of them may be missing when we sail. No wonder, I think, if the place is such an earthly paradise. He speaks of many other things likely to prove attractive to seamen. I ask if the natives are Christians. "Christians? no," he answers, with a laugh. "They would be spoilt, to my mind, if they were. They are much better as they are, as you'll agree, Mr Harvey, when you go on shore." I am inclined to be at issue with Tony on that point; but still I would fain judge of the savage virtues of which he speaks before I condemn them.

We coast some way round the island, till we reach an opening in the reef, entering through which we moor the ship in a commodious harbour. Soon she is surrounded with native canoes, laden with cocoa-nuts, bananas, bread-fruits, apples, figs, and other pleasant vegetable productions. The natives bring boughs with them, which Tom Tar tells us we are to make fast to the rigging, to show that we are friends. We now drive a brisk trade, giving beads, and trinkets, and looking-glasses, and bits of cloth and coloured calico, for fruit, vegetables, pigs, and fowls; but the captain will allow no one to come on board. He says that they are arrant thieves, and so we find them. By-and-by Phineas, with the doctor, Tony, and I, having Tom Tar to interpret, go on shore, but take ten men well armed at our heels. It is a hard matter to keep the men together: but it is not safe to let them separate. The natives are treacherous and revengeful, at least if they are like those we have already encountered. Our men might easily provoke them, especially by rude conduct to the women. Seldom have I seen more comely females. Their manners are attractive, and they know how to add to their charms, by dressing their glossy hair with flowers and shells, and such like ornaments. The country is as beautiful as it appeared a distance. The houses are mostly open at the sides, and thatched with palmetto leaves; but some are enclosed, and all are neat and clean. A house is offered to us by the chief, in which we may take up our abode while we remain on shore. It is amidst a grove of trees, with matting for the walls and floor. A sparkling torrent, rushing down the side of a hill, flows in front of it, cooling the air, while afar off is seen the deep blue sea. Provisions of all sorts are sent us by

W. H. G. Kingston

the king,—baked pig, and roasted bread-fruit, and plantains, and fish, and other articles of food, all served in large leaves. The bread-fruit is about the size of a horse-chestnut, and when baked is somewhat of the consistency of new bread. It is not fit to be eaten raw. The king and the people seem friendly; but to my mind there is no dependence to be placed on them. It is made clear to us that they are sadly depraved, nor can I describe many of the scenes which take place. Suffice it to say that, like other heathens who know not God, they give themselves up to work all manner of abominations without constraint or shame. We place a guard during the night; but when we awake there is great shouting among our party for missing articles, and it is found that we all have been robbed of articles of dress, knives, pistols, hand-kerchiefs, and pocket-books. Phineas declares that he will shoot the first savage he finds purloining, chief or not. We complain of our loss to the king, who gets back some of the articles; but Taro surmises that he has got the remainder himself.

After a bountiful breakfast we continue our progress through the island. Our surprise is great to come upon a large edifice of stone among a people supposed only able to erect huts of leaves. It is a pyramid, nearly three hundred feet long and one hundred wide, with a flight of steps on either side leading to the summit, which is fifty feet from the ground. On the top is a bird made of wood, and a fish of stone. This building forms one side of a court, the other three sides being composed of a wall of hewn stone; the enclosed area is covered with a pavement of flat stones. In this court are several altars of stone, on which are placed baskets of bread-fruit, sweet potatoes, cocoa-nuts, and other food, which we conclude were offerings to their Eatuas, or gods, which they ignorantly worship. Not far off we come upon a figure of one of these gods. It is made of wicker-work, in the form of a man; it is seven feet high, and covered over with black and white feathers. We learn that this pyramid is a temple, and that the court is a burying-place, called a Morai; the altars are called Ewattuas. While we are about to proceed on our journey we see a concourse of people collecting from all quarters, and hurrying toward the morai. We inquire of Taro for what object they are assembling.

"To offer a sacrifice to their Eatua, their god," he answers.

"Of what will the sacrifice consist?" I ask, thinking that it would be of the bread-fruit and other fruits we saw on the altars.

"You will see," he answered, with one of those gleams of savage pleasure which ever and anon pass over his countenance.

We remark that there are only men and boys among the crowd,—no women nor girls. The crowd increases,—there is expectation on their countenances, as if something of importance is about to happen. Still we can obtain no information from Taro; he only says, "You will see, you will see."

"A very well-behaved set of people are these," observes Golding. "In England, among such a crowd, there would be fighting and squabbling. I would as lief be one of these happy islanders as an Englishman, with all our religion and civilisation."

"I have an idea, begging pardon, Master Golding, that you are not yet very well acquainted with these happy islanders," observes Tony Hinks. "It strikes me that ere long you will change your opinion. Wait a bit; as Tom Tar says, you will see—you will see."

CHAPTER FOUR

A NARROW ESCAPE

The air is warm and balmy, the blue sea sparkles brightly, the lofty mountains, glowing in the sunshine, rise up majestically into the clear sky, the graceful palm-trees gently wave their boughs; all nature is smiling with life, and health, and beauty, and all the perfections which a bountiful Creator has spread over these regions. "What a paradise," exclaims the surgeon. "I agree with Golding, I should be well content to remain here to end my days."

While watching for what is next to occur, we see four chief men, so they seem by their dress and bearing, walking along the beach. Taro says they are priests. There are several men in attendance. They stop, as if waiting for some one. They are armed with clubs and knives. Among the crowd comes a young man taller than his companions, and comely in his appearance. He seems joyous and light of heart, for he sings and laughs, regardless of coming ill. The priests, watching him steadfastly, slowly approach. He stops and looks at them with an inquiring expression on his youthful countenance. "We require one quick of foot to bear a message to the Eatua," says the chief priest. The youth starts. Before he can reply, a blow from the priest's club lays him low on the sand. The others fall on him with their clubs, and drive out any life remaining. The priests, surrounding the corpse, place it with the feet towards the sea, and utter some long incantations, each priest holding in his hand a bunch of red feathers. Then they rise and place the body of their victim parallel with the line of the sea beach, and more incantations are uttered. The king, meantime, and his principal chiefs have assembled, and take their stand near the temple. Hair is now plucked from the head of the victim, and one eye is taken out and wrapped in leaves, and presented to the king. With drums beating slowly the body is now borne up by the attendants of the priests, and placed on one of the altars. The tufts of red feathers are at the feet, and rolls of cloth at the head. After this, for a quarter of an hour or more the chief priest addresses it, and pretends to give the message it is to convey to the world of spirits. The surrounding populace look on with stupid amazement, no one knowing whose turn it may be next to be slaughtered as a sacrifice to their blood-loving deity.

While the priests are chanting round the corpse the attendants dig a shallow grave, into which it is thrown with little ceremony, and covered up with stones and earth. Fires are now lighted, and dogs and pigs are slaughtered and roasted, and these being placed on the altars, the Eatua is invited to partake of the feast prepared for him. When we left the spot, I shuddering with a horror I had never before felt, the provisions remained on the altars. Taro tells us that the priests, if angered with a person, avenge themselves by selecting him as a victim, and that for fear of offending them no one ventures to interfere. The priests have thus gained more real power than the chiefs themselves. They generally, however, select some of the poorer people as their victims.

We see arranged near the morai a pile of sixty skulls, and that of the youth just slain is now added to it. They appear but little changed by the air, and Taro says that they are those of victims who have all been offered up within the last few months. He tells us that whenever one of the chiefs is about to commence an undertaking, he selects some unhappy victim, who is forthwith slaughtered and sacrificed. We have undoubted evidence, too, that they often eat their enemies, and they do this without shame or compunction. We see many of the chiefs and warriors going about with human jawbones hanging as ornaments round their necks, and we learn that they are those of enemies slain in war.

Sick at heart I accompany my shipmates. "Friend Golding, what do you now say of these pleasant-mannered, happy islanders?" I ask.

"I knock under," says he. "England is a better place; but there are thousands there who get on very well without religion, so I say religion has nothing to do with it."

"Religion has everything to do with it," I answer, in a somewhat hasty tone. "Religion influences those who have no religion themselves. The heathen world of old, with all its civilisation, was not one jot better than are these cannibals, equally given over to work all manner of uncleanness. If it were not for the true faith of some, influencing general opinion, many Englishmen would even yet be the same as these savages. I may say, as said a pious minister of whom I have read, if it were not for God's grace, we ourselves should be as are these poor barbarians; we might well see ourselves in them."

"A truce with your preaching, John Harvey. You would make us all out blacker than we are," says Phineas, walking on quickly.

"That were a hard matter," I say. "Be not offended, I include myself, remember. It is only as we see ourselves in Christ

Jesus that we are otherwise than most black, guilty, and lost."

"I understand you not, John," he answers. "But you shall not force me to acknowledge that I am not better than these half-naked savages."

"I did not say that; by God's grace, or in His providence, there are great differences, but all are sinners in the sight of God's holy law. But we will talk more of this another time."

This island of Tahiti, or Otaheite, is the largest of a group known as the Society Islands. It is about fifty miles long, consisting of two peninsulas joined by a narrow isthmus. It contains a mountain rising twelve thousand feet above the level of the sea. The other islands of the group are mostly lofty. They are Eimeo, Huaheine, Ulitea, Bolabola, and others. They are volcanic, and mostly fertile in the extreme.

We visit Ulitea, a beautiful island where there is a vast morai. Numbers of priests reside here, and it is looked on as the sacred island of the group. In reality it is more given over to horrible wickedness than any other. While on shore we witness another terrible human sacrifice. Not a week passes but some unhappy people fall victims to the bloodthirsty passions of the priests.

This my first introduction to savage life makes me feel doubly grateful to God that I was born of Christian parents, and in a land where the law of Christ, however imperfectly obeyed, is acknowledged in some sort as the standard.

The wind being fair, we sail north-east towards the Marquesas.

We have been for ten days at the anchorage of Taogou, off the island of Ohevahoa, the most fertile of the Marquesas.

W. H. G. Kingston

We have been engaged most profitably in purchasing sandal-wood, and hogs, and fruits, and vegetables of all sorts, and Phineas Golding is in high spirits, and declares that these are a people truly after his own heart. Their country certainly is beautiful, for though the mountains are not so lofty as those of the islands we have lately left, they equally please the eye, as do the groves, the valleys, and the waterfalls. The men are tall, handsome, and athletic, and the women are scarcely inferior in beauty to those of Tahiti. Alas, that I can say no more in their praise. Both men and women are most depraved, of which we have constant evidence. Hitherto we have been on good terms with these islanders. We have a strict watch kept, and whatever may be their secret disposition, they have had no opportunity of taking us at advantage. Taro warns us to be on our guard. He tells us that they are treacherous, and that if they thought they would gain by murdering every man of our crew they would do so. Taro understands their language, which is much like that of Tahiti and his own country. The men are much tattooed, their only clothing being a piece of native cloth round their loins, but the women wear a petticoat and a mantle over the shoulder. This cloth is made of the fibre of a sort of mulberry tree—not woven, but beaten into a consistency of paper. When torn the rent is mended by beating on a fresh piece. It will bear washing only once. A garment thus lasts about six weeks. The women are better treated than among most Indian tribes. Their occupations are entirely domestic—they manufacture cloth, cook, tend the house, and look after the children, but from all we hear and see, their morals are degraded in the extreme.

Having completed refitting the ship as far as is necessary, I have been able to go on shore. We form a strong body, twelve officers and men in all, with muskets. Our chief object is to visit a valley where the sandal-wood grows, to learn on what supply we can depend. High up the valley we come suddenly on a platform on which grows a large grove of bread-fruit, cocoa-nut, toa, and other trees. Amid them is a large idol of hewn stone of a man in a squatting posture. The figure is not ill sculptured. His mouth is wide, and his eyes and ears large, while his arms and legs are short and out of proportion. There are numerous other idols, of the same size and form, made out of the bread-fruit tree, arranged on either side and behind him, as if they were his ministers and attendants. To the right and left of these hideous idols are two obelisks, about thirty-five feet in height, built very neatly of bamboos, with the leaves of palm and cocoa-nut trees interwoven. At the base are hung the heads of hogs and tortoises, offerings to the idols. They are also ornamented with streamers of white cloth. A few paces to the right of the grove we see four large war-canoes, furnished with their out-riggers, and decorated with ornaments of human hair, coral, shells, and white streamers. In the stern of each sits the figure of a man steering with a paddle, and in full dress, with plumes, ear-rings shaped like whale's teeth, and all the ornaments fashionable in the country. These canoes are placed here to be blessed, we suppose, by the priests. These priests have great power, for they are looked upon as little inferior to the idols. We see this same stone idol represented in a variety of ways, made of human bones, hung round their necks, or carved on their clubs, or making handles to their fans and walking-sticks.

We find that there is no lack of sandal-wood, which raises Golding's spirits. Mine sink when I see the idolatry of these poor people, with no hope that they may be taught better. On descending the valley we pass a morai, or worshipping place, I may call it. On the ground is seated the chief, with his sons, and a large number of his attendants, or courtiers. In front of them are a number of little houses, or sheds, made of bamboo, each about two feet long and rather less in height, and ornamented with shreds of cloth. There are a dozen or more, forming a cluster like a village. The chief and the rest are singing and clapping their hands, and thus they go on for an hour or more. This they call praying to their gods,—a fit homage to gods of wood and stone. Sometimes they stop, and laugh and talk together, as if they have forgotten what they are about. We have seen no human sacrifices, but we have reason to believe that they take place, and from what we hear the people are undoubtedly cannibals. There are several tribes on the islands, in some instances two or more an the same island, who carry on devastating wars with each other, and who all slaughter and eat the captives taken in battle. Though they seem much attached to their country, they firmly hold to the belief that there is a far better land to the east, and numbers are seized with a strong desire to visit it. Year after year the largest canoes are fitted out and provisioned, and men, women, and children crowding on board, they set sail, and away they glide, never to return. Strange to say, that although those who have gone have not again been heard of, others are found equally ready to go in the same direction, believing that their predecessors have reached the happy land. The priests encourage this infatuation, as those who embark leave their property to them. This is faith, but alas! sadly misdirected. It shows a yearning for something better,—to escape from cruel wars and practices and misgovernment, to attain peace and quiet and rest. It is certain that almost all who thus embark perish horribly at sea. A few may be thrown on coral islands,— probably to die,—certainly never to return.

I must speak of the sandal-wood in which we are trading. It is a small tree, with numerous irregular branches, and which with the trunk are covered with a thick red-brown bark. The leaves, which turn inwards, are of a very dark green colour. The flowers, growing in clusters, are white, with a red exterior. The wood is of a light yellow colour, and is very fragrant. It is sold to the Chinese, who burn it as incense in their temples, and manufacture from it a variety of articles. Candles are also made from it thus: a thin sheet of the wood forms a wick, which is surrounded by a mixture of its sawdust and rice-paste.

Our traffic has continued without interruption. Tony Hinks, in command of a boat with Golding, is embarking the sandalwood, of which a pile lies on the beach. I am watching from the deck through my glass what is taking place. The vendor of the wood is a young chief: he has been examining the articles given him in barter. Suddenly he seems discontented with them, and refuses to put more wood into the boat Golding, who is on shore, threatens him. He lifts his club, and I believe that the last moment of the supercargo has arrived. Tony Hinks is in the boat; he lifts his musket, and before the club can descend on Golding's head a bullet is sent through the chiefs shoulder, and the weapon drops powerless. Howling with rage, he retreats; but it is to summon his countrymen, who with threatening gestures rush on. Golding leaps into the boat amid showers of stones cast from the natives' slings, followed by spears and darts. While some of the men shove off others fire, and load again and fire. The boat is heavily laden, and can with difficulty be moved. I fear that my shipmates will be cut off, and share the fate of Captain Cook, and many others since his day. I order another boat to be lowered, and cry out for volunteers. No lack of them. I send down to the captain—there is not a moment to be lost. I, with eight hands, leap into the boat. Away we pull. The captain comes on deck and calls us back. He points to a fleet of war-canoes coming round the point: he fears that we also shall be cut off, and that the ship, with the loss of half her crew, may fall a prey to the savages. Still I cannot without an effort see my shipmates destroyed. We dash on, —the foam flies from our bows. Hinks has got his boat afloat, but several of his men are wounded; yet they struggle bravely. We open fire, and keep the savages at bay. The

W. H. G. Kingston

war-canoes, however, approach,—Hinks' boat gets up to us. It is doubtful whether we or our enemies will gain the ship first. We pull for our lives. Simon Fuller will fight his ship to the last. Our shipmates are casting loose the guns ready for action. The savages in the war-canoes stand up ready to shower down their darts and stones at us.

"Give them a volley,—give them a volley," shouts Golding.

"It were lost time," I tell my men. "It were better get on board."

We keep ahead of the enemy, and gain the ship's side. The falls are ready,—we hook on,—the boats are hoisted up, and we hasten to man the guns. There is a favourable breeze out of the harbour, the anchor is being hove up, the sails are loosed. The canoes gather round us; the savages begin to assail us with all their weapons, shouting and shrieking terribly. The ship gathers way; the savages, grown bold, are climbing up the sides.

"Depress your guns, lads," says the captain. "Small-arm men, give it them."

The shot goes crashing in among the canoes, knocking many to pieces. Not a native clinging to the sides escapes the small-arm men. Again and again we fire, leaving the natives terrified and amazed at the power of our arms. Our guns loaded with langrage commit great havoc among them. They lose courage,—the ship is clear of them.

"And so we bid you farewell," says Phineas Golding, firing his musket at a chief with whom he had the day before been lodging. We sail out of the bay, firing shot on either side.

"We have a good supply of sandal-wood, however," observes

Phineas Golding. "But we had a narrow escape from the savages."

Not a word does he say of his merciful preservation from death; and far be it from me to hint that by my promptness I had a second time saved him, and all with him, from destruction. Tony Hinks, however, when we are clear away at sea, comes up to me and says—

"We owe our lives to you, Mr Harvey. If you hadn't come when you did, it's my belief that not one of us would have escaped."

W. H. G. Kingston

CHAPTER FIVE

AMONG THE CANNIBALS

Afar off appears above the blue line of the horizon a silvery dome clearly defined against the sky. It might be taken for a cloud, but that it never moves its position. It is the summit of the lofty mountain of Mona Roa in Owhyee, the largest of the Sandwich islands, now fully fifty miles away. There are ten of these islands, though eight only are inhabited, the other two being barren rocks on which fishermen dry their nets. As we draw near, other mountain tops are seen, those of Mona Kea and Mona Huararia. Mona Roa is a volcano, and the whole country round is volcanic. It is said to rise above twelve thousand feet above the level of the sea. It is night before we cast anchor in a sheltered bay. Next morning we are surrounded by canoes, and many people come swimming off to the ship, for they are as expert as other islanders of the Pacific in the water. We are plentifully supplied with taro, yams, cocoa-nuts, bananas, and water melons, also with hogs, which are of a large size. Friend Golding, however, finds that he cannot trade with them on the same easy terms as with other savages we have met, for many ships have visited them, and they now require firearms, and powder and shot. These people are much in appearance like those we have before seen—they are tall and athletic, and many of the chief people, both men and women, are of great bulk.

I cannot but remember that it was at this island the renowned navigator, Captain Cook, was slain; and the people have long in consequence been looked upon as very savage and treacherous. This we do not find them to be, but they are heathens given up to gross superstition, and are ignorant and immoral. They carry on bloody wars with each other, offer up human sacrifices, and are, it is reported, cannibals. But if so be they are all this, and more, surely it behoves us as Christians to teach them better things. What, however, do we do? We sell them firearms and ammunition to carry on their wars, we partake in their immorality; so far from showing them any of the graces of our religion, we make them by our lives believe that we have no religion at all, while by all those who visit these shores not a voice is raised to tell them of the truth. We find them more mild and gentle than the people of Tahiti, and very different from the fierce savages of the Marquesas. Not far off is Karakaka Bay, where Captain Cook fell.

We communicate with two other ships while lying here, and the officers all speak in favourable terms of the people. Captain Fuller, therefore, allows us to visit the shore more than he would otherwise have considered safe. We find these people very different from the wild inhabitants of the coral islands we have visited. They have attained considerable proficiency in many arts—their cloth is fine, and beautifully ornamented, as are their mats, but they excel in feather work. The helmets, and mantles, and capes of their chiefs are very beautiful. The helmets are in the form of those of ancient Greece, and are covered with bright red feathers, worked in to look like velvet, with tall plumes, and as their cloaks are of the same texture and colour, and the wearers are tall, powerful men, they have, when armed with dubs or spears, a very imposing and warlike appearance. The king alone is allowed to wear a dress of yellow feathers. The common people, however, wear but scant clothing, none being

W. H. G. Kingston

required in this favoured climate. Their great war-god is Tairi. To propitiate him human sacrifices are offered up, and his idol is carried at the head of their armies. Lesser chiefs have also their idols carried before them. One of their temples, a morai, merits description. It is formed by walls of great thickness, like that at Tahiti. It is an irregular parallelogram, two hundred and twenty-four feet long, and a hundred wide. The walls on three sides are twenty feet high and twelve feet thick, but narrowing towards the top. The wall nearest the sea is only eight feet high. The only entrance is by a narrow passage between two high walls leading up to an inner court, where stands the grim god of war, with numerous other idols on either side of him. In front rises a lofty obelisk of wicker-work, and inside this the priest who acts the part of the oracle takes his stand. Just outside this inner court is the altar on which the human sacrifices are made. Near it stands the house occupied by the king when he resides in the temple, and numerous other idols fill the rest of the space. All have hideous countenances, large gaping mouths, and staring eyes. Tairi is crowned with a helmet, and covered with red feathers. Great labour must have been expended in rearing this vast structure, and in carving all these hideous images, and sad indeed is it to consider the object for which all these pains have been taken.

The king, with whom we have been on good terms, sends to Captain Fuller to beg that he will lend him some of his ship's guns and muskets, and a few of his crew, as he is about to make war on a neighbouring island. I am on shore with Golding and Taro, and while a message is being returned, he invites us to witness the usual ceremonies which take place before war. As we accompany him to the morai, we see dragged on by the crowd no less than eleven men, whose looks of terror, show that something they dread is about to happen. Arrived before the temple, there is a cry from the multitude, who instantly set on them with their clubs. Taro tells us not to grieve; that some are prisoners taken in war, others guilty persons who have broken a taboo, and others the lowest of the people. While we stand shuddering, a concourse of people arrive bearing fruits of all sorts, and hogs, and dogs. The human victims are stripped of all their garments, and placed in rows on the altars; the priests now offer up some prayers to the hideous idol, and then the hogs and dogs are piled up over the human bodies, and the whole, we are told, are left to rot together. Sometimes, on occasions of great importance, twenty-two persons have been offered up.

The oracle is favourable, we hear, and the king sends round to all his subjects to collect at his camp with their arms—spears, clubs, javelins, and slings—ready for battle. No one dares refuse. Vast numbers assemble, but a few only of his immediate attendants have firearms. Nothing can be more fittingly hideous than their idol god of war, with his grinning mouth armed with triple rows of sharks' teeth. A hundred war-canoes are prepared. The army embarks, and, like a flight of locusts, they descend on the opposite coast. We see flames ascending from spots where lately stood smiling villages. A few days pass, and the army returns victorious with numerous captives. Some are forthwith offered up to the war-god, others are kept to be sacrificed on a future occasion. A great chief dies of his wounds, and several victims are offered at his tomb, while, as a sign of grief, his relations and followers knock out their front teeth, and fix them in a tree in his morai. His people also appear to have gone mad, committing every species of abomination, and we hear that many people lose their lives on the occasion.

The Sandwich Islanders have many more idols than those of which I have spoken. There is Mooaru, or the shark god, whose temple stands on almost every point or headland. To him the fishermen offer, on landing, the first fish they have caught that day—for they imagine that he it is who drives the fish to their shores. But the greatest of all their gods, or, at all events, the most feared, is Pele, the goddess of the volcano. She resides on the summit of Mona Roa, and descends in fire and flames to punish her enemies below. She has many priestesses, who appear in the villages with singed garments and marks of fire on their persons, to demand tribute from the inhabitants to avert her vengeance. I do not hear of one of their idols who has a mild or beneficent disposition. All the sacrifices offered are simply to avert their vengeance. The people have no love nor veneration for their idols, and they believe that their idols' chief pleasure is in tormenting and punishing them.

One of the most remarkable objects I have met with in the Sandwich Islands is what may properly be called a city of refuge. It is a sort of morai, surrounded by strong walls, with an entrance on each side. In the interior are temples and numerous houses, in which the priests and occasional occupants reside. Here, whatever crime a fugitive may have committed, if he can reach it he is safe. A victorious enemy in pursuit of foes will come up to the gates, but if the vanquished have entered they are safe. During an invasion of the territory, therefore, all the women and children are sent in here, where they may remain in security. There are several such places of refuge in the islands.

The taboo system is also very curious. The priests govern chiefly in this matter. They settle what or who is to be tabooed, and how long it is to last. To taboo is not only to set aside for a particular object, but to make sacred. The king, a hog, or a house, may be tabooed. During that time people may not do certain acts, and animals or things may not be touched or used. So important are these taboos held, that any person breaking through one of them is punished severely, often with death.

Is it not possible that some of the customs I have mentioned, though barbarous and debased, may have been derived from ancient tradition? Whence has sprung that strange expectation of the return of their long-lost god, Rona, to bring a blessing on their nation? What means that longing for a better land far away in the east, entertained by the Marquesas islanders? The king of this island seems to have great power. He is the owner of all the land, and is the lord and master of all his subjects. He rules wisely, and has the affection of his people.

I might say a great deal more about these Sandwich islanders—their history, habits, and customs, and of the events which have taken place since we have been here, but should I write all I might, my journal would be soon filled. To describe them briefly thus:—Their islands are grand and picturesque; they are very intelligent, and are physically powerful, but they seem abandoned to a debased idolatry, to cruel customs, and to a gross licentiousness. Constant and barbarous warfare, infanticide, and the diseases introduced by their foreign visitors have so rapidly decreased their numbers that the population consists of one-third less now than it did at the time of Cook. Captain Fuller, and the other masters and mates of the ships here laugh at the idea of their ever becoming Christians or civilised, and, in truth, unless they have faith in God's grace, it would seem a hard matter; but I know that He can order all things according to His will, and that, in spite of all man's theories and doubts, He will find means to accomplish His work.

Phineas Golding has just come on board in high glee. He says that he has just heard from Taro, who gets the information I know not how, that there are to the southward of this several coral islands, where abundance of mother-of-pearl and also pearls of great size are to be procured; and thus, instead of sailing west, as we had proposed, he has arranged with Captain Fuller to sail once more south towards the Hervey group, and to touch at the Friendly, Fiji, and many other islands, ere we once more steer north-west towards our destination. To complete our stores, we take in a good supply of salt, to be obtained here in abundance; and then bidding farewell to our friends the Sandwich islanders, we make sail, and steer south.

We find a young lad, the son of a chief, who had managed to secrete himself on board. We ask him why he has done so. He answers that he wishes to see the great country from which we come, and promises to do everything we require if we will let him remain. Captain Fuller consents; but I fear sometimes that he will have a hard life of it. I resolve, however, to protect him as far as I can. He gets the name of Charlie, but no other.

We have sighted several low coral islands, but at length we reach the neighbourhood of a group known as the Penrhyn Islands, about six hundred miles due north of the Hervey group, which we also purpose to visit. We sight a coral island, which we estimate as fifty feet high, nine or ten miles long and five broad, with a deep lagoon in the centre. It is as if a huge coral ring had been thrown down in the ocean. At one end there is an opening, through which a boat can enter the lagoon. The island is covered with groves of cocoa-nut, pandanus, and other trees; and, from the number of huts we see, and the people moving about, it seems to be thickly populated. While the ship is hove-to, I take charge of a boat to carry the supercargo, and Taro, and Charlie; with six men, on shore. We pull round, but find that there is so heavy a surf running that we cannot land on the outside. To save time, Taro and Charlie swim on shore to communicate with the natives. I anxiously wait off to receive their report. After some time we see them running, pursued by many natives. They leap into the water, and dash through the surf. Some of the natives attempt to follow, but our shipmates distance them, and are taken safe on board.

They say the natives, though looking very wild and fierce, were kind in their manners, and invited them up to their houses, and brought them food; but that they soon pressed round them, and began to strip off their clothes, and to take possession of everything they had. Seeing them preparing some hot stones with which to heat an oven, they believed that they were to be cooked and eaten, and so starting up, they rushed headlong for the shore, so completely taking their entertainers by surprise, that no one at first attempted to stop them. They report, however, that they saw pearl-shell ornaments, and even pearls, worn by the savages; which so excites Golding's imagination, that he insists on our attempting further communication with the people. Finding at length the opening into the lagoon, we approach the mouth, the surf breaking over the rocks on either side with great violence. There is a narrow lane of clear water; we pull in; a strong current carries the boat along with fearful speed, and several seas break into her. It seems as if we were in a whirlpool. The rudder has lost its power, and we are spun round and round helplessly; about every moment it seems to be hove on the rocks. She violently rises and falls, and then we are cast, as it were, into the smooth water of the lagoon, though still carried upward for some distance. It strikes me at the moment that we are like mice caught in a trap, and that it must depend on the pacific disposition of the natives whether or not we escape.

At length we steer for the shore, where we see several Indians collected. They retire as we draw near. We again send Taro and Charlie on shore with looking-glasses and trinkets; they go not very willingly. The savages stop, and cast at us glances of suspicion. Then they make a rush forward, seize all the articles they can lay hands on, and again run off. Our two interpreters now come down shaking their heads, and saying that there is no hope of trading with these savages. Still Phineas will not give up the attempt; he has seen the pearls, and is longing for them.

"Why, such a necklace as that would be worth a hundred pounds, or more," he exclaims. "We must have the fellow dead or alive."

He stands up in the boat with his piece, ready to fire. I sternly draw him back, crying out, indignantly:

"I will not allow murder to be committed; for murder it would be, if the men were ten times more savage than they are. They have souls immortal as ours, which we have no right to drive out of their bodies before their time."

"Souls or not, mate, you have made me lose my pearl necklace," says the supercargo, angrily.

"It were better to lose a dozen pearl necklaces, or all the pearls the bottom of the sea can produce, than commit a great crime," I answer, more hotly than usual; and then, knowing that another sort of argument would have more weight with such a man, I added, "Remember, too, we are yet inside the trap. If we kill one of these people, their countrymen may assemble at the entrance, and slaughter every one of us."

This silenced Golding. We pull some way up the lagoon. The water swarms with fish, and the shore seems more fertile than any of the coral islands we have visited. In all directions we see signs of inhabitants, and in some places small canoes hauled up, but none approach us. We now pull back towards the passage by which we entered; but the tide still runs in like a mill-stream. Suddenly we run aground. The men jump out and lift the boat off. We are in a wrong channel. We at length get into what we believe to be the right passage. The men track the boat along, but we make little way. Night comes on rapidly. There will be a moon, but it has not yet risen, and without its light we cannot escape. We secure the boat to the rock, and wait anxiously for that time. Few of us can sleep, for we know not any moment whether the savages may be upon us. Both Taro and Charlie declare, from what they saw on shore, that the people are cannibals. There was also the remains of a wreck burnt on the beach, and they declare their belief that some ship has been cast away there, and the unfortunate crew destroyed. We wait anxiously. Golding says very little; he is evidently ill at ease. I write it, not to boast, but my own mind is far more at ease; for I can say, "In God put I my trust: I will not fear what man can do unto me." Thus, through God's grace, I have always been allowed to feel when in positions of great peril. My shipmates I have heard speak of me as the bravest man among them. So I verily believe I am; but then I am brave not in my own strength, but in the strength of Him who is strong to save. There would be many more brave men in the world, if all knew on whom they may leap confidently for support. There is a kind of bravery that is natural to some, and is a constitutional fearlessness; but a far higher and surer courage belongs to those who have committed their souls to their God and Saviour, and who feel that whatever may befall them, when in the way of duty, must be for the best.

These thoughts pass through my mind as I keep watch while the men are sleeping around me. Still the night continues dark; but as I peep through the obscurity, I fancy that I see against the sky some objects flitting here and there over the rocks. I step cautiously back into the boat, rouse up the men, who seize their arms, and with the oars ready to shove off, if necessary, we wait prepared. The figures approach silently in great numbers, but cautiously stealing along, as if not aware

W. H. G. Kingston

that we are awake. We make no sound. On they come over the rocks, with more ease than we could advance in daylight. In less than a minute they will be upon us. I wish to save bloodshed. There is a faint light in the sky: it is the looked-for moon about to rise. Suddenly the silence is broken by loud unearthly yells, and hundreds of naked forms spring up as it were from the ground upon us.

CHAPTER SIX

SAVED BY A STORM

Never have I heard yells more terrific than those with which the Penrhyn Islanders set on us. We are assailed also with showers of darts and stones, which wound many of our people sorely. Golding, brave as he is on most occasions, utters a cry of terror, and nearly leaps overboard on the opposite side of the boat I give unwillingly the word to fire. Many of the foremost savages fall—the rest hang back. We shove off. The oars are quickly got out. The moon rises. I distinguish the channel. It is almost slack water. We pull for our lives. Golding and Taro stand up and fire. The savages either do not see their comrades fall or do not dread the bullets, for they rush along the rocks still within a few yards of us hurling their stones and darts. I feel assured that if we strike a rock our lives will pay the penalty. The rising moon gives me more light to steer, and allows Golding and Taro to take better aim. It shows us, however, more clearly to the savages. There is still the narrowest channel to pass. The savages are making for the point when, Golding and Taro firing together, two of their chief men fall. It is as I thought, they had not before noticed who had been struck. Now they stop, and with loud howls lift up the bodies of their chiefs. Our men bend to their oars—we dart through the narrow opening, and though many of the savages spring after us,

W. H. G. Kingston

they fail to reach the point in time. Golding and Taro continue firing without necessity. The poor wretches have received punishment enough, and why thus slaughter them when our own safety does not sternly require us to kill? The lights on board our ship greet our sight, and we pull gladly towards her—Golding still uttering his regrets at the loss of his pearl necklace. We reach the ship, and stand off for the night, Golding insisting that he will try his luck to-morrow. The morrow comes, but when we pull in the aspect of the people on shore is so hostile that even Golding acknowledges that we are not likely to get pearls from them this visit. Captain Fuller, therefore, resolves to steer south for the Hervey Islands, according to orders, although, from the accounts I find in Captain Cook's voyages, I doubt much whether our supercargo will be satisfied with the traffic we may chance to open up with the natives.

The first island we made is that of Atiu, the same which Captain Cook calls Wateeoo. It is about seven hundred miles west of Tahiti. We passed not far from the low island known as Hervey Island, which gives its name to the whole group.

We now sail round this island of Atiu, in hopes of finding a landing-place, but none appears—a coral reef surrounds the whole. Still our bold supercargo is anxious to land, and so while the ship stands off and on, I take him, with Taro as interpreter, towards the shore, in the long boat, in which we have a gun mounted. We pull in as close as we may venture outside the surf. Numerous natives are on the shore. Taro beckons, and three small canoes are launched. They paddle swiftly through the surf, and come alongside. Those on the shore stand waving green branches as a sign of amity, so Golding determines to land with Taro. Away they go, and as I may not quit the boat, I watch them anxiously. They land in safety, and vast numbers of the natives instantly close round them. I see them borne up by the throng away from the beach, and then lose sight of them. Two hours pass away, and they do not appear. I begin to dread that they have been cut off. I wait another hour. Just as I am about to return to the ship, the canoes are launched. As they approach, to my disappointment I do not see our shipmates. "The Indians are just thinking that they will knock us on the head," I hear one of my men say. "It will be our fault if we let them," I answer, not feeling, however, altogether satisfied that the man was wrong, yet unwilling to show any fear; "we'll let them know what we can do if they play us tricks. Hand me the slow match." There was a clump of palm-trees close down to the beach. I step forward to the gun, and have the boat's head put towards the shore. On come the Indian canoes paddling rapidly through the surf—the men shouting and shrieking, and whirling their paddles round their heads. I am unwilling to injure the poor wretches. I aim instead at the trees. The white splinters start off on either side from a palm-tree struck by the shot. The effect is like magic, the Indians' threatening shrieks are changed to cries of terror, and in hot haste they dash back through the surf towards the shore. Still we are left in doubt as to the fate of our friends. It is clear that we cannot land to go to their assistance. But I resolve not to give them up. We rest on our oars watching the beach. At length we see a concourse of people coming over a ridge of sand which shuts out the view of the interior from us. Golding and Taro appear in the midst of them. The savages seem to be paying them great respect, and Golding bows with infinite condescension now on one side, now on the other. Canoes are launched, they step into them, and the obedient natives come paddling off to us through the surf. Golding steps on board and signs to the Indians to return. "Now, Harvey, get on board as fast as we can," says he. "It has been a question in my mind all day whether we were to be treated as gods, or to be cooked and eaten; and even now I don't feel quite comfortable on the subject. Your shot turned the scale in our favour, for notwithstanding all Taro's boastings, they had no

W. H. G. Kingston

great opinion of us when they found that we could not bring our big boat through the surf." Taro at length bethought himself of boasting that we could make thunder and lightning, and set off a few cartridges he had in his pocket to convince them. The effect was considerable, but not as great as was hoped for. There was the lightning, but the thunder was wanting. On the hill-side were some ovens with fire in them heating. Taro looked at them suspiciously, not quite satisfied that he might not before long be put inside one of them. Turning about, he saw some warriors walking round and round with huge clubs in their hands. He had no longer any doubt of their intentions. Golding saw them also, and became not slightly uncomfortable. Just then our gun was fired. Many of the natives fell flat on the ground, others rushed hither and thither, while some of the braver examined the trees which had been struck, and reported the effects of the white man's thunder and lightning. Instead of knocking our friends on the head and eating them as they had purposed, the savages came crouching down before them in the most abject manner, as if they were beings altogether of a different nature. Still, as Golding says, the look of those ovens made him glad to get down to the beach, lest the Indians should again change their minds about him.

Two days after this we sight another island. Again Golding goes on shore with Taro, and the captain, and Tony Hinks.

I cannot be surprised if some day Golding is cut off by the savages. He is bold and daring, and far from cautious. Aitutaki is the name of the island. Natives come off to us in great numbers singing and shouting. They are tattooed from head to foot. Never have I seen wilder savages. Some of their faces are smeared with ochre, others with charcoal, and are frightful to behold. We keep on our guard, for we know not any moment that they may venture to attack us. As Taro is on shore we cannot understand what they say. Festing and I allow only a few at a time to come on board. They attempt to climb up the sides, but we keep them off by striking at their hands with boarding pikes, and pointing to the gangway, showing that they may only enter there, a few at a time. Still they persist, when Festing taking up a musket ready at hand, fires it over their heads. They look around for a moment, as if not certain whether they are standing on their heads or their feet, and then leap headlong, some into their canoes and some into the water. They paddle to a distance, but then stopping, look back and threaten us. Festing insists that the only way to make these countries of any use is to sweep the people off into the sea. As to civilising them, that, he says, is impossible. I differ from him. We wait anxiously as before for the return of the captain and our other shipmates. Hour after hour passes by. However great the danger in which they may be placed, we cannot go to their assistance. We begin to fear that they have fallen victims to the savages.

"You and I, Harvey, will have to take the ship home, I suspect," observes Festing; "I am sorry for the old man especially, as we can do nothing to revenge his death."

"That were small consolation," I observe; "nor is that as God wills it."

Festing looks astonished. He would be very angry if he were accused of not being a Christian, and yet, it seems to me, that he encourages feelings and ideas very much opposed to the rules Christ our Master laid down for the government of His disciples.

Evening approaches. With thankfulness I see the boat putting off from the beach. We stand in as close as the reef will let us to meet her. She makes for a narrow channel between the breakers. It is a question whether she will get through. The spray, as it curls upwards, completely conceals her. Or—I

W. H. G. Kingston

look through my glass—has she been capsized by the breakers? No, she is seen again. Her crew give way. She is soon alongside. All have come back safe, though they have been in great peril of their lives.

Captain Fuller has a curious story to tell of the inhabitants of this lovely spot. They are the wildest savages he has ever seen. More like wild beasts than men, yet not so cruel as some of the islanders we have met. As an example. It appears from what Taro has learned on shore, that a vessel calling off here but a few days back, landed a number of natives from another island, who, instead of being killed and eaten, have been kindly treated. The name of the island is Raratonga, but whereabouts it lies Taro could not learn, for the vessel appeared off the coast at early dawn on the east side, and no one saw whence she came. They are young women, and have a pitiable tale to tell of the cruel way in which they were kidnapped by these monsters in human shape. Probably to prevent disputes among his crew, the captain landed these poor creatures, certainly from no motives of humanity if the account Taro gives of them is true.

The vessel only left the island three days ago, so that we may chance to fall in with her. Both Captain Fuller and the supercargo declare that they will give the master a bit of their mind. "Suppose," say they, "we had chanced to call off that island directly after those fellows had perpetrated this rascality, not suspecting harm, what would have been our fate? Without doubt we should have been clubbed."

"So we might, indeed!" I observe, but I think to myself, what may other voyagers say who follow in our footsteps. Have we not shot down the poor savages, who have been defending their own shores? Well may the islanders be ready to destroy any white men they can get into their power.

Captain Fuller says that he never was in greater danger of losing his life than on this morning. If one of the party had wavered, the savages would have been encouraged to rush in on them and club them. He and Golding talk of looking for Raratonga in the hopes of trading with the natives, but we can by no means learn in what direction it is to be found. There is another group we hear of to the south of the Society Islands called the Austral Islands, but it would take up too much time to visit them, and so we shape a course for the Tonga or Friendly Islands. Rumours have reached us that the people do not quite deserve the character given of them by Captain Cook.

Steeling west, we again sight land. We stand in, and heave-to off the coast. It is Savage Island, justly so-called by Captain Cook. Several canoes, with uncouth, fierce-looking savages, come off to us, with painted faces and long hair, even more brutal than those of Aitutaki. Taro ascertains from them that another vessel with two masts has just called there, but gone away,—undoubtedly the brig which carried off the poor people from Raratonga, the unknown island. We may therefore overtake her. A calm comes on,—the savages surround the vessel, and contemplate an attack on us, it seems. The guns are loaded with langrage, and Captain Fuller issues orders to prepare for our defence. Their numbers increase. Taro warns us that they are about to commence an assault on the vessel. He signs to them that they had better not make the attempt; but by their gestures they show their contempt and boldness. Again with loud shouts they come on, shooting their arrows, and hurling darts, and spears, and stones.

"Depress the guns, and fire," cries Captain Fuller.

The order is obeyed. In an instant the sea is covered with the forms of human beings, some swimming from their canoes

W. H. G. Kingston

cut in two, others having jumped overboard through terror. The sea is red with the blood of those wounded. The captain orders that the guns be again loaded. Shrieks, and groans, and cries rise from the water. It is fear, I feel sure, prevents the poor wretches moving. I wish that I might beg the captain not again to fire; but he would not listen. He is about to lift his hand when I see the topsails fill, and the vessel glides out from among the crowd of canoes.

"Hold," cries the captain; "they have had enough of it."

Away we sail, following the setting sun. "A pretty day's work," I think to myself, as I get into my berth. "Yet how is it to be avoided?"

I drop asleep. I know that I am asleep, and yet I fancy that I am looking over the side of a vessel,—not the *Mary Rose*, though,—and I see the ocean covered with the forms of men, their skins brown, and white, and black, swimming towards all points of the compass. They swim strongly and boldly; each on his head wears a crown of gold, and in his right hand carries a book,—an open book. I look again,—it is the Bible. They read the book as they swim, and it gives them strength to persevere; for sharks rise up to threaten them, and other monsters of the deep. And now land appears, the very island we have left, and two or more swim towards it, and the savage inhabitants come out in their canoes to attack them, and I tremble for their fate; but the swimmers hold up their Bibles, and the savages let them pass, and follow slowly. Soon the swimmers land, and numbers collect round them and listen attentively while they read. Weapons are cast away,—the countenances of the islanders are no longer savage. They kneel,—they clasp their hands—they lift up their eyes towards heaven,—their lips move in prayer. They soon appear well clothed, parents with their children dwelling in neat cottages, and lo! a large edifice rises before my eyes: it is a house of God. A bell sounds, and from every side come men, women, and children all neatly clad; and then the words of a hymn strike my ear. The music is sweet, but the words are strange. It grows louder and louder, till I hear the cry of "All hands shorten sail!"

I spring on deck. The ship has been struck by a squall; she is almost on her beam-ends. It is blowing heavily, the thunder rolls along the sky, the lightning flashes vividly. Not without difficulty the canvas is got off her. Once more she rights, and now away she flies before the gale. The sea rises covered with foam. Still she flies on. We prepare to heave her to; for thus running on, with coral islands abounding, may prove our destruction. It is a moment of anxiety, for it is questioned whether the canvas will stand. It requires all hands, and even then our strength is scarce sufficient for the work. We, under circumstances like these, see the true character of men. Golding, hitherto so daring and boastful, trembles like an aspen leaf. He believes that the ship is going down, and dares not look death in the face. I may write what I feel: "Whoso putteth his trust in the Lord shall be safe," as says Solomon, and as his father David had often said in other words before him. It is this knowledge makes the truly bold and brave seaman at all times.

This night is one truly to make a stout heart sink not thus supported. At the main-mast-head appears a ball of fire. Now it descends,—now it runs along the main-yard-arm,—now it appears at the mizen-mast-head,—now there is a ball at each mast-head. The men declare that it is a spirit of evil come to guide us to destruction. Often while the foaming seas are roaring and hissing round us, and the wind is shrieking and whistling through the shrouds, and all is so dark that a hand held up at arm's length can scarcely be seen, flashes of lightning burst forth making it light as day, and revealing the pale and affrighted countenances of those standing around.

　　　　　W. H. G. Kingston

Day dawns at length. As I looked to leeward, not half a mile away, I see a vessel. She is dismasted, labouring heavily. We are drifting slowly down towards her. Now she rises, now she falls in the trough of the sea, and is hid from view. She is a brig, as we discover by the stumps of her two masts, and we do not doubt the very vessel of which we have lately heard. A signal of distress is flying from a staff lashed to the main-mast; but, with the sea now running, what help can we render her hapless crew?

We watch her anxiously; even Phineas Golding, his thoughts generally running on dollars, seems to commiserate the fate of those on board, especially when Tony Hinks remarks in his hearing that such may be ours ere long. The men are at the pumps, and we can see them working for their lives; but, by the way she labours, there seems but little chance that they will keep her afloat. We are gradually dropping down towards her; we can distinguish through our glasses the countenances of the crew, their hair streaming in the gale. What looks of horror, of hopeless despair are there! They know that we cannot help them, though so near. The vessel is sinking lower and lower; the crew desert the pumps, and hold out their hands imploringly towards us as we drive down towards them. Their boats have been all washed away: it were madness in us to attempt to lower one. Some with hatchets are cutting away at the bulwarks and companion hatch to form rafts, others run shrieking below to the spirit-room, or rush bewildered here and there; not one do I see on bended knees imploring aid from heaven. The vessel now labours more heavily than ever; a huge sea rolls towards her,—she gives a fearful plunge. Many of our people, rough and hardened as they are, utter cries of horror. I pass my hands across my eyes, and look, and look again. She is gone!—not a trace of her remains but a few struggling forms amid the white foam. One by one they disappear, till one alone remains clinging to a plank. We see him tossed to and fro, looking wildly towards us for help. Not another human being of those who stood on the deck of the foundered vessel remains alive. Will this one be saved? I feel a deep pity for him. As I watch him, I lift up my heart in prayer to God that he may be saved.

The gale has been decreasing, and the ship lies-to more easily. We hope in a short time to make sail. The seaman still floats in sight. At length I believe a boat would live. I ask Captain Fuller leave to go in search of the man, and sing out for volunteers. No lack of them. We must have drifted some way to leeward of the man; but still, as I took the bearings when I last saw him, I believe that I can find him. Away we pull; the seas are heavy, but long, and do not break much. I look out in vain for the seaman.

"He must have gone down before this," I hear one of the crew remark.

"But the plank would be floating still," I observe. "That man has a soul, whoever he may be. If we save his body, by God's grace his soul may be saved."

This thought encourages me to persevere. Often the boat is half full of water, but we bail her out, and pull on. Already we are at some distance from the ship, when I see a dark, speck rise on the crest of a sea and then disappear. My hopes rise that it is the person of whom we are in search. We hear a faint cry. He is still alive. The crew cheer, and pull lustily towards him. The stranger gazes at us eagerly: he if a youth, with long light hair hanging back in the water. His strength is evidently failing. I urge on my men. Even now I fear that he will let go his hold ere we can reach him. Again he cries out imploringly. A sea striking the boat half fills her with water, and I lose sight of the lad.

W. H. G. Kingston

"He is gone, he is gone!" some of the men cry out. But no; I see his hair far down, close under the stern of the boat I plunge in, and diving, grasp it and bring him to the surface. The boat has forged ahead. With difficulty I get him alongside, and we are hauled on board. The young man has still life in him, but cannot speak. We pull back to the ship, more than once narrowly escaping being swamped. It is some time before the stranger can speak. Even then he does not seem willing to say much. He does not mention the name of the brig to which he belonged, nor whether he was serving before the mast or as an officer; but he speaks like a lad of education. He is, however, so much exhausted, that it would be cruel to ask him questions. Indeed, from a remark he made, I suspect that he believes himself to be dying. I fear that he may be right; but, alas! it is without hope that he looks on death,—only with dark horror and despair. I speak to him of One who died to save all sinners who look to Him for salvation and repent; but my words seem to fall unheeded on the young man's car.

CHAPTER SEVEN

A LAND OF HORRORS

The young man we picked up two days ago is better. He takes more to me than to any one else, yet he is reserved even to me. His name is, he says, Joseph Bent, and the brig was the *Wanderer*. I suspect that he is one of those castaways who have fled from the restraints of parents, or pastors and masters, and that he has been reaping the fruits of his folly, and found them bitter. The brig undoubtedly visited the island of which we have heard, and her crew were the men who committed those black deeds of which I have spoken, but do not here again describe.

How soon are they all sent to their dread accounts except this youth! Great is his astonishment when I speak to him of what was done, and of the poor natives so barbarously carried away.

"The vengeance of a pure and just God quickly finds out the doers of such deeds," I remark. "And, Joseph, my friend, where would you now have been had you not been rescued by the hand of mercy from the jaws of death?"

"In torment—in torment!" he shrieks out; "in everlasting torments! Rightly condemned—rightly condemned!"

W. H. G. Kingston

"But, think you not, that the same loving hand which saved your life from destruction will preserve your far more precious soul from death eternal if you will but believe in His power and will to save you? Do not have any doubts on the subject. The most guilty are entreated to repent and to come to Jesus—the loving Saviour—the Friend of sinners."

"These are strange words you speak, mate," said the young man sitting up and looking earnestly at me.

"Not strange, friend," say I. "Thousands and thousands of times have they been spoken before to the saving of many a perishing soul. Let them not be spoken to you in vain."

Thus do I continue for some time, till I see tears starting into the eyes of the young man. The knowledge of a Saviour's love softens his heart, while his sins still make him afraid.

"I remember to have heard words like those you have been speaking, mate, long, long ago," he observes. "I forgot them till now. They sound sweetly to my ears."

"Never forget them again, friend," I answered, having now to go on deck to keep my watch.

Joseph Bent lives, and is gaining strength, but as he does so he seems to be hardening his heart, and avoids religious subjects; yet he speaks of the doings of his late shipmates at Raratonga. What must have been their feelings when their ship was going down, and the thoughts of their late evil deeds came rushing on their minds. If people would but reflect each morning as they rise, and say to themselves, "For what I do this day I must most assuredly account before the judgment-seat of the Almighty," how many a sin might be avoided; and yet, surely, the love of Jesus, the dread of grieving our blessed Master, will do more than that. With me love is the constraining power—with some men the fear of judgment may have more effect; fear may prevent sin, but love surely advances more the honour and glory of Christ's kingdom. It is love to his blessed Master which will make a man give up home and country, and go forth to preach the unsearchable riches of Christ to the perishing heathen; fear will keep him strictly observant of his religious duties at home: fear rules where the law exists; love reigns through the liberty of the gospel. Yes, I am sure, that love, and love alone, will make a man a persevering missionary of the truth.

We bring up at length on the north shore of Tongatabu, at the same spot where, many years back, Captain Cook anchored his ships, when he called the island Amsterdam. It is the largest by far of all the Friendly Islands, being some twenty miles long and twelve broad, and it is very beautiful, though not rising anywhere more that sixty feet above the level of the sea. Its beauty consists in the great variety of trees and shrubs with which it is covered, while few spots on the earth's surface are more productive; added to this there is a clearness and brightness in the atmosphere which is in itself lovely. Captain Cook bestowed the name of the Friendly Islands on this group, on account of the friendly way in which the natives received him. Captain Fuller says that he has heard certain reports which make him doubt as to the friendliness of the natives. They come off to us in large double canoes, unlike any we have before seen. They consist of two canoes secured side by side, though at some distance apart, by a strong platform, which serves as a deck. In the centre is a house with a flat roof on which the chiefs stand. The sail is triangular, and formed of matting, and long oars are also used, worked on either side. These canoes carry a hundred men or more, and make long voyages, often to Fiji, on the east, and lo! the Navigators Islands, on the north. When sailing forth for war covered with armed men, blowing conch-shells and flourishing their clubs and spears,

W. H. G. Kingston

they have a very formidable appearance. Many smaller single canoes came off to us ringing fruits and fowl of all sorts. They are a very fine race of men, taller than most Englishmen, and well formed and of a light healthy brown colour. They come on board in great numbers, and laugh, and appear to be well disposed. The Captain's suspicions are soon lulled, and so are Golding's. He wishes to trade with them for cocoa-nut oil and other articles. Several of our men ask leave to go on shore, and the captain allows them.

Just as they have gone off, Joseph Bent comes on deck. He has, he tells me, been living on shore here for some time, and knows the people. Notwithstanding their pleasant manners and handsome figures and countenances, they are treacherous in the extreme. He tells that of which I have not before heard, that missionaries have already been sent out to these seas; that some were landed on this very island, of whom three were killed, and the rest driven away. Some, strange to say, were in King George's Islands while we were there, but we heard not of them nor they of us. Indeed, I fear that our captain would have taken but little interest in the matter, though he might have shown those poor banished ones, as countrymen, some of the courtesies of life. Thus I see that people may visit a place, and fancy that they know all about it, and yet be very ignorant of what is going on within. Other missionaries have gone, so says Bent, to the Marquesas Islands. We heard nothing of them; indeed, our captain laughs at the notion of such savages being turned into Christians.

"Who can this Bent really be?" I have asked myself more than once. For one so young he knows much about these seas, and what has taken place here. While I have been thinking how good a thing it would be to have missionaries sent out among them, I find that people at home have already done so, though as yet to no purpose, as far as man can see.

The people seem everywhere sunk in heathen darkness. When Bent sees that some of our men are going on shore, he urges that they may be at once recalled; but Captain Fuller says that the supercargo, Taro, and Tony Hinks, will take care they do not get into mischief. The half-naked chiefs, with their clubs in their hands, and many other people are wandering about the deck, examining everything they see, and now and then standing and talking, as if expressing their wonder. I observe Bent moving quietly among them. Soon afterwards he comes up to me.

"Mate," he says, in an ordinary tone, as if there was nothing the matter, "These men are plotting to take the ship. The fellows on shore will all be murdered, and so shall we unless we manage well. My advice is to get the chiefs into the cabin on pretence of giving them a feast, and then seize them and hold them as hostages. Directly that is done, run the after-guns inboard and clear the decks. It will be better to knock away the bulwarks than to be clubbed."

The captain seems unwilling to believe this.

"I have little to thank you for in saving my life if you do not now take my advice," says Bent, earnestly. "You, and I, and all on board may be numbered with the dead before many minutes are over. Look at those men's arms, and at their heavy clubs. Whose head would stand a single blow from one of them?"

I urge the point with the captain, for I am convinced that Bent is right. He is still irresolute, when we see some more canoes coming off from the shore. This decides him. Fortunately the men's dinner is ready. The captain sends for it into the cabin, and the steward covers the table with all other food he has at hand. We then fix upon four of the leading chiefs whom Bent points out, and by signs invite them to feast below. They look suspicious, and, we are afraid, will not come. Bent stands by to hear what they say. He whispers to me that one of them proposes coming, as it will throw us more off our guard. Again, by signs, we press them to come below. When at length they comply, we endeavour not to show too much satisfaction. We treat them with great courtesy seemingly, keeping our eyes, however, constantly fixed on them. We have the steward and two other men concealed with ropes ready to spring out and secure them. The captain, Festing, and Bent, go below, while I remain in charge of the deck, and Festing hands me up a brace of pistols and a cutlass, through the companion hatch. The crew have been prepared, and stand ready to run in the after-guns and to slew them round the instant the chiefs are secured. I listen for the signal, anxiously watching the proceedings of the savages. Now I see them talking together; now they handle their clubs, and look towards the cabin, as if waiting for the return of their chiefs to begin the work of death. They eye our men askance. It is clear that both parties mistrust each other. The suspense is painful in the extreme. There is a sound of struggling, and shouts from the cabin; the savage warriors press aft. Just then the captain cries out that the chiefs are secured. I order the guns to be slewed round, and sign to the natives to keep back. They are about to make a rush, when Bent springs on deck, and shouts to them in their own language, warning them that if they move our war-fire will burst forth on them, and that their chiefs will be killed. The men, looking grim and fierce, stand match in hand at the guns. Bent now orders the savages to return to their canoes. Sulkily, and with many a glance of defiance at us, they stand, unwilling to obey, till Captain Fuller brings on deck, bound, one of their chiefs, holding a pistol to his ear. The chief speaks to them, and one by one they go down the ship's side. Bent now tells them that unless all our companions return in safety the lives of the chiefs will be taken. I bethink me of writing a note to the supercargo, telling him what has occurred, and urging him to return instantly. I give it to the last savage who leaves the deck, and Bent explains to whom the paper is to be delivered. We now use all haste to get ready for sailing. We have for the present escaped a great danger, but we tremble for the fate of our shipmates, and we are convinced that fear alone will keep these savages in order. The chiefs, finding that Bent can speak their language, endeavour to persuade him to let them go. "When our friends return you will be set at liberty," is his answer. It seems at present very doubtful whether they ever will return. Bent says that these people are treacherous in the extreme, worshippers of devils, offerers up of human sacrifices, and cannibals, though not so bad as the people of Fiji, the next islands we are to visit. The chiefs all this time are kept in durance below. I have seldom seen four finer men in figure and feature. The children, Bent says, are often quite white, like English children, but as heathens they are born, and as heathens they die, without hope.

A boat is now reported coming off from the shore. A large canoe follows. In the boat are fewer men than left the ship. What has been the fate of the rest? They come alongside, and we order the big canoe to keep off. The supercargo and Taro make their appearance on deck. Their escape has been most miraculous. Already had the clubs of the natives begun to play on the heads of their companions, and five had fallen. Golding tells me that he expected every moment to be his last. The man next him had been struck down, and lay writhing on the ground, when a cry was raised, and the canoes were seen hurrying away from the ship, the savages refrained from letting drop their uplifted clubs, and watched the approaching canoes.

When the messenger with the note arrived there was a long consultation. Golding says he never felt so uneasy. It was handed to Tony Hinks, who, unable to read, gave it to

W. H. G. Kingston

Golding. He assumed a tone of authority, and through Taro told the savages that if all the survivors were not released their chiefs would be carried away captives. They seemed to hesitate. Golding believed that they were balancing in their minds whether they loved their chiefs or the blood of the white strangers most. At last they decided to let Golding and Taro with three other men go, and to keep Tony Hinks, whom they take to be a chief, as a hostage. Tony was very unhappy at being left, and tried to escape, but the savages held him fast, and Taro, it seems, who owes him a grudge, would not help him. Thus we are placed in a difficulty to know how to get Tony back without first liberating the chiefs. If it were not for the boatswain, the captain says he would hang all four at the yard-arm. At last it is decided that one alone shall go, and Bent is instructed to tell him, that unless the boatswain instantly returns alive and unhurt, the other three shall be hung up. I put him on board a canoe, which comes out to meet our boat as we pull in.

Some time passes, and at length Tony appears on the beach. We make signals that he must be brought off in a canoe. As he steps into the boat, stout-hearted fellow as he generally is, he sinks down, overcome with the terror he has been in. Several of the crew cry out that now we have got him back, we must hang the savages we have in our power in revenge for our shipmates who have been clubbed. The captain says that we are bound to let one go. I plead that all should be let go, that on the faith of this Tony was returned to us, and that it is both our duty, and wise as a Christian and civilised people, to show clemency to the savages. With difficulty, however, I prevail, and Bent tells the chiefs that they may order a canoe to come alongside, and may go free. They appear very much astonished, and doubtful whether we are in earnest. I watch their eyes when they fully understand that they are free to go. Savages though they may be, there is human sympathy between us; they are grateful for the way we have treated them; and I feel sure that we should be far safer on shore should we return, than if we had hanged them as proposed. "We are well quit of these savages," observes Golding, as we get free of the reefs, and stand out to sea.

There is another group to the north of the Tongas called Samoa, or Navigators Islands. The people, Bent tells me, are very like those of the Tonga group. Of this Tonga group which we are leaving there are numerous islands—the first collection to the north, called the Haabai group, while further north is that of Vavau—all governed by different chiefs, who spend their time in fighting with each other.

While I am on deck in charge of the watch that night I see a bright light burst forth to the north-east, rising out of the sea and reaching to the sky. There is a noise at the same time as if there was distant thunder. I fancy at first that some hapless ship has caught fire, and I send below to ask leave of the captain that we may steer towards her to pick up any of the crew who may have escaped. The captain bids me come and examine the chart, and I see several islands with burning mountains on them marked down. The fire we see proceeds undoubtedly from one of them—Koa, perhaps. The matter is settled by finding our deck covered with fine ashes fallen from the sky.

Four days after leaving Tonga we find ourselves among islands of every size and shape and height, many of them having lofty mountains in their centres, while coral reefs are in all directions. Never has my eye rested on scenes of greater loveliness than these islands present; they are apparently fertile in the extreme, green gems dotting the blue ocean. If men could be perfectly happy and gentle and contented, loving each other and being loved, it would, I should think, be here. Each island looks like a paradise—the abode of peace and innocence. We are standing in towards a

W. H. G. Kingston

secure harbour formed by a coral reef, a native town appearing on the beach, with a hill covered with graceful trees rising above it, down which a waterfall tumbles and glitters in the sunbeams, forming a clear pool, from which we expect to fill our casks. I remark on its beauty to Bent.

"No doubt about that, Mr Harvey," he answers. "But we have more need to be on our guard against the natives here than in any islands of the Pacific. A more treacherous, fierce, and determined race of cannibals is not to be found. Of all the islands we see scattered around, and of many score more, the inhabitants of one dare not visit their nearest neighbours, for fear of being entrapped and killed and eaten. Their great chiefs and warriors boast of the number of people they have killed and devoured; and if they have no captives in their hands when they wish to make a feast, they will kill some of their own slaves, or will send a party of their warriors to any small island near, to knock as many people on the head as they may require."

I fancy that Bent is joking, though it is not a lively subject to joke about. The captain, however, says that he will be on his guard, and a strong party, well armed, will alone be allowed to go on shore. Still, as we require water and fuel and fresh meat and vegetables, we must put in here to obtain them.

We drop our anchor in a calm bay, with scarce a ripple on the surface of the clear blue waters, while against the outer edge of the coral reef the sea rolls in and breaks in masses of white foam. There is a town in sight, surrounded by a ditch and bank, and bamboo stockades, and full of cottages with high-thatched roofs. Above the town, on the hill, is a separate tall building with an exceedingly high-pitched roof, also thatched, the ridge-pole extending out on either side. It is a temple, Bent says, where human sacrifices are offered, and many other abominable things done. The god may be a whale's tooth, or a piece of cloth, or a hideous wooden idol. Soon after we have furled sails, two large double canoes make their appearance inside the reef, running for the town. They have vast mat sails, and on the deck of each are fully a hundred black warriors armed with clubs and spears and bows. They are painted hideously. Several have huge heads of hair, and all are gesticulating violently, as if recounting their deeds of valour. They pass close to our vessel, but do not seem to heed us much. We have our guns run out and the crew at quarters ready for them.

As I look through my glass I see in the bows of each some twenty dead bodies arranged in rows—men, women, and children. "Alas! were these taken in war?" I ask. The canoes reach the beach, and crowds come down with loud shouting and wild leaps, and the canoes are hauled on shore, and then the dead bodies are dragged up the hill towards the temple, all the men shouting and shrieking louder than ever. They appear truly like a horde of evil spirits let loose on earth. I accompany the captain and supercargo with Bent, Taro, and a boat's crew, all well armed, on shore. Taro explains that we come as friends, and as the people see that we are well prepared for war, no opposition is offered. We enter the house of a chief who has just died; his body lies at one end of a long hall full of people. Among them are some twenty women, most of them young and fine-looking persons. Their hair is adorned with flowers, and their bodies are oiled. Some look dull and indifferent to what is taking place, others are weeping, and others look well pleased. Taro tells us that they are the wives of the king. Several men stand near them; ropes are cast round their necks, and suddenly, before we have time to rescue them, as we feel inclined to do, five of them are strangled, and fall dead corpses on the ground. Their bodies are quickly carried off, with that of the chief, and all are buried in one common grave. The new king now appears, and the crowd come to do him honour. He is a tall, stout young man—every inch a savage. We look with horror at what we witness—the bodies are dragged up the hill, and thrust into huge ovens. Some of the captives not yet dead are blackened and bound in a sitting posture, and thus, horrible to relate, are placed *in the ovens to be baked alive.*

It is too sickening to write what afterwards follows. None of us can longer doubt that these people are the most terrible of cannibals. I feel inclined to charge forward to rescue them, but the captain orders us all to stand fast, or we may chance to be treated in the same way ourselves.

We now, through Taro, tell the chief that we require water and fruit and vegetables and hogs and fowls, and that we will pay for all. He receives the message somewhat haughtily, and informs us with the air of an emperor, that though he is one of the greatest sovereigns on earth, and that all men bow down to and fear him, he will grant our request. There he sits, a naked black savage, benighted and ignorant in the extreme; and yet such is his opinion of himself. I cannot help thinking, as I look at him, that I have seen civilised men almost as well contented with themselves with as little cause. We do not find any of our men inclined to straggle, after what they have seen. We hurry down to the beach. The boat has been left hauled off at some distance, under charge of three men, well armed. They pull in when they see us, and say that they are not a little glad to find us safe, for that many canoes with fierce-looking savages have been paddling round and round them, the cannibals showing their white teeth, and making signs that they would like to eat them. Whether this is only the fancy of our men I cannot say. Even Golding, when we get on board, looks pale and says little. It seems to me as if Satan had truly taken possession of the people of these islands, for Bent tells me that the scenes we have witnessed are only such as occur constantly.

We keep a watchful look-out all night, ready for action at a moment's notice. Again we visit the shore, armed as yesterday. Preparations are making to build a house for the new chief. The four uprights for the corners are already placed in large holes dug deep into the earth. In each hole stands a living man bound to the post, with upturned eyes gazing at the light of day. What is our horror to see parties of savages begin to throw in the earth upon them. It covers their breasts, their shoulders, and rises up, the hapless wretches still breathing, till the tops of their heads are concealed, and then with eager haste the murderous wretches stamp down the ground over them. Taro tells us the savages say that the spirits of the dead men will guard the house, so that no evil will befall its inmates. Truly I shall be glad to be clear of this land of horrors, yet it is a fruitful land, and one producing a variety of articles for barter. With cocoa-nut oil alone we could quickly load our vessel, and with the population these islands possess, what numberless other tropical productions might they not furnish, if means could be found to civilise the people!

CHAPTER EIGHT

IN PERILS VARIOUS

Again we go on shore, armed as yesterday. The men cast uneasy glances around, and show no inclination to separate from each other. We meet the chief, who looks taller and fiercer than ever. His black hair is frizzled out in the most extraordinary manner, and on the top he wears twisted round it a piece of smoke-coloured native cloth like a turban. He has rings round his arms and legs, and a small piece of cloth round his loins, but otherwise this great king, as he believes himself, is entirely naked. He carries in his hand a richly carved black club—so heavy, that to strike with it is to kill. He receives us in the same haughty manner as before, as if he wished to impress us with his importance. As he strides along, the people fly on either side, or bow down before him, though he does not in the slightest degree heed them. He is on his way to witness the launching a large new war-canoe, and which, now decked with streamers, we see at some distance from the beach. Conch-shells are sounding, and there is much shouting and dancing. As we draw near, a band of prisoners, with downcast looks of horror, are driven along towards the canoe. Men stand ready with long ropes to drag her to the water. Before she is moved, the captives, bound hand and foot, are cast down before her; then loud shouts arise—the men haul at the ropes—the canoe moves, and is dragged over the bodies of the slaves, crushing them to death. No one pities them. This night the cannibal chiefs will feast on their bodies. Even now the ovens in the great square are heating to cook them. It strikes me that these people take a pride in showing to us the enormities they dare to commit.

As later in the day we are passing through the town, we see two people, a man and woman, wrangling. The man grows more and more angry. A young child is near them; it runs to its mother's arms, but the man seizes it, and in an instant he has killed the poor little creature, and with a fierce gesture thrown the yet panting body on the ground. He gazes for a few seconds moodily at the dead child. The mother does not attempt to touch it; then he orders her to bring a spade. He digs a hole in the floor; the still warm body is thrust in; the earth is thrown back; both stamp it down, and then return to their seats as if nothing had happened.

We see another day a young man buried alive by his own parents. Taro says he had grown weary of life, and they did it to please him. We see very few old people, and we hear that when people get weak and ill from age, their children either strangle them or bury them alive. Bent tells me that human sacrifices are often made to their gods, when the priests and chiefs feast on the victims. We see many people with fingers cut off, and we hear that they have been devoted as offerings to their chiefs who have died, or may only have been ill. No crime is more common than that of killing children, especially girls, indeed, it is remarkable that these people do not seem at all sensible that they are committing crimes. At all events they glory in their shame.

I might note down many more things we see and hear during our stay in this group, but I feel sick at heart as I write and think of all that is told me; and every day, as I tread these blood-stained shores, the very air seems polluted, and the shrieks of the wretched victims of their fellows cruelty, ring in my ears. Wars seem never to cease among them. One tribe is always attacking another, and those inhabiting islands within two or three miles of each other cannot live at peace. The desire to retaliate is the great cause of all their quarrels. If a man is killed by those of another tribe, his friends are not content till they have killed some of that tribe; then the people of that tribe do not rest till they have avenged the death of their relations; and so it goes on, each murder producing another, till there is not a man among all their tribes who does not feel that there are numbers ready to take his life, while he is also on the watch to kill certain people with whom he is at feud.

Of another thing I hear, which, had I not seen so many horrible things they do, I could scarcely credit. If the people of a small island offend a chief, he does not kill them at once, but he takes away all their canoes, so that they cannot escape. Then, whenever he wants victims to offer in his temples, or to feast any friendly chief who may visit him unexpectedly, he sends and brings off one or more families, or parts of families, from the doomed island. No one knows who will be next taken, but they live on with the full consciousness of what their fate will be. They see their relatives and friends taken and carried off to be baked, and they know that, perhaps, their turn may come next. Bent was some time among them, protected by one of their chiefs, to whom he made himself useful, yet he says that he never felt sure of his life an hour together; and whenever he saw the chief handling his club, he could not help fancying that it might come down on his head.

Dreadful as these accounts are, we can speak of little else on board. "It would be as easy to wash a blackamoor white, as to make these men Christians," observed Phineas, one evening, as we sit in the cabin. "What say you, Mr Bent;

would you like to make the attempt?"

Bent casts his eyes on the deck, and does not answer. Golding looks at me. "I'll tell you my opinion," I reply. "If man alone had to accomplish the work, I would say, it is impossible. But man works not alone. God's Holy Spirit is on his side. We are all by nature vile; we have all gone astray. All our natural hearts are of stone. God's grace can alone soften our stony hearts, can alone bring us back to Himself, and as He surely is all-powerful, to my mind He can just as easily shed His grace on the hearts of these black heathen cannibals, and soften them, and bring them to love and worship Him, as He can work the same change in any white man; and so I see no reason to doubt that if the gospel is put before them some will hear it gladly and accept it."

The captain, as I speak, begins to grow angry. Golding bursts into a fit of laughter.

"You're talking Greek to me," says he. "How could these black savages, who have never seen a book in their lives, understand the Bible, even if you gave it them? It's hard enough for civilised white people to comprehend, eh, Captain Fuller! You find it a tough job? I'm sure I do."

"As to that, I don't pretend to much learning in that line—like my second mate here, but I always leave such matters to the parson."

What the captain meant I cannot tell. On looking up, I see Bent's eyes full of tears, and he says nothing. I do not press the subject now as it will only provoke hostility, but I resolve to speak privately to Bent whenever I can. Yes, I am sure, by God's grace, and through the instrumentality of human ministers and His book, these dark heathens may become enlightened worshippers of Him.

W. H. G. Kingston

We hear that there is a port at the great island of Vanua Levu, where sandal-wood is to be procured, and we accordingly forthwith sail there.

Truly it is dangerous work navigating these seas among coral banks in every direction, some just above water, others three, four, and fifteen feet below it. It is only when the sun is shining and the sea blue that we can distinguish the coral, which gives a green tinge to it, under water. One of us is always stationed aloft to pilot the ship. We have hitherto escaped. I pray we may, for if we were to wreck the good ship, these savages would spare the lives of none of us.

Once more we drop our anchor, and canoes come off to us. We make known that we have come for sandal-wood, and have axes, and knives, and nails, to give in exchange. The natives seem so ready to trade that Golding is quite enamoured of them, but the captain wisely will allow no one to go on shore. We keep a careful watch as before. The natives, however, seem very peaceable. They tell Taro that they wish to trade with us, and be our friends, and tempt us to come back again. The first mate, Tony Hinks, and others, declare that the captain's regulations are too strict, and that they ought to be allowed to go on shore.

Two days pass by, and we are almost ready once more to sail. I am below talking with Bent and the doctor. Most of the men are forward at their dinner, the captain, and the first mate, and the watch only being on deck. There is a loud sound like a blow given on the deck, then a shout and a piercing shriek. Something is the matter. We seize cutlasses and pistols, and any weapons we can lay hands on, and spring on deck. Upwards of a dozen savages are collected there with heavy clubs in their hands uplifted, and our men are righting desperately with them, but almost overpowered. The first mate lies dead on the deck near the companion, and further forward are Tony Hinks and a seaman with their heads beaten in. The supercargo is defending himself with a capstan-bar against several savages, while the captain stands in one of the quarter boats, which has been lowered partly down, pointing a telescope at the savages, who look at it as if they think it some sort of firearm. Most of the cannibals turn upon us, and advance furiously with their heavy clubs. We have, I deem, but little chance of contending with numbers so overpowering. I hand a cutlass and a pistol to the captain, who springs out of the boat on deck. Bent stands wonderfully cool, and levelling his pistols kills two of our assailants almost at the same moment. The rest hesitate; they have not thought of putting on the hatches, and to our great relief we see the crew springing up from the forepeak armed with axes, knives, and harpoons. With loud shouts and threats of vengeance they rush at the savages, some of whom they cut down, others they hurl overboard; we from aft join in the onslaught, till the savages take fright, and in another instant our decks are clear. The guns are always kept loaded—the captain orders them to be depressed and fired at the canoes, towards which our late assailants are swimming. Many are struck, and several of the canoes are knocked to pieces. The greater number of the people swim to the shore with the greatest ease, diving when they see the guns fired, or the levelling of the muskets. We make sail and stand out of the harbour to the west, intending to bury our chief mate and boatswain in deep water, out of sight of these cannibal regions.

Truly it makes me sad to think of these two men thus suddenly cut off, utterly unprepared to go into the presence of a holy God. They trusted not to Him who alone could washed them clean. They were good seamen, but they were nothing else. The captain comes on deck, as their bodies lie near the gangway, lashed in their hammocks, with that of the other man killed, and covered up with flags. We read a

W. H. G. Kingston

portion of the burial service, and commit them to the deep, till "the sea shall give up her dead."

The next island we make, sailing north, is Tutuila, one of the Navigators', or Samoan group. The harbour we enter is Pango Pango. It is the most curious we have seen. It runs deep into the land, and on either side are high precipices, some a thousand feet high, with two or three breaks, by which the waters of the harbour are approached from the shore. The people come off to us with great confidence in their large dug-out canoes. They are a brown race, like those of Tahiti. They are evidently a better disposed people than those we have just left. We have no fear about going on shore, and meet with civil treatment. Yet they are great thieves and beggars—the greatest chiefs asking for anything to which they take a fancy. They are also debased idolaters; and Taro says they worship fish, and eels, and all sorts of creeping things. They are also savage and cruel, and constantly fighting among each other. As to their morals, they are undoubtedly superior to the people of Tahiti, yet, from the style of their dances, we cannot argue much in their favour.

There is much wild and beautiful scenery in the islands of this group, and as far as we are able to judge, the climate is good. We keep as usual on our guard, and from what we hear, not without reason, for numerous articles of dress, and carpenters tools, and iron work, and chests, and parts of a vessel, have been seen among the people, which leaves no doubt that some unfortunate ship's company have been wrecked on their shores or put off by them. Indeed, it is worthy of remark that, with the exception of Tahiti, there is not a single group at which we have touched where we have not had evidence that ships had been attacked or wrecked, and a part, if not the whole, of the ship's company cut off. In some, only boats' crews have been destroyed, as was the fate of Captain Cook and his companions, but at several of the islands several ships' crews have been captured, and the greater number of the people killed and eaten. Indeed, such is the barbarous heathen and debased condition of the countless inhabitants of this island-world of the Pacific, that the navigation of these seas is indeed an undertaking of great peril. No man can tell when he is safe, or at what moment the treacherous islanders may not turn round and destroy him, just as they did Captain Cook, and just as they have treated many other unfortunate Englishmen since his time. Truly, it may be said, that these islands lie in darkness and in the shadow of death. There is but one means by which they can be changed—the sending to them the gospel. Yet my brother seamen and the traders laugh at such a notion, and people at home, who ought to know better, call it fanatical nonsense. I do not wish to set my opinion up against that of others, but there are certain points where a man can feel that he is right and others wrong, and this is one of them. The gospel has power to change the evil heart. Nothing else can do it. That never fails if accepted. God has said it. Why should we doubt?

We hear that the people of this place are carrying on war with those of another island. Some of the chiefs come and invite Captain Fuller to help them, but he replies, that if they wish to fight, they must fight among themselves. I would rather he had tried to dissuade them not to fight at all. We make sail out of the harbour, and are becalmed not far off a fortress on the summit of a high cliff which is to be attacked.

It is crowded with the whole population of the island. With our glasses we can see clearly what is taking place. Soon the canoes from Pango Pango, and of other tribes, their allies, appear. The people land, and begin to scale the rock. Numbers are hurled down and killed, but others climb up. Higher and higher they get. They seem determined to

W. H. G. Kingston

conquer. I tremble for the fate of the hapless defenders if they succeed. We can hear their shouts and cries. Some of the assailants have gone round on the land side. We observe the multitude inside rushing here and there. Those scaling the rock on our side have reached the summit; several fall, but now the rest break through the stockade, and rush with their clubs and spears against the shrieking crowd. The rest of the invaders have succeeded in gaining an entrance on the opposite side. The work of death goes on. All are indiscriminately slaughtered—men, women, and children. The warriors hold together, and fight despairingly. One by one they fall before the victors' clubs. A breeze springs up, and we stand clear of the reefs and once more out to sea. In the last glimpse we obtain of the fort the fighting is still going on, and thus it continues till the scene fades in the distance.

"Such is the warfare carried on among these savages," observes Bent. "Those who are victorious to-day will be attacked by other tribes before long, and in like manner cut to pieces. In a few years not one of these numberless tribes will remain. War kills many; but in war, crops are destroyed, and famine ensues, and kills many more; and disease, with no sparing hand, destroys numberless others also. A few years hence, those navigating these seas will find none alive to welcome them."

The carpenters declare the ship in such good condition that the captain and supercargo resolve to explore the Loyalty and New Hebrides, and other groups in that direction, before seeking our final port. These islands are especially rich in sandal-wood, with which it is resolved we shall fill up. The first land we make is Mare—one of the Loyalty Islands—a low coral island, about seventy miles in circumference. The inhabitants are almost black, and a more brutalised savage race we have not yet seen. There are four tribes constantly at war with each other—the victors always eating their captives.

Hence we steer north, and bring up in a fine harbour in the island of Fate, or Sandwich Island. It is a large, mountainous, and fertile island, with great beauty of scenery. The inhabitants are tall, fine-looking people, but most debased savages and terrible cannibals. Here sandal-wood is to be had in abundance, and very fine, so that Golding is highly delighted, and declares that it is the finest country he has yet been in. More than once, however, our suspicions are aroused with regard to the natives, who are, we think, meditating an attack on us on board, or when we go on shore to bring off the wood. While here I will write down a brief account of some of these numberless islands in the Western Pacific, among which we are cruising.

The largest is New Guinea, to the north of Australia, the inhabitants of which resemble the negroes of Africa, but are more barbarous. Next, to the south-east of it, is New Caledonia, also a very large island, with barbarous inhabitants. To the south-east is the Isle of Pines, and to the north-east is the Loyalty group, of which Mare is one, and Livu, and Uea. North-east again, we come to the considerable islands of Aneiteum, Tana, Eromanga, and Fate. North again, we fall in with the Shepherds' Islands and the New Hebrides, of which Malicolo and Espiritu Santo are the largest; and then there are the Northern New Hebrides and the Santa Cruz group, and the Solomon Islands, and New Britain, and New Ireland, between where we now are and New Guinea. Then there are the Caroline group—the isles as thick as the stars in the milky way; and the Ladrone Islands, and Gilbert Islands, and many others, too many indeed to write down. I do not say, however, that the countless inhabitants of these islands do not differ from each other in appearance, and manners, and customs. Some are almost jet black, and others only of a dark brown, but in one thing they are similar—they are all equally fierce heathen savages, and mostly cannibals.

W. H. G. Kingston

We have now a full cargo, and Golding rejoicingly calculates that he will make several hundreds per cent, on the original outlay. He does not, methinks, reckon the lives of those who have been lost in the adventure. Having laid in a supply of yams, taro, bread-fruit, cocoa-nuts, and other roots, fruits, and vegetables, we raise our anchor for the last time we hope till our voyage is over. The captain and Golding can talk of nothing but their plans for the future—how they will return and load the ship with sandal-wood and other valuables. Whether the captain is thinking more of his speculations than of our reckoning I know not. He has insisted that we are clear of all danger, and we are running on at night under all sail before a fresh breeze, when the cry of "breakers ahead" makes me spring from my berth. Before the ship can be rounded to she strikes heavily. Again and again she strikes, and I can hear the coral grinding through the bottom; the masts go by the board, and the ship lies a helpless wreck on the reef. The wind has fallen, and, being sheltered by another part of the reef, we have no fear of her yet going to pieces. We wait anxiously for day, not knowing whether we may not be near one of those cannibal islands from whose inhabitants we may expect little mercy.

Another day has passed. We find a sand-bank some eighty yards across, close inside the reef. On this, having saved one small boat, we are landing our stores, and provisions, and arms.

We set to work to build a small vessel. The men labour diligently, though they grumble. We, the officers, keep watch over the spirit casks. Our great want is water. We dig deep, but the little we find is brackish.

The schooner is finished, and Captain Fuller proposes steering for Port Jackson, where there is a convict settlement.

The schooner is launched, but when we search for a passage to take her over the reef, none is to be found. In vain we make the attempt. Everywhere we are baffled. Some of our people almost go mad with despair. I propose building a large flat-bottomed punt from the deck of the ship, which can pass over the reef. All agree.

Our punt is almost completed. We see three objects in the distance, which prove to be canoes. We are discovered, for they approach. They are filled with black savages, who keep at a little distance, shouting and flourishing their spears. We make signs of friendship, but they still come on. We stand to our arms, and as they begin to hurl their spears at us, we are compelled to fire; several fall. With loud howls they paddle off to a distance, watching us. We have little doubt that they will return.

The punt is completed and provisioned. We get her over the reef, and try again to get the schooner across. In vain. We abandon her on the reef. It is time to be away, for we see a fleet of canoes approaching from the north. We hoist sail. The sea is smooth, and we glide rapidly over it, but on come the canoes still faster. They may overwhelm us with their numbers. Much of our powder has got wet. The men do not know it though. Happily the savages catch sight of the schooner and our tent left on the sand-bank. Their eagerness to secure the plunder from the wreck overcomes every other consideration, and they dash over the reef, and allow us to proceed unmolested.

* * * * *

We have been many days at sea; frequent calms and little progress made. The men are becoming discontented, and several are sick. We have avoided nearing any land. Several islands have been seen, but were we to touch the shore, our

W. H. G. Kingston

prospect of escape would be small indeed. Far better, we agree, to trust to the fickle ocean. No, strange as it may seem, there is not among all these rich and lovely islands one on which we dare set foot.

* * * * *

Several of our men have died; the rest are in a state of insubordination. We are on a short allowance of water, and we fear that our provisions will not hold out. Our frail punt has been so damaged by a gale that we can never cease baling.

* * * * *

[Port Jackson.] When almost despairing that one of our company would escape to tell the tale of our disasters, a ship hove in sight, took us on board, and brought us hither. Thus ends our voyage, and all the bright anticipations of wealth enjoyed so long by Golding and our old captain—not a log of sandal-wood, not a string of pearls preserved. ... Bent has told me his history. He feels his heart warmed with gratitude to the Almighty, who by His grace has preserved him from death of body and soul, and his whole mind is bent on going home with me forthwith, and returning to carry the gospel of salvation to the perishing heathen of the wide-spreading islands we have visited. Surely he could not devote his strength and life to a more glorious purpose.

CHAPTER NINE

A NOBLE RESOLVE

I must ask the reader to return to the scene described in the introductory chapter, where we commenced hearing the extracts from the sea journal of old John Harvey. It will be remembered that at our family gathering at my father's house my brother John was the reader.

"Father," said my brother John, pausing awhile after he had finished reading our uncle's journal, "God willing, and with your permission, I will go and preach the gospel to the heathen of those Pacific Islands."

"Go, my son," said our father, promptly. "You shall have my prayers that your preaching may not be in vain."

"What! go off at once, dear John, and leave us all?" exclaimed several of the younger members of the family in chorus.

"I think not," answered John, calmly, with that sweet smile and gentle voice which gained him so many hearts; "I have much to learn and much to do before I shall be fitted for the office of a missionary. It is not a task to be undertaken lightly and without consideration. When a man charges among a host of foes, he must be armed at all points. A missionary, too, should be like a light shining amid the surrounding darkness; he should be able to show the heathen how to improve their moral and physical, as well as their spiritual condition. He should be fairly versed in the most useful mechanical arts, and possess especially some knowledge of medicine and surgical skill."

"Well, it will take you a good many years before you can do all that, and perhaps you will change your mind before the time comes," said one of the younger ones, who did not, as indeed they could not be expected to do, enter into John's thoughts and feelings on the subject.

I may say from that very moment John devoted all the energies of his mind and body to preparing himself for the high and holy calling he had undertaken. Long, I know, that night he knelt in prayer for grace, and wisdom, and strength to direct, fit, and support him for the work. Besides giving much time to his studies at the theological college, he gained a considerable knowledge of medicine and surgery, and was to be seen now with saw and plane labouring with a carpenter,—at the blacksmith's anvil, with hammer in hand, forming a bolt, or hinge, or axe,—and now at the gardener's, with hoe or spade, planting or digging, or pruning. Many wondered how his mind could take in so many new things, or his slight frame undergo so much labour. Few could comprehend the spirit which sustained him. He grew indeed stronger and more robust than any one would have supposed he would become.

I had since my childhood wished to go to sea, and my father allowed me to follow the bent of my inclinations. I now and then thought that I ought to go forth as a missionary also; but when I compared myself with John, and considered his great superiority to me, I gave up the idea, which I had mentioned to no one, as preposterous. My first two voyages were to India and China, and when I came back from the second John was still at college. I remember thinking that he was losing a great deal of time in preparation. He, however, said that he was gaining time. "A blunt tool can never properly perform the work. I am getting sharpened, that I may be used to advantage," was his remark.

On my return home from my third voyage, he had gone to the Pacific. Where he was to be stationed was not known. He had not gone alone, for he had taken a wife to support and solace him. I had never seen her; but I was told that her heart was bound up with his in the work in which he was engaged.

Having now become a fair seaman, I determined to seek a berth as a mate. An old shipmate and friend had just got command of a fine ship bound round Cape Horn; and though I had had no previous intention of going to the Pacific, I was glad to ship with him as third officer. My sisters had copied out our uncle's journal for John; they now kindly performed the same task for me. My ship was the *Golden Crown* a South-sea whaler, and Mr Richard Buxton was master, belonging to Liverpool. Things had changed greatly since the days of my uncle John. We had a definite object: no supercargo was required, and every spot we were likely to visit was well known, and mapped down in the charts. We had several passengers—two missionaries and their wives, newly married. I thought them inferior to John; but they were good men, humble too, with their hearts in the work. We had also another gentleman, a merchant or speculator of some sort. What he was going to do I could never make out. His heart was in his business, and he seemed to consider it of greater importance than anything else. This made him look down with undisguised contempt on the missionaries and their work, nor could he comprehend their objects. "If people want to go to church, let them," he more than once remarked:

W. H. G. Kingston

"but I don't see why you two should be gadding about the world to teach savages, who would know nothing about chapels, nor wish to build them, if you would let them alone, and stay quietly at home and mind a shop, or some other useful business."

The missionaries seldom answered his remarks. They continued perseveringly studying the language of the natives among whom they were to labour, and prayed with and expounded the Scriptures to all on board who would join them. I am writing an account of certain events, and not a journal, so I must suppose the Horn rounded, Chili visited, and Raratonga, where we were to land the missionaries, reached. This was the island whose very position was unknown when my uncle visited those seas, and for long afterwards lay sunk in heathen darkness. It had now become the very centre of Christianising influences, whence rays of bright light were emanating and reaching the farthest islands of the Pacific Ocean.

I have seldom seen a more attractive-looking spot than Raratonga appeared as we came off it. In the centre rise mountains four thousand feet above the level of the sea, with lower hills and beautiful valleys around them, clothed with every variety of tropical tree and shrub. At the foot of the hills is a taro swamp, and then a belt of rich country covered with cocoa-nut, bread-fruit, and banana trees; and then a broad white sandy beach, and a band of blue water; and next a black broad coral reef, like a gigantic wall, against which the swell of the Pacific comes thundering, and rising majestically to the height of twenty feet, curls over and breaks into masses of sparkling foam. The openings in the reef are few and narrow, so that no ship can anchor near the coral-girt isle. Canoes, however came off to us with natives on board, well clothed, and gentle in their manners, who welcomed the missionaries with a warmth and affection which must have been very gratifying to them.

I accompanied the captain on shore to obtain supplies. We took with us a chest of suitable goods for barter. An officer met us on the beach, the appointed salesman of the place, and putting out his hand, said, "Blessing on you." He then led us to the market-house, where we found collected a large store of all the chief productions of the island,—cocoa-nuts, bananas, potatoes, yams, pumpkins, hops, fowls, eggs, and many other things. We selected all we required, payment was made, and the salesman engaged four canoes to carry them off at once to the ship.

I was but a short time on shore, but I saw enough to wonder at. Everybody was well clothed,—the men in jackets, shirts, waistcoats, and trousers, with straw hats, and many had shoes and socks; the women in gowns, shawls or mantles, and bonnets. There were many stone cottages, neatly furnished, and others of a less enduring character. There was a handsome stone church, and an institution, a substantial stone building, for training native youths for the ministry, surrounded by cottages, the residences of those who were married; while gardens and cultivated fields were seen on every side. Such, I was assured, was the condition of the whole island, there being ample church and school accommodation for all the inhabitants, provided entirely by themselves. I saw also an excellent printing-press, at which several editions of the whole Bible had been printed, as well as commentaries, and numerous other works, and issued well bound, almost the whole work being performed by native youths, whose fathers were wild savage cannibals, as indeed were all the natives when first visited by the Reverend J Williams, in 1823, and such they would have remained, had not Christian missionaries arrived among them.

I have fallen in with many seafaring men who have abused

W. H. G. Kingston

the missionaries in no measured terms, and I have read books written by educated men who have done the same, and I was not quite decided whether they were right or wrong till I went to the Pacific. Then I discovered why those men abused the missionaries. Where the missionary has laboured faithfully, the natives will not desecrate the sabbath, and will not pander to the gross desires of their civilised visitors. That is the secret of their dislike to the missionaries.

Again, however, I have met many masters of whalers and numerous officers of the Royal Navy who have spoken and written in the highest terms of the missionaries, and acknowledged that the change which has been wrought through their instrumentality has been most beneficial to the cause of commerce as well as humanity; and that whereas where formerly, if a ship was wrecked, the destruction of her crew was almost inevitable, now through nearly the whole of Eastern, and a considerable portion of Western Polynesia, they would receive succour, and sympathy, and kindness. Still there are many—very many—dark places both in Eastern and Western Polynesia, and no Christian soldier need sigh, like Alexander, that no more worlds remain to be conquered.

During our voyage to Raratonga I learned a great deal more about the progress made by the missionaries of the gospel in these seas, which, while the *Golden Crown* lies off the island, I will briefly describe.

The London Missionary Society was established in 1795, and in the following year it sent forth, on board the *Duff*, a band of twenty-nine missionaries, who landed at Tahiti, one of the Society Islands, March, 1797. Some went on to Tongatabu, the chief of the Friendly Islands, and two to Christina, one of the Marquesas. The savage character of the inhabitants of the two last-named groups prevented success.

At Tongatabu three missionaries were murdered, and the rest made their escape, as did those at the Marquesas. At Tahiti they were received at first in a friendly way by the chiefs and people; but for several years very little real progress was made in instructing the people in the truths of Christianity. Indeed, at one time all the missionaries, in despair of success, in consequence of the unceasing wars of the natives, sailed for New South Wales. Favourable reports, however, reaching them, some returned, and from that time forward slow but steady progress was made, though it was not till the year 1815 that Christianity was firmly established, and idolatry almost completely abolished. The year 1817 was memorable on account of the arrival of two of the most distinguished missionaries who have laboured among the isles of the Pacific—the Reverend J Williams and the Reverend W Ellis.

Mr Williams, who combined a wonderful mechanical talent with the most ardent zeal for the propagation of the gospel, soon after took up his abode at the island of Raiatea where by his example he advanced the natives in the arts of civilisation, at the same time that he instructed them in the truths of Christianity. The natives of the Society Islands having sincerely accepted Christianity, became anxious to spread the good tidings among their heathen neighbours. A considerable number prepared themselves for the office of teachers. Some went forth to the Paumotu Group, or Low Archipelago, to the east; others to the Austral Isles, to the south; and others, among whom was Papehia, accompanied Mr Williams on a voyage to the Hervey group. His first visit was to Aitutaki, where some native teachers were left, by whose means the natives became Christians.

After paying a second visit to Aitutaki, Mr Williams sailed in search of Raratonga, of the position of which even he was uncertain. He was accompanied by Papehia, and by some

W. H. G. Kingston

natives of Raratonga, who had been carried away by a trading vessel from their own island, and cruelly deserted on Aitutaki. Among them was Tapaeru, the daughter of a chief, who had become impressed with the truth of Christianity. At length Raratonga was discovered, and the native teachers were landed; but had it not been for the courage and constancy of Tapaeru, they and their wives would have been destroyed on the first night they were on shore. Sadly disconcerted, they returned next morning on board, and the enterprise was about to be abandoned, when the devoted Papehia stepped forward and volunteered to return on shore.

"Whether the natives spare me or kill me, I will land among them," he exclaimed. "Jehovah is my Shepherd—I am in His hand." Clothed in a shirt, with a few yards of calico in which he had wrapped some portions of the holy Scriptures, the intrepid pioneer landed alone among a host of heathen warriors, who stood on the reef with their spears poised ready to hurl at him. He had not trusted in vain. He persevered, and soon a powerful chief, Tinomana, turned to the truth, and burned his idols.

Again Mr Williams came to Raratonga—this time to remain for many months, to see Christianity established, to erect a large place of worship, and to perform one of the most wonderful tasks I have ever heard of a man single-handed doing. It was to build in three months a schooner of eighty tons, without one single portion of her being in readiness. He taught the natives to cut down, and saw, and plane the wood; then he erected a bellows and forge for the smith's work, which he performed himself; a lathe to turn the blocks, a rope-making machine, and a loom to manufacture the sail-cloth. All the time he laboured, he taught the wondering natives in the truths of Christianity. In three months from the day the keel was laid, this prodigy of a vessel was safely launched, and named "*The Messenger of Peace*." She proved a seaworthy, trusty little vessel, and from island to island, across many thousand miles of water, she was the means of conveying numerous missionaries of the gospel of peace to their benighted inhabitants.

First, several islands of the Hervey group were visited by her, and then she sailed for Raiatea; whence, after remaining some time, she once more sailed with a party of English missionaries and native teachers on a long voyage, calling at the Hervey Islands, then at Savage Island, where an unsuccessful attempt was made to land teachers. Next, she called at Tongatabu, already occupied by missionaries of the Wesleyan Missionary Society. Then she steered north for Samoa, known as the Navigators Islands. Here Mr Williams and his companions met with a most cordial reception from the chiefs and people, and teachers were soon established on several of the islands. The Wesleyans had before sent some missionaries to Samoa, but in a truly Christian spirit, worthy of imitation, they agreed to yield the group to the care of the London Missionary Society, while they devoted their exclusive attention to the Friendly and Fiji groups. They had made great progress among the Friendly Islanders, and the king himself had become a Christian, when it was resolved to attempt the conversion of the Fijians. Between Tonga and Fiji a constant intercourse was kept up, and thus the way seemed opened to carry the gospel to the latter group. There was also no lack of interpreters, an important advantage at the first. The first missionaries to Fiji were established on the island of Lakemba, where, in spite of great opposition, they laboured on faithfully and steadily, extending their efforts to other islands, till finally the Cross was triumphant even at Mbau, the blood-stained capital of the group, where the cannibal monarch himself, the dreaded Thakombau, became a Christian.

In the meantime, the inhabitants of the Sandwich Islands had heard of the gospel from English and American ships visiting the group. No sooner did King Rihoriho ascend the throne than he decreed that idolatry should be abandoned, because he had discovered that his idols could not benefit him; but he knew little or nothing of the Christian religion. At that very time, however, the American Board of Missions had sent out a band of missionaries to them, who on arriving to their joy heard that the idols of Hawaii were overthrown. They were, I believe, chiefly Episcopalians.

While these glorious events were taking place in Eastern Polynesia, the Church Missionary Society had sent forth missionaries among the fierce cannibals of New Zealand. They were joined by several Wesleyans, who together laboured with so much perseverance and success, that a very large number of the inhabitants became acquainted with the truths of the gospel. Numerous well-trained native teachers have gone forth from Tahiti and Raratonga to the surrounding isles, and many of them to the Loyalty and New Hebrides groups, and other parts of Western Polynesia. Following this example, the Bishop of New Zealand has brought natives from a large number of the islands in Western Polynesia, which he has visited, and having instructed them, at a college he has established near Auckland, is sending them back, to spread among their countrymen the truths they have learned. Thus Christianity has begun to spread among the dark-skinned races of those almost countless islands. To carry the gospel to them had been one of the energetic Williams's darling schemes; and it was while carrying it out that, landing at Eromanga, he, with a young missionary, Mr Harris, was barbarously murdered by the savage natives. Still the Society persevered, and missionaries have been established at several of the islands, and many of the natives have become Christians. Among these islands several Presbyterian missionaries have been established, who have laboured steadily and successfully in the Lord's vineyard. Thus several sections of the Protestant Church have been engaged cordially together in instructing the heathen nations of the Pacific in a knowledge of the truth, and in many instances the Holy Spirit has richly blessed their efforts. Still there are many hundred islands the inhabitants of which remain in gross darkness, while a large portion of those who have been converted require instruction, support, and the correction of errors. Much is done through native agency, but still the superintendence of well-educated and well-trained English missionaries is required at even the most advanced settlements to act as overseers or superintendents.

Having now given a very brief account of the progress of Christianity since those midnight hours when my uncle sailed in these seas, I may commence my personal narrative. It must be understood that I have somewhat anticipated events in the above account. At the time my narrative commences, Christianity, though advancing, had not made the great progress it has since done, and many of the islands which are now entirely Christian, were then only partially so, heathen practices prevailed, and the heathen chiefs had still influence and power. It is daylight over these regions, but nearer the dawn than noon. Many a year must pass away before the full blaze of the light of truth will shine from east to west across the vast Pacific. I must not forget to mention the impediments which the priests of Rome, chiefly Frenchmen, endeavour to throw in the way of the progress of the pure faith in Christ. To gain an influence with the natives they wink at many of their vices, they teach them an idolatrous faith, and try to prejudice them against the Protestants.

Having performed our contract at Raratonga, landing the missionaries and their goods, we sailed for our fishing ground in the south, where we were tolerably successful.

W. H. G. Kingston

Whale catching is very hard work, and at length it became necessary to return north, to obtain fresh provisions and to recruit our crew. Our captain had resolved also to try his fortune on the fishing grounds in the neighbourhood of the New Hebrides and the other Western Archipelago.

"A sail on the starboard bow," cried the look-out man, from aloft. I was officer of the watch. We were far away from land, and meeting with a strange sail is always a matter of interest in those seas. I went to the mast-head with my glass, and made out that the sail was that of a large double canoe. We kept away for her, not doubting that she had been driven far out of her course. Of this the sad spectacle which met our eyes as we drew near convinced us. On her deck were numerous savages—some grouped together in the after part, others lying about in different places, or leaning against the mast, and some apart in every variety of attitude. Many appeared to be dead or in the last stage of existence. Some few lifted up their hands imploringly towards us. Others shook their spears and clubs, which they held in their fast-failing grasp, possibly unconscious of what they were doing—the ruling passion being, with them as with others, strong in death. The ropes of their mat sail had given way, and it no longer urged them on. It was necessary to approach them cautiously, for, though the savages had but little strength left, they might, in their madness, attack us. We lowered two boats, and, with our men well armed, pulled up to them. As we got nearly alongside, some of the people in the after group rose from their seats, and one endeavoured to drag himself towards us. He was a young man—a light-coloured Indian—tall and handsome, and, unlike most of the rest, clothed in jacket and trousers. The others moving, showed us a young girl of the same light hue, reclining on a pile of mats. She was clothed; her head was adorned with a wreath of coral, and her arms and ankles with strings of beads. She struck me at once as being very beautiful, though, as I saw her nearer, I perceived that her eye had lost its lustre, and that her face was wan and emaciated. The canoe was a very large one, capable of carrying a hundred and fifty people, though not more than sixty were on board, and of that number nearly half lay dead or dying on the deck. It was easy to divine what had become of the rest. The young man made a sign that he would speak, and pointing to the girl, he said, in a husky voice, "Save her, save her! she Christian!" and then sunk exhausted on the deck.

CHAPTER TEN

THE DESTRUCTION OF THE IDOLS

The canoe, it was evident, had met with some severe weather, and she could scarcely, we considered, have held together had she encountered another gale. We lost no time in getting the survivors into the boats. The suspicions of the warriors were soon calmed by the explanations of the young man, and they allowed us without resistance to lift them on board. The chief's daughter, or young princess, she might have been called, was less exhausted than many of the strong men. I lifted her up with care, and placed her on her mats in the stern sheets, and pulled back as fast as we could to the ship, that the sufferers might have the advantage of our surgeon's assistance. Having removed the sinnets, mats, and other articles with which she was loaded, we abandoned the ill-fated canoe, and stood on our course. I asked the doctor what he thought of the state of the Indians. "The princess and her attendants require careful nursing, and so does that young man, but for the rest who are still alive I have no fear," he answered. "The greater number died for want of water. They had no lack of food, I suspect." I looked in his face, and shuddered at the answer he gave. Several days passed by before the young man who had addressed us in English was again able to speak. He spoke but a few words of English, but enough to let me understand that his name was John Vihala, that he was related to the young girl, daughter of the chief or king of one of the islands; that her name was Alea; that she had become a Christian; but that her father and most of the family remained heathens. She had been betrothed (as is the custom, at an early age) to a powerful chief of a distant island, still a heathen and a cannibal; and, notwithstanding all her prayers and entreaties, her father insisted on her fulfilling the contract. She, in due state, accompanied by several of her relations and female attendants, was placed on board the canoe, which sailed for its destination. At first the wind was propitious, but a fierce gale arose, which drove the canoe out of her course for many days before it, till those on board were unable to tell in what direction to steer to regain their own island. Another gale sprang up, which drove them still farther away, and then famine began, and sickness, and then water failed, and death followed, and despair took possession of even the bravest. Alea's chief relations died, but she and Vihala were wonderfully supported. While their heathen companions lost all hope, they encouraged them, spoke to them of their own religion, and endeavoured to teach the truths of the gospel.

Much to my satisfaction, Captain Buxton agreed, on hearing their story, to take them back to their own island. I do not mention the name of the island for reasons which will appear. It took us some days to beat up to it. It was a lovely spot, of volcanic formation, with lofty mountains in the centre, and in most parts clothed with the richest vegetation. Alea and her female attendants were by this time able to come on deck. Her astonishment at seeing her native island was very great, but her satisfaction was less than I expected. I asked Vihala the reason of this. "She expects to be sent again to her intended husband," he answered, in a melancholy tone. I suspected that Vihala loved his young cousin, nor was it surprising that he should do so. They were of the same faith, and pity for the sad condition to which she

W. H. G. Kingston

would be reduced if the wife of a heathen chief, would have made him wish to free her. We anchored the ship in a secure harbour, and at once sent Vihala and several natives on shore as a deputation to the chief, to inform him of the arrival of his daughter.

After some time, they returned with the announcement that the chief would receive us, and that his daughter would be welcome. We found him seated under a wide-spreading tree, on a bundle of mats, in great state, with numerous lesser chiefs and attendants standing on either side of him. His only clothing was a piece of native cloth wound round his body, and he looked every inch the savage. We expected Vihala to act as interpreter, but when we approached the chief, a person whom we supposed to be a native, though he had a rougher and more savage appearance than the rest, and had on as little clothing as they, advanced a few steps, and informed us in undoubted English, or rather Irish, that he had the honour of being the king's prime minister, and that it was his duty to perform that office. His name was Dan Hoolan (a runaway seaman, we found), and he had been fifteen years on the island, and was married and settled with a family.

After we had made our statement, poor Alea was allowed to approach her father, which she did in a humble posture, with fear and trembling. He manifested very little concern at seeing her, and directed her to be conducted to her mother's cottage. I was anxious to know how Alea and Vihala had become Christians, and asked Dan if he had taught them. "No, indeed, I have not," he answered drawing himself up. "I hope that I am too good a Catholic to teach them the sort of religion they know. There is a sort of old missionary fellow comes over here who has taught them, and he has left a native teacher here, who does nothing but abuse me because I do not make the king here *lotu*, and do not *lotu* myself, as they call it, and give up my wives, and make myself miserable." From this speech of Dan Hoolan's, I had no difficulty in understanding the state of the case. The wretched man would not give up his own sins, and, therefore, tried to keep the chief in heathen darkness. It would, however, be impolitic to quarrel with him, or, rather, wrong, because the so doing would have increased the difficulty of bringing him round. I should explain that the term *lotu* means becoming a nominal Christian.

"But I thought, friend Hoolan, you said that you were a Christian," I remarked quietly, looking fixedly at him.

"So I am inwardly, of course, mate," he answered, with a wink he could not suppress. "That is to say, a right raal Catholic, as my fathers were before me, with nothing of your missionary religion about me; but just on the outside, maybe, I'm a heathen, just for convenience sake, you'll understand."

I did not press the subject then, but being interested about poor Alea, I inquired if he could tell me how her father would treat her.

"Why, send her on to her husband, of course, mate," he answered, with the greatest unconcern; "it's the right thing to do."

"But the chief to whom she is to be given is a heathen and a cannibal, and old enough to be her grandfather," I remarked.

"Maybe, but it's the rule; we don't set much value or women in this part of the world," observed the prime minister; "I might have married her myself for that matter, but it would have brought on a war with the old chief for whom she is intended, so I did the right thing, do ye see, mate, and let it alone."

I now turned the subject, and asked what assistance he could give in refitting the ship and supplying fresh provisions. He was immediately in his element, and showed himself in worldly matters a shrewd, clever fellow. Everything now seemed to go on smoothly, and the repairs of the ship progressed rapidly, while we had no lack of fresh provisions. We soon discovered that another double canoe was fitting out to carry Alea to her intended husband. My heart bled for the poor girl, and I would have done anything to save her, I thought over all sorts of plans. They were, however, needless, for the next morning I heard that she had disappeared. No one knew where she had gone. At first I feared that her father had sent her off secretly; but Hoolan's rage and undisguised fears of the consequences which might occur when the old chief discovered that he had lost his bride, convinced me that such was not the case. I suspected that Vihala might have had something to do with it when I found that he had disappeared about the same time. We were at first suspected, but I convinced Hoolan that we had had nothing to do with the matter.

Several days passed, and not a clue was gained as to what had become of the young princess. One evening, when the men had knocked off work, as I was sitting under an awning on deck, I saw a large canoe entering the harbour. It struck me that it might contain the old chief come to claim his bride; so, as it was not my watch, I jumped into a boat and went on shore to see what would happen. As the canoe drew near, however, I saw that instead of her deck being crowded with tattooed, naked, and painted warriors, dancing, and shouting, and sounding conch-shells, all the people on board were well clothed, while in the after part stood a venerable-looking man with long white hair escaping from under his broad-brimmed hat, and by his side a young lady, both evidently Europeans. I at once naturally walked towards the part of the beach where they would land, and waited for them. No sooner did the canoe touch the shore than several natives from the crowd rushed forward, and lifting the strangers on their shoulders, bore them, with every demonstration of respect, to dry ground. I at once went forward and addressed them in English, and was warmly greeted in return. The old man said he came from a station about fifty miles off. The young lady was his daughter. They had come over on a periodical visit to the Christian converts of this island, and were much concerned to hear that Vihala and the young princess had disappeared.

"They should have abided the storm," the old man remarked. "I will go see this heathen chief, and try again if by God's grace his heart may be softened."

I undertook to get Pat Hoolan out of the way, as it was evident that all his influence was exerted to prevent his master from becoming a Christian. I had fortunately arranged to transact some business with him about this time; so, leaving the missionary addressing the people under a cocoa-nut tree, I hurried up to the king's village, and without much difficulty persuaded Hoolan to accompany me on board. I kept him there as long as I possibly could. Meanwhile the missionary sought out the chief, and found him willing to listen while he unfolded the story of the gospel. A long time the two conversed; and for the first time the benighted savage heard the message of salvation. Gradually the truth interested him, and he began to turn a more favourable ear to the missionary's exhortations than he had ever before done.

"Ah, would that I had Vihala with me," he would frequently exclaim to the missionary. "When you are gone he would instruct me further in the wonderful things I hear." But neither Vihala nor Alea were to be found. He had driven them forth, there could be no doubt, by resolving to unite his daughter to a heathen chief; and yet was Vihala free from

W. H. G. Kingston

blame in carrying off the young princess? The heathens said that they had committed suicide, and were drowned, but judging from Vihala's generally consistent character, I felt sure that that was not the case.

From the first I had felt myself drawn very much towards the venerable missionary. His gentleness, yet firmness of manner, his utter negation of self and devotedness to his Master's cause were very remarkable. His tender love for his daughter, too, was very beautiful. She returned it with the deepest affection and devotion. Accustomed as I had been to the endearments of a happy, well-ordered home, I was sensibly touched by it, and took every opportunity of being in their company. It may appear curious that three days had passed before I learned the name of the good old man. Everybody called him the missionary, spoke of him as the missionary,—thrice-honoured name! In the same way he knew me only as the mate. He had a house assigned to him by the chief, which, by being partitioned off into three chambers, was made tolerably habitable. I was one evening drinking tea there with him and his daughter, when I happened to mention my name.

"What! are you any relative to that devoted missionary, John Harvey?" he asked. When I told him that I was his brother, "Ah, that accounts for your having so friendly a feeling for missionaries," he observed.

"I learned to respect missionaries, and to see the importance of their work, long before my brother became one," I answered; and I then told him of my uncle's journal, which I promised to bring on shore to show him. He was evidently much interested, and made many inquiries about it.

"Does he mention the name of Joseph Bent?" he asked suddenly.

I remembered well several circumstances connected with that person.

"I am the very man," he exclaimed, grasping my hand. "Oh, how much do I owe to that excellent man! He saved my life; but he did far more,—he brought the truth before me,—he showed me my own vileness by nature; and thus, by his instrumentality brought by grace to trust in Jesus, has my soul been saved. Can one man owe a greater debt to another than I owe to him? I had begun to like you for your own sake, and for that of John Harvey I shall ever regard you as a son. Your uncle was an example of the good a true Christian layman can effect in his ordinary course in life. Those on board every ship in which he sailed benefited by his presence, not so much from what he said as from what he did, from his pure and bright example; for he was a man of few words under ordinary circumstances, though he could speak on occasion, and well. Many by his means were brought to know Jesus, and to serve and love him as their Lord and Master. When John Harvey left the sea and went to live on shore, he devoted his whole time to doing God's service, and great has long since been his reward."

This was indeed an interesting discovery. It was gratifying to me to hear the fine old man speak thus of my uncle, as I was sure the praise was not undeserved. As I looked at him, too, I felt how great is the power of grace. I saw before me the drowning youth snatched from the very jaws of death, and of eternal death, too, and allowed to spend a long life in making known to the heathen the inexhaustible riches of Christ. From that day I naturally looked on Mr Bent as an old friend, and was more than ever with him. Indeed, I confess that I was thus drawn into a more intimate acquaintance with his daughter Mary than would have been otherwise the case, and to discover and admire her many excellences.

　　　　　W. H. G. Kingston

The missionary was never idle during his visit to the island, and in a week after his arrival the king declared openly that he could no longer withstand the arguments he brought forward in support of his religion, and that he was resolved to lotu. Hoolan, who had been tipsy for some days, or as he called it, enjoying himself, was very indignant when he recovered and heard this, and hastily going to the king, advised him to wait till the arrival of some Roman Catholic priests, who were the proper persons to whom to lotu; but the king replied, that the advice of a man who had been making himself no better than a hog was not worth having; that he had heard what he was sure was true from the missionary, and that therefore he should become of the missionary's religion. To show his sincerity, he resolved to destroy his gods and burn their moraes, or temples. His great regret was that his daughter and Vihala were not present to see the work done. The missionary urged him to lose no time. It was impossible to say what a day might bring forth. It was not a thing to be done lightly. The missionary visited the king the evening before the ceremony, and many hours were passed in prayer and in reading the Scriptures.

The next morning the king, attended by some of his principal chiefs, and all those who had already professed Christianity, assembled at an early hour, armed with axes and clubs, and firebrands, and ropes, and proceeded to the principal morae, or temple. The heathens also assembled, and stood at a distance trembling, in the expectation that something dreadful would happen. As the king approached the morae, some of his own followers even drew back, and formed a knot at a distance. They had been taught that their gods were full of revenge and hatred, delighting in doing harm to mortals. As Mr Bent considered it to be most important that the natives should destroy their idols themselves, we also stood some way off watching proceedings. The king advanced, exclaiming, "Jehovah is the true God—these are but senseless blocks of wood. See!" As he uttered the last word he struck the principal idol a blow which brought it to the ground. He then rushed at another, several of his chiefs following his example, and in a few minutes every idol was overthrown. [See Note 1.] All the time it was interesting to watch the attitudes and gestures of the heathen, who were evidently under the expectation that fire would come down from heaven, or that the earth would open and destroy their impious chiefs. Their astonishment was proportionably great when nothing of the sort happened, and when the icono-clasts, fastening ropes round the senseless logs, dragged them ignominiously forth, while others of the king's followers applied their torches in all directions to the morae, and set it on fire. While the conflagration was at its height several of the idols were thrown into it, and speedily consumed; others were dragged down to the sea, where blocks of coral were fastened to them, and they were put on board canoes, ready to be carried into deep water and sunk; while the remainder we secured, to be sent home as trophies won by the soldiers of Christ. The king and the chiefs dragged them up to us, shouting as they did so, "The reign of Satan is at an end—the reign of Satan is at an end." So far I could agree with them that his kingdom was shaken to the foundation, as it always is where the free gospel is introduced.

Just at this juncture Hoolan, who had remained on board all night, came on shore. His astonishment gave way to rage, and walking up to the king, he shook his fist in his face, and asked him how he dared lotu to the missionaries, and not wait for the arrival of the Catholic priests whom he expected? The chief, accustomed to the eccentricities of his late prime minister, answered calmly:

"Because the reign of Satan is over. The missionaries told us news which we know to be good, and we have believed

W. H. G. Kingston

them. When the priests you speak of come, will they tell us better?"

Hoolan had nothing to say; he soon got calm again, and observed, as he turned on his heel, "Well, I only hope that you'll be after getting on as well under your new system as you did under mine, that's all."

The king made no reply. He steadily progressed in his knowledge of the Scriptures, and gave very hopeful signs that he was really converted. No men could be more scrupulous as to receiving converts in name as really converted than were all the missionaries I met; and I boldly declare that very many of the newly converted could give a better reason for the faith that was in them than can, alas! a very large number both of young and old with whom I have conversed on the subject in England. There still remained, however, a strong heathen party in the island, under the leadership of a warlike and fierce chief, who was very likely, we feared, to give the king a good deal of trouble. It was necessary, however, for Mr Bent to return to his station. He says that, although called by the natives a missionary, he was not employed by any society, but felt it a privilege to help on the good work, supporting himself by trading, and supplying necessaries to the ships that touched at the island where he had fixed his residence. On asking him about some of the places mentioned in old John Harvey's journal, he said he could tell me of wonderful works of God which he had either witnessed himself, or of which he had heard from those in whose reports he could place the fullest confidence. I need scarcely say how much I felt the idea of being parted from him and his daughter, and I bethought me that I would ask permission from the captain to carry them back in our largest boat. It was at once kindly granted, as a much safer mode of conveyance than a native canoe. I was very happy at being able to pay this last mark of attention to those I so much esteemed; and having made every arrangement I could think of for their comfort during our short voyage, I received them on board at the earliest dawn, in the hopes that we might reach the station before night fell. How true is the saying, "Man proposes, God disposes." Oh that men would therefore throw all their cares on the Lord, remembering alway that "He careth for us."

* * * * *

Note 1. In the early Missionary Reports wonderful narratives are given of the speedy destruction of idolatry in many of the islands. With too sanguine hopes, some of the missionaries spoke of these revolutions as the result of religious zeal, and even quoted the prophecy of "a nation being born in a day." A few years' experience taught them that in many instances the first profession of Christianity was due to various influences, and that the people with impetuous impulse followed the example of their chiefs. Not without prayerful labour and long patience did the missionaries at length obtain precious fruits of spiritual conversion from the good seed sown in these regions. The statement in our narrative only expresses what was often true as a historical fact. In "Brown's History of Missions," volume two, will be found some of the more remarkable instances of the sudden overthrow of idolatry.

W. H. G. Kingston

CHAPTER ELEVEN

VIHALA'S NARRATIVE

The missionary and his daughter were on the beach attended by a number of natives, among whom was the chief, so lately a fierce heathen, now deeply affected at the thought of parting from his friend. As the boat drew near, they all knelt down and offered up prayers, reminding me forcibly of the departure of Paul the apostle from Miletus. It was a deeply interesting sight. In the centre was the venerable missionary with his silvery hair, his daughter kneeling by his side, while around were the king and other chiefs and people, with many women and children. My men without my orders lay on their oars till the prayers had ceased. We then pulled in, and my friends embarked, when the natives burst forth into a hymn, and as we rowed away from the land, we continued to hear it still growing fainter and fainter, till the sound was lost in the increasing distance. We then set our sails and glided swiftly and pleasantly over the sparkling waters. I felt very happy. I would not think of the separation to take place, and determined to enjoy the society of my friends to the utmost. This, perhaps, prevented me from observing as carefully as I might have done the signs of a change in the weather. I believe, however, that Mr Bent, who had more experience as a seaman in this ocean than I possessed, had perceived but he said nothing. The wind suddenly dropped, then it sprung up again, then once more dropped, and the boat scarcely moved through the water. At last it fell altogether, and the sun's rays struck down with intense violence. My men, however, willingly took to the oars, and we proceeded slowly on our course. Still the island was far away, and I lost all hopes of reaching it before dark, though I could not persuade myself that there was any danger to be apprehended. Mr Bent, however, more than once cast a look round the horizon, anxious more on his daughter's account than his own. We had lowered the sail, for it was useless keeping it set. Suddenly Mr Bent exclaimed, "Here it comes, round with her head, David." I looked up, and saw a foam-covered sea rolling towards us. I placed the boat's head so as to receive it, while the men pulled on steadily as before. The question was whether they would be able to continue so doing. The gale was coming from the west, and should it blow with the same fury for any length of time, we might be driven far away to the east without falling in with any land where shelter could be found. I was thankful that my friends were not on board a native canoe. It would have fared much worse with them. We had the means of finding our way, and might beat back when the weather moderated. Mary behaved with beautiful composure when the sea came seething and hissing up alongside us. "This is only one of the trials and dangers to which missionaries are exposed," she observed. "We should bear it patiently and trustfully."

"Trustfully!" How seldom employed, how still less frequently made a practical use of. That one word described much of her character.

The gale soon reached its height; the sea, lashed into fury, seemed one mass of foam, and broke over us so frequently that every instant I expected the boat to be swamped. Two men baling could scarcely keep her free. Our only chance was to run before it, for the strength of the crew no longer

W. H. G. Kingston

availed to keep our small craft's head to wind. The danger of getting her round was very great; should a sea strike her on the beam, it would have rolled her over helplessly. I gave exact orders what was to be done—one man to hoist the foresail, two to pull round with the starboard oars, the rest to spring aft so as to throw the greatest weight into the stern of the boat, thus allowing her head to come round more rapidly. I waited till a heavy sea had rolled past, and then before we had sunk to the hollow I gave the word. For the first time Mr Bent and his daughter turned pale. The boat flew round, and seemed to be climbing up the ascent towards the crest which had just hissed by, and then on we darted with the small patch of sail we could show to the gale.

On, on we went, the huge seas rolling up astern of us, and appearing as if they would come down and overwhelm us. During all my nautical career I had never been in an open boat exposed to such a gale, though frequently in a big ship, and even then I have felt the helplessness, the nothingness of man. Still more sensibly now was it brought before me—"He commandeth and raiseth the stormy wind, which lifteth up the waves thereof. They mount up to the heaven, they go down to the depths; their soul is melted because of trouble. Then they cry unto the Lord in their trouble, and He bringeth them out of their distresses." The missionary was repeating those lines, which come so home to the Christian sailor's heart; and at his exhortation, we offered up our united supplications for protection in our sore distress. To the few solemn words which he spoke, the seamen listened earnestly. They knew that at any moment they might be summoned away. I felt an unusual calmness. I may say that I had no fear: I knew the danger, and yet I believed that we should be preserved.

On, on we drove, farther and farther to the east, our view now confined to the sides of the two seas, in the dark trough between which we floated, seemingly about to be swallowed up, and now lifted on the summit of a foam-crested billow to the tumultuous mountain masses of water which madly leaped and danced one beyond the other till lost in the line where the murky sky sunk over the seething caldron. We had an abundance of provisions on board, but for many hours anxiety prevented any one of us from wishing to partake of them, even the rough seamen seemed indifferent about the matter. At length, however, Mr Bent and I agreed that Mary ought to take some food, which, after a blessing had been asked for, she did, the rest of the party following her example.

We all felt wonderfully refreshed, and hope revived in the hearts of the most desponding. Still we could scarcely dare to conjecture by what means we should be saved. We could not conceal from ourselves that the gale might continue to blow for many days, and that we might be driven far away to the east, whence a long time would be occupied in returning, or that we might be thrown on one of the numberless coral reefs of those seas, or hurled against some rocky shore and be dashed to pieces, while we knew that any moment some cross sea might strike us and send us to the bottom. I have heard of people's hair turning grey in a single night. The anxiety I began to feel the moment I allowed myself to dwell on our too possible fate would quickly have turned my hair grey, and yet directly I turned my gaze upward, and put my trust in Him who said to the waves, "Peace, be still," all my anxious fears vanished, and hope came back strong as ever. The missionary all the time maintained the most perfect and beautiful equanimity, not speaking much, but occasionally offering a few words of encouragement to his daughter. She looked up in his face and smiled.

"I have no fear," she said, calmly. "We cannot be separated, dear father. Should the ocean overwhelm us, we shall together begin a joyful eternity. You have taught me that our Redeemer liveth. 'I know in whom I have believed, and am persuaded that He is able to keep that which I have committed unto Him against that day.'" This hope gave her courage when others would have shrieked with fear.

The gale continued, the boat driven before it. The night approached. Darkness came down on the face of the waters. Oh, the horrors of that night. The sea roared and hissed, and we knew that those mountain waves were following us as before, though the sight could scarcely distinguish the vast watery masses which, in the obscurity, seemed doubled in height. That a delicate girl should exist through the time appeared indeed surprising; yet, anxious as I was, I could discover no failing of strength or energy in her.

When the sun went down, the missionary had called on us all to join in prayer. At midnight he did so again, thereby comfort and consolation being brought to the souls, I believe, of all of us. He then offered to take the helm, to allow me a short sleep, which nature much required. The instant my hand was off the helm, I dropped down and was fast asleep, too soundly even to dream. I was awoke by a cry from the men, and starting up, I beheld a sight sufficient to alarm the stoutest heart. Before us in the direction the men were gazing, as we rose to the summit of a sea, appeared in the grey light of morning a long row of breakers unbroken apparently for miles, the sign of a coral reef. The sea, hurled against it, rose to a height so great in a wall of foaming water that it was impossible to see beyond whether there was land or not; indeed that was a matter of indifference I felt, as the boat must be dashed to pieces and overwhelmed the instant it reached those fearful breakers. These were the thoughts which flew rapidly through my mind as with the first impulse of waking I looked ahead. My next was to turn round, when I saw the venerable missionary standing up on the after seat gazing earnestly ahead, while his daughter clung to his legs in her anxiety lest he should be thrown overboard with the violent movement of the boat.

I could not help being struck, even at that moment, with the appearance of the old man, so calm and collected, and so earnest as he kept his eye fixed on some object ahead. "Courage, courage, friends! God will find us a way to escape," he cried out, at length. "An opening appears in the reef; yes, yes, the boat is heading in for it." As he spoke, I observed a dark spot in the wall of foam which an unpractised eye would not have discovered. As we rushed on towards the breakers, it increased in width till I felt assured that it was indeed an opening, and now beyond it appeared the tops of palm, pandanus, and other trees of those regions, giving us the assurance that we should find land and a haven where we might rest secure from the storm. Still, humanly speaking, our peril was fearful. The greatest skill and judgment were required to guide a boat in a direct course across the tumultuous sea on which we floated. But looking up at the calm countenance of the missionary, as he called me to his side, I had no doubt about the result. On we flew. On either side appeared those walls of foam; one narrow space alone was to be seen where the waves rushed in unbroken by the resistance of the reef. We mounted to the summit of a vast billow—it seemed as if it were about to hurl us on the reef. In another instant we must be struggling helplessly amid that foaming mass of water I heard a cry of despair from more than one of my men. But no, the boat's head again turned towards the opening, and gliding down the billow we dashed through it, and saw on either side a comparatively smooth lagoon extending between the reef and the shore. The sheet was immediately hauled aft, and we ran along parallel with the beach in search of a favourable place for landing. We could scarcely judge of the size of the island, but we supposed it to be about three miles in length,

W. H. G. Kingston

and a mile or two in width, but Mr Bent did not know its name nor the character of its inhabitants.

The question now arose as to whether they were the treacherous savages and cannibals most of the islanders of those seas were till the introduction among them of Christianity, and would attempt our destruction as soon as we landed, or whether they would receive us with kindness and hospitality. As yet we had seen neither houses nor people; but a smooth beach appearing, with a natural quay of rocks, we resolved to land. We stood in towards the shore, and soon found a calm dock, into which we ran the boat and secured her. With thankful hearts we stepped on the dry land, when the missionary exclaimed, "Let us, dear friends, return thanks to God for the merciful deliverance He has vouchsafed us." Following his example, we all knelt in prayer, bursting forth at the end in a hymn of thanksgiving. While we were thus engaged a sound made me look up, and I saw emerging from among the cocoa-nut trees a band of unclad Indians with long hair and beards, and armed with spears, and bows, and clubs. That they were still savage heathens there could be no doubt. However, as emerging from the wood they saw us kneeling, they stopped, apparently watching us with the greatest astonishment. Not till we rose from our knees did they again advance. Flourishing their weapons, however, with frightful gestures, they rushed towards us. Happily they did not shoot their arrows. Mr Bent called out to them, but so loud were their shrieks and cries that his voice was not heard. We had a couple of muskets and a fowling piece in the boat; but so completely wetted had they been, that I doubted if they would go off, even had there been time to get them. We waved our handkerchiefs and lifted up our hands, to show that we were unarmed, and desired their friendship; but they disregarded all our signs, and came rushing on. Our destruction appeared inevitable.

"It's hard lines to lose our lives by these savages, after escaping all the dangers of the seas," exclaimed one of my men near me.

"Friend, God knows what is best for us," said the missionary, calmly. "His will is never really hard, though we may think it so. Trust in Him."

Mary was clinging to her father's arm, ready to share his fate. I stood by her side, resolved to defend her to the last. The savages were close upon us, when another person appeared from the wood, flying at full speed towards us, shouting at the same time in a loud voice to the savages. He was fully clothed in native fashion, and at first I thought that he was a chief, till, as he came nearer, I recognised in him our missing friend Vihala, the Christian teacher. The natives stopped when they became aware of his approach, and, finding that we made no resistance, contented themselves with standing around us, till he, rushing through them, cast himself down at the feet of the missionary, sobbing with joy at again seeing him. He then turned round to the natives, telling them that we were their greatest friends, and had left our homes and come from a far-off land to do them good. He spoke in a manly, authoritative tone, and greatly to our relief the savages at once retired, watching us at a distance. Mary's first inquiry was for Alea, in whom she took a great interest. "She is here, and safe," answered Vihala; and he then briefly recounted the way in which they had been brought to the island.

When first escaping, their intention had been to visit Mr Bent, and to get him to intercede with Alea's father, and to try and conciliate the heathen chief to whom she was betrothed: but the small canoe in which they had embarked being driven out of its course, they were unable to find their way back, and finally reached this island. The weather had

W. H. G. Kingston

greatly moderated before they got near it, or their frail canoe would in all probability have been dashed to pieces on the reef. They found a passage similar to that by which we entered, and with fear and hesitation approached the beach. Still they had no choice; their water and food was expended, they were suffering from hunger and thirst, and their limbs were cramped and chilled, and they must land or perish. Their chief hope was that the island was not inhabited; for they knew too well the savage character of the people of most of the islands surrounding their own to have much hope of escaping without being either killed or made slaves. They had little doubt that there were inhabitants, from the fertile appearance of the country, and as their canoe touched the beach a number of savages darted out of the wood and surrounded them. They cried out that they had come with no evil intent, and that they had some news of great importance to announce to them. Notwithstanding this, the savages showed an inclination to maltreat them, and were proceeding to rifle their canoe, when another party appeared on the stage. Vihala at once saw that they were chiefs or people of consideration, and immediately thereupon cried out, and entreated that their lives might be spared. The chiefs, for such they were, came forward, and with some interest asked numerous questions in their native tongue, and soon there commenced a most affectionate rubbing of noses all round, and Vihala discovered with great satisfaction that the chiefs were his own relatives, who had left their native island some years previously, and were supposed to have been lost. Alea, as the daughter of the king, they treated with even more consideration than Vihala.

Most providential was the influence the young people were thereby enabled to gain over their savage countrymen; nor did they fail to endeavour immediately to exercise it for good. This was clearly one of God's ways of working, and one which has been more than once employed in Polynesia.

They had glorious tidings to give,—to describe the new and beautiful religion brought to them by people from a far-off country, who had left their native land, their homes, and their families for love of their souls, in obedience to the loving, merciful God whom they served. Some listened, rejoicing in the news; others would not understand, and many turned aside altogether. A small band had, however, been taught by the Spirit to acknowledge Jesus as their Saviour, and they now welcomed heartily the missionary who had at first brought the glad news into that region. Vihala was able to repeat many of the words of truth, which were dropped as seeds in the hearts of the people. The conduct of Alea, even in her living in a different part of the island from Vihala, excited their curiosity and gained their attention. So admirable an example had they set, and assiduously had they laboured, that many of those who had become Christians were already well instructed in the faith, and could give a reason for the hope that was in them. Even the heathen party appeared to have no enmity towards them; when they heard that we were people of peace, and anxious only to do them good, they showed their friendly disposition by bringing us provisions, and in preparing a house for our reception under the direction of Vihala.

Alea was on the other side of the island when we arrived, so that we had been on shore some time before she appeared. The meeting between Mary and her was very affecting. She threw herself into Mary's arms, and sobbed aloud with joy, exclaiming, "Oh, my sister, my sister,—my more than sister,—my teacher, my mother, my soul's friend!—and have I found you again? Do I once more hear that dear voice,—do I once more kiss those sweet lips which have told me such holy truths? Ah me! I have gone through much pain and terror, and sorrow and suffering of the spirit, and I have done very wrong, I fear; but I think that I am forgiven, because that I am allowed once more to see you in this wonderful way."

Often have I since thought of the words uttered by that young unsophisticated child of nature, so lately a child of Satan, and the remarks made by the venerable missionary to me:—"'My soul's friend!' Do we, with all our learning, and knowledge, and religious privileges, thus measure the value of our friends? How many of our friends are our soul's friends? Oh, as we value our souls, let us try and find out and cling to those which are so. Do we value most the lips which tell us holy truths or those which speak to us pleasant words,—flattering words? Let us seek, my friend, those only whose lips ever speak to us holy truths,—who will tell us of our faults,—who will not flatter with their tongues."

I will not repeat more of his remarks, but I may mention that, like all faithful pastors of the Lord's flock, he never lost an opportunity of inculcating the truth, of exhorting of advising. He knew the value of a soul in his Master's sight. The chiefs assured us that our boat would be safe; so having unloaded her, we hauled her up on the beach, and left her in charge of some natives, with whom it was arranged my men should lodge till we were again able to put to sea. I took one of them with me well armed, as I was myself; for I own that I did not like altogether to trust the missionary and his daughter alone among the savages, the greater number of whom were still heathen in all their notions and customs.

CHAPTER TWELVE

A LOVING WELCOME

We now set off with Alea and her friends through the woods to the other side of the island. The natives kept at a respectful distance, the children peeping at us out of the entrances to their huts or from behind the trees, we being the first white people they had ever seen. We reached at length the shore of a beautiful sandy bay, where in a grove of cocoa-nuts we found Vihala busily employed in forming divisions in a large native hut to suit our requirements. So assiduously had he and his Christian converts worked, that it was almost ready for our reception. The people began immediately to assemble round us, expecting that the missionary would address them, as Vihala had been accustomed to do, but he told them that we were weary from our long voyage and needed rest, as indeed we did. "No, no, my friend," said Mr Bent, "do not send the people away till we have bestowed on them some portion of the bread of life." On this, greatly fatigued though he was, the missionary spoke to them in plain and simple, yet in tender and glowing words, of the great love of God for a perishing world, which caused Him to send His only Son down on earth, that all who believe in Him should not perish, but have life everlasting. Many wept and cried out that they were sinners, and entreated that he would talk to them again of this matter as soon as he was able.

W. H. G. Kingston

After an ample repast, provided by the natives, we retired to rest without fear, for we felt that we were watched over by One who never slumbers nor sleeps. I do not believe that I ever slept more soundly in my life.

The next morning the people again assembled to hear the missionary deliver his message, his glad tidings of great joy, and glad tidings indeed they were to many of those long-benighted beings. They had never dreamed of a God of love; their only notion of a superior power was one which inspired them with awe and terror. I have frequently observed that the unsophisticated minds of savages grasp the simple and glorious truths of the gospel with an avidity and a power of comprehension which would be surprising to those who have been accustomed week after week and year after year to set the same truths before those to whom they are familiar. As I heard Mr Bent and Vihala addressing the people, whose upturned eager earnest countenances I watched, my heart glowed within me, and I longed to be able also to spread the same glad tidings among a race so eager to receive them. Mary Bent was not idle either, for she had collected round her a number of young women and girls, to whom she was telling the same truths in a way calculated to fix them on their memories.

I deeply regretted that we could not remain on the island till some at least had been thoroughly instructed in the doctrines of Christianity, but it was clearly my duty to return as soon as I possibly could to my ship. "Find out what is right and do it, independent of all other considerations," was a maxim in which I had been instructed. Mr Bent, although more anxious to remain for some time longer even than I was, saw things in the same light I set to work, therefore, with my crew to prepare our boat for sea, so as to commence our return voyage directly the storm should cease and the sea become calm.

A week, however, elapsed before I considered that we might safely venture to put to sea. When the natives heard that we were about to take our departure, they entreated with tears that we would remain some time longer. Finding that they could not prevail, they then of their own accord begged that Vihala might be left with them. This was a sore trial to him, for Alea had been convinced that it was her duty at once to return to her father, and the separation was grievous to both. Still the path of duty seemed clearly marked out for them. There was no hesitation. Vihala felt that he could not abandon those who had been so lately taught to know the truth, and who so much needed further instruction. The young people consoled themselves that they might soon again meet to be united for ever. "Fear not, dearest," said Vihala. "Let us put our trust in God. We are doing our duty. He always protects those who do that." Still, though they thus bravely spoke, they were both deeply affected at parting.

A large multitude of the natives accompanied us to the beach, and earnest prayers were offered up for our safety. Mary and her friend were already in the boat, when there was a cry among the crowd, which opening in the centre, several men appeared dragging by ropes what looked like logs of wood. "Here, take these things," they shouted. "These were once our gods—we are ashamed of them; but they will serve to show the people of other lands that we are no longer what we were, trusting to blocks of wood and stone, but disciples of the true God, who made the heavens, and the earth, and all things therein. Take them—take them with you, or cart them into the sea, so that we may never behold them again." The boat was already fully loaded; but we could not refuse this request, so fixing one at the stern, and another at the bows, and some smaller idols under the seats, we, thus freighted, pulled out through the reef and made sail for the mission station.

W. H. G. Kingston

The wind was light, and we could scarcely expect to accomplish the voyage within three days. As however the boat was large, we were able to fit up a small shelter, in which Mary and Alea could sleep with tolerable comfort while the weather was fine. The conversation of Mr Bent I found of unspeakable advantage. He and I kept watch and watch, though I insisted on keeping five to his three, not to run the risk of fatiguing him overmuch. I remember, during a midnight watch, feeling some uneasy sensations come over me with occasional shivering, but at the time thought little of it.

The second morning dawn had just broken, when I saw in the distance an object, which, as we neared it, proved to be a large double canoe. Where she could have come from, and what was the character of the people on board I could not tell, and this caused me no little anxiety. Still, without going much out of our course, it would be difficult to avoid them. I awoke Mr Bent, and we agreed to sail directly on, taking no notice of them, unless the people showed a friendly disposition. In a short time we got near enough to ascertain without doubt that she was crowded with heathen warriors, who were indulging themselves in every conceivable variety of violent gesticulation. We had too much reason to believe that they would attack us. Our men loaded the firearms, but I hoped that we might avoid having to fight for our lives. Providentially the wind was light. Under sail the canoe could beat us hollow, but we could pull faster than she could. I accordingly ordered the oars to be got out, so as to avoid her if necessary. Suddenly, however, as she got close to us down came her sail, and all the warriors prostrated themselves on the deck, where they remained as we glided by. Had we been alone we should have boarded them, but with Mary and Alea on board, we felt it more prudent to avoid them.

The wind soon again springing up, on we sailed, and as long as we could distinguish the people on the deck, they were seen still lying down as they were when we passed. The cause of this strange behaviour did not till then strike me, when my eye fell on the hideous idol in our bow, and I found many months afterwards that I was right in my conjectures, when I met with one of the men who had formed the crew of the canoe. He and his companions were among the most ferocious of the cannibals of the Pacific. On seeing us they had borne down upon us intending our destruction. When, however, they saw the two hideous idols stuck up at either end of the boat, they were impressed with the idea that some powerful gods were on a cruise, or about to visit some new country, and completely awestruck, they dared not examine us further. Thus were we delivered from another great danger. It was not till we were out of sight of the war-canoe, that Mary and Alea awaking, we told them of what had occurred. The Indian girl trembled, as well she might, for there was much reason to suppose that it belonged to the heathen chief to whom she was betrothed, and that had she been discovered she would have been carried away as a prisoner. Again a feeling of illness came over me, for which I could not account, but I exerted myself and succeeded in overcoming the sensation.

Our voyage continued prosperous though our progress was slow, and it was not till the morning of the fourth day that we sighted the high land above the missionary station. As we sailed in through an intricate passage, under the guidance of Mr Bent, we saw people collecting on the beach. He stood up and waved to them with his daughter resting on his arm. A minute passed, when it was evident that he was recognised, for there was an immediate hurrying to and fro—numbers rushing down to the beach from all quarters, clapping and stretching out their hands, and leaping, and dancing, with other demonstrative gesticulations; and as we got closer we could hear them shouting forth their welcomes, and then a

W. H. G. Kingston

song of gratitude and praise arose from the mouths of the many hundreds collected together. The reception was truly touching and gratifying. "Oh, how they love my father!" said Mary. Those words spoke volumes. I did not propose allowing myself more than an hour on shore, intending to start immediately for my ship.

Scarcely, however, had I walked ten paces than I tottered, and should have fallen had not Mr Bent and some of the natives caught me; and I found myself carried away to his house. My impression was that I was dying, and Mr Bent insisting that he would not allow me to undertake the voyage, I begged that my men would return to the ship. As the coxswain was a steady fellow, and the wind was fair, I had no anxiety as to their finding their way. The boat, therefore, immediately sailed, and I was left alone at the missionary station. I have ever felt that it was providential my illness seized me when it did, for had I embarked, I do not believe, humanly speaking, that I should have survived. I use the term providential, at the same time that I believe nothing happens to us which is not subject to God's providing care. For many days Mr Bent believed that my life hung by a thread, as the expression is, and it was owing, as far as human means were concerned, to his and his daughters watchful care that I recovered, and to his knowledge of medicine.

I do not wish to trouble the reader of this narrative with more than is seemly of my personal affairs, but I must briefly refer to what proved the happiest event of my life. After having seen so much of Mary Bent, I felt that no pain could be greater than that of having to part from her, and I found also to my joy that she had given me her affection. We at once told all to Mr Bent.

"My only regret, if I have one, David, is, that you are not a missionary," was his reply. "I had wished Mary to have become the helpmate of one entirely devoted to the glorious service of our Lord and Master."

"But, sir, surely without being set aside exclusively for the work of a missionary, I may labour not without effect in the Lord's vineyard," I answered, promptly, for I had often read and often felt how much might really be done by a Christian layman in the cause of Christ.

"True, true, David, and I pray God that you and many more like you may thus labour in whatever course of life you are called," answered the missionary. "I believe you, indeed I may say that I know you, to be (as far as one man can judge another) a true and sincere Christian, or no consideration would induce me to entrust my child to you. I do, however, give her to you with confidence that you will watch over her spiritual, as I am assured you will over her temporal welfare."

I will not repeat more that Mr Bent said to me on the occasion. The exhortation he then uttered I have repeated often to others. Husbands and wives, do you watch over each other's spiritual welfare? Are you each jealously watchful over every word and action which may lead the other into sin? With whom do you associate? In what sort of amusements do you indulge? What sort of places do you prefer to visit? In these matters your consciences do not accuse you. Very well. But do you pray together, and pray aright? Do you read the Scriptures together? Are you constantly pointing out to each other the heavenward way? Do you more earnestly desire each other's salvation than all the wealth the world can give, than all earthly blessings? Have you assured yourselves that you will meet together before the great white throne clothed in the bright robes of the Lamb? Surely those alone are truly happy and fitly

W. H. G. Kingston

matched who can answer yes, yes, in a joyful chorus, to such questions.

It would be profitable if I could repeat many of the remarks made to me from time to time by Mr Bent. "How sad it is that seamen are generally so ignorant of their awful responsibilities, and of the immeasurable amount of good they have it in their power to effect in the Christian cause during their visits to foreign lands," he one day observed to me. "Ay, alas! and to think of the immeasurable amount of harm they by their too general conduct produce. Thousands and thousands of professed Christian seamen are found every day in the year at seaports inhabited by heathens. Into what disrepute do they too generally bring Christianity, instead of exhibiting its beauty and excellence by the propriety and correctness of their lives—I will not say, as I could wish, by their purity and holiness.

"It is impossible to calculate the amount of harm nominally Christian seamen have produced among these islands of the Pacific. There have been bright exceptions, especially among the British ships of war happily commanded by Christian officers; Sir Everard Home, Captain Waldegrave, and others—names that will ever be honoured among the isles of the Pacific. Several masters of whalers and merchantmen also have come here and done credit to the Christian character; but the larger number, with their crews, have done incalculable mischief to the hapless natives, and when they have found their evil practices opposed by the missionaries of the gospel, they have wreaked their revenge by spreading on their return home reports intended to injure them, and to prevent the spread of Christianity among the isles of the Pacific. God ever protects those labouring earnestly in His cause; and although these reports have done little harm at home, they will have to render up a tremendous account for their own doings among the inhabitants of Polynesia. The missionaries and their supporters only desire that those at home should read their statements as well as the reports of their traducers, feeling assured that every impartial judge will pronounce a verdict in their favour. The missionaries to the Pacific desire that their fellow-men should approve their proceedings, not for their own sakes (for to their Master they joyfully and confidently commit their cause), but that their so glorious cause may not suffer, and may obtain the required support."

But to return to my narrative.

CHAPTER THIRTEEN

THE ROMANCE OF MISSIONS

I have not described the mission station where I had spent the last few weeks. It was beautifully situated on gently rising ground backed by lofty hills wooded to their very summits. Here and there dark and rugged masses of rock might be seen peeping out from amid the trees and streams of sparkling water falling down their sides far away below into basins of foam, and then taking their course in rapid, bubbling rivulets towards the blue sea. The windows of the house, which were very large to admit a free current of air, and were shaded by a deep-roofed verandah, looked on one side up towards the hills, and on the other over the boundless ocean. The interior was a pattern of neatness. The furniture, though simple, was pretty and well made, with snowy white curtains to the windows and beds, and green blinds to keep out the glare of that hot clime. The verandah ran completely round the house, and a thick thatch of leaves formed a roof which effectually prevented the sun's rays from penetrating below. In front was a pretty flower-garden, and in the rear a well-stocked kitchen garden, producing in perfection all the native vegetables, fruits, and roots, as well as many from Europe. The islanders there saw even their own fruits and roots increased in size, and improved in flavour by careful culture. Near it was a cool grove of cocoa-nut palm and bread-fruit trees, through which a fresh current of trade wind was continually blowing.

The church, although built by the natives of wood—under the direction of course of Mr Bent—was a commodious and imposing edifice. The school-house was also a large and neat building. In its neighbourhood was a long street of cottages inhabited by natives, constructed after the plan of the teachers' dwellings—some of stone or rather rock coral, and others of wood—all having both flower and kitchen gardens, while round the settlement were extensive fields where the chief food for the support of the community was produced. Of the many missionary stations which I have visited, all are more or less like the one I have described. The missionaries have thus not only taught the natives of these wide-scattered islands the truths of the gospel, but by practically showing them the very great advantages which civilised men possess over savages, they have induced them to become industrious, and to learn those elementary arts by which alone their civilisation can be advanced and secured. However, it must be remembered that very few communities are so favourably placed that they can advance far in civilisation unless they have the means of exchanging the produce of their labour with that of other people, and on this account Mr Bent was very anxious to obtain another vessel in lieu of one which had been lost, so that he might enable the natives under his special charge to trade with other islanders, and might at the same time convey missionaries and teachers wherever they might desire to move.

I offered to assist in building such a craft—a schooner which could be easily handled—and afterwards to take command of her should the *Golden Crown* not return for me. In the event of her appearing, I hoped that still Captain Buxton would give me my discharge; but should he be unwilling to comply with my wish I purposed returning out to the island as soon

W. H. G. Kingston

as possible, that I might marry Mary Bent, and then commence the very important undertaking I had proposed.

That no time might be lost, we forthwith drew out the plan of our vessel. I was still unable to move about to assist Mr Bent; he, however, at once set the natives to work to cut down the necessary trees, and to prepare the timber. When we remembered how much that great and good missionary, Williams, had accomplished single-handed, we agreed that we ought not to be daunted by any difficulties which might occur. We had already an ample supply of tools, a carpenter's and a blacksmith's workshop, and several of the younger natives had become, if not perfectly skilled, at all events very fair artisans; indeed, fully capable of performing all the rougher work, both of wood and iron, which would be required. Indeed, I may say, that in a great degree they made up for their want of skill by their teachableness and anxiety to do their work in a satisfactory manner. They understood as clearly as we did the importance of the undertaking, both on account of the worldly advantage it might prove to them, and the benefit of a religious character the vessel might convey to others. The more I saw the work progressing as I lay helpless on my couch, and the more I thought of the benefit, not one alone, but a fleet of such vessels, might prove to the Pacific isles, the more eagerly I prayed for my recovery, that I might take my share in it. It was indeed a joyful day when at length I was able to go out and join the rest, even although only for a short time, in the work.

I had brought my uncle's journal with me that I might lend it to Mr Bent, as I felt sure that he would be interested in reading it. "The perusal of that manuscript has caused me tears of joy and thankfulness," he observed, as he returned it to me. "Wonderful, under God's providence, are the changes which have been wrought among the inhabitants of a large portion of Polynesia since the time of which he wrote. They have indeed truly been called from out of darkness into light; and even those who have not been converted, benefit by the light which shines among them. The description he gives of their spiritual condition and of the scenes which were constantly enacted among them is indeed most true. You see what they have become; you see order and civilisation prevailing among those who were considered the most savage and debased; places of worship, educated and enlightened ministers, well-regulated schools, a large proportion able to read the word of God in their own tongue; but you are not acquainted with the means by which this glorious change has been wrought—with what may be called 'the transition state' of Polynesia. One of the chief reasons why people at home are incredulous as to the present condition of these islands is, that they are ignorant of the events which have occurred, and of the nature of the instrumentality which has been employed. They say that man could not have done it, and, therefore, that it cannot have been done. They are right in saying that man could not have done it, but it has been done by the Holy Spirit of God working by means of human agency; weak things have indeed been employed to confound the strong."

I was seated with Mr Bent and his daughter at our evening meal—the labours of the day being over—enjoying the cool sea breeze, which blowing through the room afforded us that strength and refreshment which our frames, exhausted by the heat, greatly required. I assured him how thankful I should be to have the account he offered, confessing that except with respect to the islands at which we had touched, and where I could judge of the changed state of the people, I was still very ignorant of the condition of the principal part of the inhabitants of Polynesia. Indeed, I owned, that had I believed the accounts given in two works we had on board, I should have supposed that the inhabitants had rather suffered than benefited by the advent of missionaries among them, and

W. H. G. Kingston

that from being light-hearted, happy beings, they had become morose, discontented, and inhospitable. I mentioned Kotzebue's "Voyage round the World," in which work the author abuses the missionaries in unmeasured terms, and another by a Mr Beale, the surgeon of a South-Sea whaler, who, in a book full of valuable descriptions of whales, and the mode of catching them, loses no opportunity of showing his dislike to missionaries, and the principles they have inculcated on their native converts.

"Yes, indeed," said Mr Bent; "I might mention several other works of a similar character, which, I believe, have prevented many persons from supporting missions to these seas, or served as an excuse to them for not doing so; but I also have many works written by men of high standing, and thoroughly unprejudiced as witnesses, who do full justice to the labours of my missionary brethren, or rather, I would say, to the results which by their instrumentality have been produced. The Hon. Captain Keppel (now Admiral Yelverton), of HMS *Meander*, who visited these islands in 1850, will, I know, speak in favourable terms. Captain Erskine, of HMS *Havannah*, has done so in a very interesting work on the `Islands of the Pacific' Captain Wilkes, of the United States navy, in his `Voyages round the World,' speaks most favourably of the result of missionary enterprise; and so indeed do many other naval officers of both nations. I myself must be considered as an impartial witness to the magnitude of the work which has resulted from the labours of the agents of the various societies which have sent the gospel of peace to the islands of these seas. On being rescued from more than death by your uncle I was received back as a returned prodigal by my family, and was enabled to pursue a course of studies which would fit me for the work to which I had resolved to devote myself. My father, when he consented to my wishes, made the proviso, however, that I should not connect myself with any religious body for the purpose, or act as the agent of any missionary society, but that I should go forth by myself, relying on the funds which he would place at my disposal. While he lived he supported me liberally, enabling me to marry and to bring out a wife to be the sharer of my toils, and on his death he left me an income which has been sufficient, with that derived by my own labours, for all my wants. I have thus been able, by means of the little vessel I spoke of, to move about among the islands as I judged best, and often to render assistance to brother ministers of various denominations, whose work had become too great for their strength. I do not speak of the mode of proceeding I adopted, to induce others to follow in the same course, but simply to explain how it is that you find me unattached to any missionary society, and yet acquainted with the transactions of all those labouring in this part of the world. I propose, my young friend, that you may the more clearly understand the present spiritual condition of these Pacific isles, to give you a brief sketch of what I consider the four great prominent events which have taken place connected with them, and almost immediately, I may say, under my own eye—events of importance unspeakable, as marking the signal overthrow of Satan's power. First, the declaration by the king of Tahiti, one of the Georgian Islands, of his conviction of the truth of Christianity, and of his desire to become a servant of the true God, on the 12th June, 1812, just fifteen years after the arrival of the missionaries in that group, followed imme- diately by the open profession of several natives of Tahiti. The second event occurred in November, 1819, when King Rihoriho, of Hawaii, one of the Sandwich Islands, in one day breaking through the most revered of heathen customs, set fire to the temples, and destroyed the idols, a few months before the arrival of the missionaries, who were then on their way to attempt the conversion of his people. The third event occurred in 1829. It was the conversion of a powerful chief of the Friendly Islands, who afterwards became King George

W. H. G. Kingston

of Tonga. Some time before this, two Tahitian teachers connected with the London Missionary Society, on their way to Fiji had resided with Tubou, chief of Nukualofa. Under their influence and instruction Tubou gave up the Tonga gods, destroyed the spirit house, and erected a place for Christian worship, in which he and his people, to the number of two hundred and forty, assembled to listen to Divine truth in the Tahitian language, on the 4th of February, 1827. He was not, however, baptised till 1830. A fourth event, which appears still more wonderful to those who know the man than any I have before mentioned, was the conversion of the fierce and proud cannibal, King Thakombau, of Bau, the most powerful among the chiefs of Fiji, on the 30th April, 1854. He may, indeed, be considered the king of all Fiji, for all the other chiefs are either his vassals, or vassals to those who acknowledge him as their chief. Although a large number of the inhabitants of the group, of all ranks, had embraced Christianity before the king, yet his conversion more especially marked the triumph of the truth in Fiji, and proves the power of the gospel to change the heart of a man, however benighted, savage, and bloodthirsty he may have been.

"To these more prominently important events may be added the establishment of a church at Raratonga, in May, 1833, ten years after the landing of the first native teacher, which went on increasing till the entire population had been brought under Christian instruction.

"Still more important than the former events was the arrival of Messrs. Williams and Barff at Samoa, with a band of native teachers, in 1830, at the moment when Tamafaigna, a despot, who united the supreme spiritual with great political power, and whose boundless sway presented a most formidable barrier to the introduction of the gospel, had just been slain, and their cordial reception by Malietoa, a chief of an acute and inquiring mind and amiable disposition, who himself, with his sons, and their wives and children, soon afterwards renounced their superstitions, and destroyed the only idol found in Samoa. The population, when the missionaries landed, amounted to forty thousand, who, though not so cruel and bloodthirsty as that of other groups, were still sunk in the lowest depths of pagan ignorance and misery.

"I have watched too the partial establishment of Christianity among the native inhabitants of New Zealand, and its extension thence northward, as also from the east among the islands of Western Polynesia—the New Hebrides, New Caledonia, and the Loyalty and Britannia Islands. Still the great work is progressing. New labourers are appearing in the field. From all directions the heathen are crying out for instruction in the wonderful gospel, and more and more labourers are required to supply their urgent wants. A very remarkable feature in this great work is the mode in which it has been accomplished. The number of educated white men engaged in it has been comparatively very small. The most unexpected results, the greatest triumphs have been brought about through native agency. The natives of the Society Islands and Hervey group especially, instructed by English missionaries, and inspired by the Holy Spirit, have, with love in their hearts for their perishing brethren and a burning desire for their conversion, gone forth, braving all perils, some to the surrounding, others to far distant islands, and their language being similar, they have at once been able to address their heathen inhabitants. Many have died from sickness, others have been murdered by those they came to help, but the remainder have persevered till they have seen the cause of the gospel triumphant.

"Oh, Mr Harvey, I wish that others were impressed as I am with the awful thought that day after day thousands upon thousands of heathen are perishing in darkness and sin who might, did their Christian fellow-men use more exertion, have had the glorious gospel preached to them, and have been brought to see the light. I will illustrate the remarks I have made," said Mr Bent, "by examples as they occur to me, keeping, as much as my memory will allow, to the sequence of events."

* * * * *

To the testimonies referred to in the foregoing chapter may be added that given by Dr Seemann, in "Viti: An Account of a Government Mission to the Vitian or Fijian Islands in the years 1860-61." He was sent out by the English Government to ascertain the fitness of the group for the production of cotton. He was absent only thirteen months from England, and had time not only to sow the seed, but to pluck the cotton which it produced. Speaking of the missionaries to the group, he says: "It was all up-hill work; yet results have been attained to which no right-minded man can refuse admiration. According to the latest returns, the attendance on Christian worship in 1861 was 67,489, and there were 31,566 in the day-schools. For the supervision of this great work the Society had only eleven European missionaries and two schoolmasters, assisted by a large class of native agents who are themselves the fruits of mission toil, and some of whom, once degraded and cannibal heathens, are becoming valuable and accredited ministers of the gospel." Dr Seemann is a naturalist, and certainly is not prejudiced in favour of the Wesleyans, or of any other religious body. His evidence is therefore of more value. A description of the condition of Fiji as it was is sickening; and yet it is necessary to show the depth of depravity to which human nature can sink, and the glorious change which the gospel can work even in savages such as these. They were constantly at war with each other, and often fought for no other purpose than to procure people for their ovens. They have been known even to bake men alive. Often a town was attacked, and all the inhabitants, sometimes four or five hundred in number, were slaughtered. When the son of a great chief arrived at manhood, it was the custom to endue him with his *toga virilis* on the summit of a large heap of slaughtered enemies; and the whole population of a town was ruthlessly murdered for no other purpose than to form such a heap.

When a chief received a visit from a brother chieftain, if he had no captives ready to kill, he would kill some of his own slaves, or send out to catch some men, women, or children from a neighbouring island, or from among his own people. Indeed, no man, whatever his rank, was safe; and hundreds thus lost their lives every year, that the cannibal propensities of the chiefs might be gratified.

Infanticide was common among the chiefs as well as among the lower orders; and mothers, abandoning all natural affection, considered it no crime to kill their children. It was an ordinary matter for children to bury their aged parents alive; and fathers and mothers have been known to bury alive their grown-up sons who might complain of illness, or have become weary of life, stamping down on their graves with the greatest unconcern.

On the death of a chief his favourite wives were invariably strangled with him. Numerous slaves also were killed, to form his band of attendants to another world; and a great cannibal feast was also held. Human victims were offered to their obscene deities by their priests in their temples, groves, and high places. When a house was to be built for a chief, four live slaves were placed in deep holes to support the corner posts, when the earth was filled in on them, that their spirits might watch over the edifice. When a large canoe was to be launched victims were clubbed, or the canoe was drawn

W. H. G. Kingston

over their living bodies like the car of Juggernaut, crushing them to death. For the slightest offence a chief would club to death one of his wives, or any of his people, and feast afterwards on their bodies.

But enough has been said to show the character of the people of Fiji. They are, especially the chiefs, tall, handsome men; and though their skin is black, they have not the features of negroes. They are also very intelligent, active and energetic.

Dr Seemann says, page 77 of his work, "Until 1854, Bau, which is the name of the metropolis as well as of the ruling state, was opposed to the missionaries, and the ovens in which the bodies of human victims were baked scarcely ever got cold. Since then, however, a great change has taken place. The king and all his court have embraced Christianity; of the heathen temples, which by their pyramidical form gave such a peculiar local colouring to old pictures of the place, only the foundations remain; the sacred groves in the neighbourhood are cut down; and in the great square, where formerly cannibal feasts took place, a large church has been erected. Not without emotion did I land on this blood-stained soil, where probably greater iniquities were perpetrated than ever disgraced any other spot on earth. It was about eight o'clock in the evening; and, instead of the wild noise which greeted former visitors, family prayer was heard from nearly every house.

"To bring about such a change has indeed required no slight efforts, and many valuable lives had to be sacrificed; for although no missionary in Fiji has ever met with a violent death, yet the list of those who died in the midst of their labours is proportionately great. The Wesleyans, to whose disinterestedness the conversion of these degraded beings is due, have, as a society, expended 75,000 pounds on this object; and if the private donations of friends to individual missionaries and their families be added, the sum reaches to the respectable amount of 80,000 pounds."

Dr Seemann describes a visit to the island of Lakemba, hallowed as the spot on which the first Christian mission was established. Mr Fletcher, the resident missionary, conducted him and his companions through a grove of cocoa-nut palms and bread-fruit trees to his house, a commodious building, thatched with leaves, surrounded by a fence and broad-boarded verandah, the front of the house looking into a nice little flower-garden, the back into the courtyard.

The ladies gave them a hearty welcome, glad to look once more upon white faces, and to hear accounts from home. Though the thermometer ranged more than 80 degrees Fahrenheit, the thick thatch kept off the scorching rays, and there was a fresh current of trade wind blowing through the rooms. It was pleasing to see everything so scrupulously neat and clean; the beds and curtains as white as snow, and everywhere the greatest order prevailed.

"There are the elements of future civilisation,—models ready for imitation,—hallowed homes which no Romish priest can afford," observes the Doctor, "the yard well-stocked with ducks and fowls, pigs and goats,—the gardens replete with flowers, cotton shrubs twelve feet high, and bearing leaves, flowers, and fruit in all stages of development. These missionary stations are fulfilling all the objects of convents in their best days, and a great deal more; for their inmates are teaching a pure and simple faith in Jesus, which those of the convents did not."

Mr Fletcher showed them over the town, the first spot in Fiji where Christianity was triumphant and a printing-press was established, from which was issued an edition of the whole Bible in the language of the people, and several other works.

W. H. G. Kingston

There exist, indeed, two versions of the Bible in the language of Fiji. The church in the town is a substantial building, capable of holding three hundred people. There are some thirty other churches in the Lakemba district alone.

From Lakemba, occupying a week on the voyage, they proceeded to the island of Somosomo, till lately one of the strongholds of idolatry and cannibalism. Golea, the king, was a heathen, but his chief wife, Eleanor, was a Christian, and they believed a sincere one, judging from the almost frantic manner in which she endeavoured to obtain a Fijian Bible seen in their possession. She exhausted every argument to get it, and her joy was indescribable when her wishes were acceded to.

Dr Seemann writes: "If the Wesleyan Society had more funds at its disposal, so as to be able to send out a greater number of efficient teachers, a very few years would see the whole of Fiji Christianised, as all the real difficulties now in the way of the mission have been removed. On my representing the case in this light, his Majesty the King of Hanover was graciously pleased to subscribe his first gift of 100 pounds towards so desirable an object, at the same time expressing his admiration for the labours of the individual missionaries I named."

CHAPTER FOURTEEN

FROM DARKNESS TO DAYLIGHT

"My dear young friend," said Mr Bent, addressing me, in continuation of the subject on which he had before been speaking, "we should never despair while God is with us of the success of our labours among the heathen. In my experience I have known numerous instances in which, when it appeared that profound darkness rested on the land, light has burst forth and spread far and wide around.

"I believe that thirteen years had passed after the *Duff* had made her most successful voyage to these seas in 1796, and landed a large body of missionaries at Tahiti, before one single acknowledged convert to Christianity was made. Still the diminished band of missionaries laboured on. They obeyed God's express command to preach the word to all creatures, and they knew that His word would not return to Him void. God works through human agency, and it must be confessed that many of these missionaries were not fitted by education for the work they had undertaken. It may be said with justice that therefore they did not succeed. Still they laboured on, teaching many the principles of Christianity although none turned to the truth.

"Pomare, the king of Tahiti, although he was friendly to the missionaries, for long remained as determined a heathen as any of his people. At length, however, attacked by his own subjects, he could not protect the missionaries, and the larger number were compelled to retire to the island of Huahine, where they hoped to be in safety. So little progress did they appear to be making even here in their undertaking, that, with one exception, the following year they left Huahine and retired to New South Wales, thus bringing the once promising mission to the Society Islands to a termination. I refer to this time to show you how necessary it is that missionaries should not under any circumstances despair of success. Nothing could be more hopeless than this mission now seemed. Pomare, although he befriended the missionaries, remained still seemingly as dark and determined a heathen as at first, and he had now indeed no longer the power of helping them. He had, however, received a considerable amount of instruction from them. He had acquired the arts of reading and writing his own language, and had learned the first principles of Christianity.

"The seed had not, as was supposed, been sown on stony ground, though it took long in growing up. Adversity caused Pomare to think. He had been told that Jehovah is a God of purity and holiness, and he began to reflect that the life he and his people led must be very distasteful to such a God, and might be the cause of the sufferings he was enduring. The Holy Spirit seemed to apply the truth, so that he at length comprehended the nature of sin, and especially felt his own great sinfulness. He, therefore, wrote letter after letter, entreating the missionaries to return. With joy they accepted his invitation. On their arrival, the king and several of his people professed their belief in the new religion; but a coalition of heathen chiefs being formed against them, some severe fighting took place. The heathens were defeated. Pomare treated them with great leniency, allowing no one to be injured, and even sending the body of a chief killed in battle back to his own people to be buried. So great was the effect of this conduct that the heathen party became anxious to know more of the new faith, and in a few months the idols of Tahiti were thrown to the ground. Although Pomare and some of his chiefs, as well as the lower orders, had embraced Christianity in spirit as well as in name, the mass of the people remained, as might have been expected, ignorant of its principles, and indulged in habits the very reverse of those it inculcates. Still the true faith went on taking root downwards and bearing fruit upwards. In 1817 a large number of missionaries arrived from England at Eimeo. Among them came two whose names are known far beyond their spheres of action—William Ellis and John Williams. The following year some of them removed to Huahine, the principal of the Leeward or Society group, and soon after John Williams and Mr L Threlkeld, invited by Tapa and other chiefs of Raiatea, settled in that island. Similar invitations were received from the chiefs of other large islands, while native teachers were sent to the smaller islands which were also occasionally visited by the missionaries. Thus in a few years the entire population of the Georgian and Society Islands had renounced idolatry, and were in general outwardly very strict in their religious observances. I say outwardly, because many of those who attended religious worship and refrained from all work and amusement on the sabbath, still continued in the practice of heathen vices. Yet I believe that at that very time the great mass of the people were not more ignorant of Christian truth, nor more vicious, than are too many communities of like size in so-called Christian Europe. We should judge of people who have lately been brought out of a savage state, not by a standard which we should wish them to attain, but by other people who have long been considered civilised Christians; and thus judging of the inhabitants of Tahiti and the neighbouring islands, I am certain that they will not lose by comparison with many of those who have claimed for centuries to be civilised, and whose religion has long been nominally Christian. I say this with confidence, but after all it is not saying much in their praise. One thing, however, is very clear. A few years ago they were ignorant barbarians, savage and debased, not knowing right from wrong. Now they abstain from their former cruel and sanguinary practices, they go about clothed and live in neat cottages, and industriously cultivate the ground; they can generally read and write their own language, and have learned many mechanical arts; they understand the principles of Christianity, attend Divine worship, and respect the sabbath, while undoubtedly some, and perhaps many, have been 'created anew in Christ Jesus unto good works,' and not a few have risked their lives, and laid them down for the gospel's sake. A large number of the native teachers who have gone forth among the savage tribes of the wide-scattered islands of the ocean to carry to them the glad tidings of salvation, have come from Tahiti and other parts of the Georgian and Society Archipelago.

"Great as was the change, after all allowances are made, in the islands of which I have been speaking, that produced by the promulgation of the truth in Raratonga was still greater. You know how John Williams, after founding the church in Huahine, moved to Raiatea, in the Hervey group, and thence sailing forth, discovered the then savage Raratonga, where the devoted Papehia landed to commence the work which he was afterwards enabled to perfect. Papehia began his ministrations by telling the people about the power and purity of God, and His love to mankind, and contrasting His attributes with those of their idols. By teaching both old and young portions of Scripture, and the latter to read, they began to perceive the follies of heathenism.

"Thus the old religion was undermined, and a way prepared for the introduction of the new faith. The priests were the most inveterate opponents of Christianity, yet the first person who destroyed his idols was a priest. Several others followed his example. Soon another native teacher from Tahiti joined Papehia to aid in the work which so rapidly progressed. The first chief converted was Tinomana. After a lengthened conversation with Papehia, in spite of the expostulations of priests and people, saying, `My heart has taken hold of the word of Jehovah,' he ordered a servant to set fire to his idol and his temple. The Christians now united, with Tinomana at their head, to live together in one community, numbering four or five thousand. Not fifteen months after Papehia landed, they erected a chapel three hundred feet long, with a pulpit at either end, from which each teacher addressed nearly fifteen hundred wild, naked savages at once, without inconvenience. This wonderful change had been effected, you must remember, by two native teachers alone, in less than two years and a half from the day of their landing in Raratonga, and who were themselves born heathens and trained in idolatry in an island nearly seven hundred miles away.

"Four years after the discovery of the island, John Williams took up his abode there with the Reverend C Pitman, they being afterwards joined by the Reverend A Buzacott. Laws were now formed, and the first Christian community divided into two separate villages. A chapel of a substantial character was next planned. A site was cleared, large trees were cut down, coral lime was burned, the timber was sawn, and in two months from the commencement an edifice an hundred and fifty feet long and fifty-six feet wide, the thatched roof supported on either side by seven iron-wood pillars twenty-five feet high, was erected. There were ten doors, three at each side and two at each end, and twenty windows, with large Venetian blinds. This chapel was a substantial proof of the zeal of the Christian converts; but the heathens were still numerous and powerful, and at length, hoping to overthrow the new faith, they attacked the settlement, and burned the

W. H. G. Kingston

chapel and many of the Christians' houses. A fearful storm and flood and a severe epidemic followed, carrying off hundreds of the natives. Though severely tried, the missionaries were not cast down. The heathen retired, the epidemic ceased, the damage caused by the storm was repaired, and the work of civilisation proceeded.

"It became expedient to form a new village for the immediate followers of Tinomana. A site was fixed on, the land was cleared, and in a few months the village was completed. It was nearly a mile and a half in length; a wide and straight road, gravelled with sea-side sand, was made from one extremity to the other, on either side of which were rows of the tall and beautiful tufted-top 'ti' trees. The houses were built of lime and wattle, each about forty feet long, twelve high, twenty wide, and divided into three or four rooms. They stood back some fifty yards from the road, and were that distance from one another. About the centre, on one side of the street, was the chapel, and on the other the school-house. A belt of trees protected the settlement on the sea-side, while inland rose ranges of picturesque mountains, the intervening space being occupied by pastures and fields cultivated or in the course of cultivation. I remember the scene well. It gave me an indescribable feeling of satisfaction when I first saw it, for it proved that a very great change must have been wrought in the habits of the people, and I trusted that their spiritual condition had likewise been much improved. This was the first on the same plan of many villages which were erected as Christianity spread among the people. At each village, or even where there was a chapel alone, a school-house was erected, where the elements of reading, writing, arithmetic, and geography, were taught to adults as well as to children, and only eight years after the landing of Papehia, two thousand children and one thousand six hundred adults were under instruction. Although many of the adults could never be taught to read, they learned portions of Scripture, and as they willingly listened to the teachers, the truth gradually spread among the whole population.

"A printing press was during this year of 1831 introduced into the island, and the first native Raratongan teacher went forth to carry the glad tidings of salvation to the people of the Samoan group, then lying in darkness. `Teava' was one of the first converts made by Papehia, and a devoted imitator of the noble example he set. He wrote earnestly, praying to be allowed to go Samoa, thus expressing himself: `My desire is very great to fulfil Christ's command when He said, "Go ye into all the world." My heart is compassionating the heathen, who know not the salvation which God has provided. Let me go. Why this delay?' He was conveyed to Samoa, and gained a position among its then savage people at Monono, where he has proved one of the most consistent pioneers to the European missionaries, and one of the best native assistants both in the schools and in translating the Bible and other works. A letter he wrote to his friends in Raratonga a few years afterwards is worthy of note. In it he says: `When I left you, the good work had not taken much root, but now I hear it has spread over the land. All the people have received it. My friends, be diligent in the use of the means, in learning, in reading, in hearing, in prayer; search the word of God. But I will ask you, Do you expect to be saved by your works? No; no man can thus be saved. Salvation is obtained through Jesus. There are two kinds of scaffolding, one of banana stalks and the other of iron-wood: those who trust in their own works are resting on the banana stalks, and will fall; but let our minds be fixed on Jesus alone, and we shall be safe.' Such are nearly the exact words he used. They prove the soundness of his knowledge and faith. The glorious work progressed wonderfully in Raratonga. Churches and schools were built at all the settlements, and several works printed by natives, under the superintendence of the missionaries, issued from the press. I was present on the arrival of the *Camden* from England with an edition of five thousand copies of the New Testament in the language of the people, and several missionaries. Crowds came from morning till night to purchase the book, and for many days the missionaries house was more like a bazaar than a private dwelling.

"One day a messenger at full speed arrived from the old chief Tinomana. Seating himself cross-legged on the floor, he asked if a missionary had arrived for his part of the island. On one being pointed out to him as destined to labour in his settlement, he sprang up with an expression of joy, and hastened back at full speed with the intelligence to his chief. This was at Avarua, where a chapel had been erected worthy of description. It was built in a frame, a hundred and forty feet long and forty-five feet wide, filled up with wattle and lime plaster, white as snow. It was well floored, surrounded by a gallery, and had a pulpit and desk at one end. On the day I was there it was filled with sixteen hundred natives, mostly clothed in home-made cloth, the greater number really thirsting for religious knowledge. Next to the chapel stood the school-house filled in the morning with seven hundred children, each class of ten or twelve having its teacher. Near it was the missionaries' cottage, neat, clean, and commodious; and not far off that of the chief, which was large, well-built, and convenient. It was thoroughly furnished with chairs, sofas, tables, and beds, and the floors covered with mats; while on the tables were several books, which he could read with fluency. Ten years before this he and his people were naked savage cannibals. Missionary meetings were held in the island to assist in sending the gospel to other lands. Thus spoke an aged native at one of them to the young people: `Exalt your voices high in praise of God. He has saved you from the pit of heathenism. We your fathers know the character of that pit; some of us were born there. The place on which we are now met was once a place of murder; spears and the sling and stone were our companions; we ate human flesh, we drank human blood. Let us do what we can to send the word of God to those who *are* as once we *were*.' That year three thousand pounds of arrowroot were subscribed for missionary purposes.

"More effectually to carry out this object, it was resolved to establish a missionary college. A piece of ground was purchased, a number of neat stone cottages for the students and a house for resident missionaries, and lecture-halls, one of which was for female classes, were erected. The latter were under the charge of the missionary's wife. Here one hundred men and women have been instructed, a considerable proportion of whom were married couples. Some have been employed on the home stations, and others have gone forth to the Western Islands to prepare the way for European teachers. A boarding-school was also established, where some forty boys have received instruction. At the college the students go through a course of theology, church history, Biblical exposition, biography, geography, grammar, and composition of essays and sermons. For three hours in the morning they are employed in the workshop, and in the afternoon in study, in class, or examination.

"In the Hervey group ten or more stations are well worked by these native teachers; in Samoa four of them have stations; they have introduced the gospel to the Maniiki group; and in Western Polynesia they have successfully preached the truth in the language of the inhabitants, and braved, and several have suffered, martyrdom for the gospel's sake. What should you suppose is the total expense of instructing, clothing, feeding, and lodging these most valuable missionaries? Only five pounds a year; while the entire outlay of their providing for twenty students does not amount to the sum of three pounds a week, or less than a hundred and fifty pounds per annum. Comparatively very few of those educated at the college have fallen away or proved unworthy of the confidence placed in them. Of course there, as elsewhere, the faith of the missionaries has been tried. Storms, and floods, and disease have visited the island; evil-disposed persons have come from other lands and endeavoured to introduce drunkenness, and to turn the unstable to their own bad courses. Still I may safely say, that there are not twenty persons in the island, and very few in the whole group, who do not attend Christian worship.

"A large edition of the whole Bible has been purchased by them; and I may also venture to assert that, in consistency of conduct, in civil and social propriety, in commercial industry and honesty, and in zeal and liberality, they are not behind any other community in the world. The gospel has been introduced and completely established in the Penrhyn Islands, or Maniiki group, as they are more properly called, entirely by native teachers from Raratonga. But I wish to describe to you the progress made by the gospel in Samoa. Before I do so, however, I will give you a sketch of the way in which some of the missionaries I have met, whose duties require them to be stationary, spend their time.

"The missionary in some instances attends the early morning adult service, those present having then to go forth to their daily duties in the field or on the water. In other instances he devotes the hour from six to seven o'clock in dispensing medicine to the sick; from eight to nine he is either at the children's general school in the village, or attending to private advanced classes at home, or discussing public matters with neighbouring chiefs. From nine to eleven he lectures in the class-room; thence till noon he is in the workshop, where the students or the boys at the boarding-school are learning the use of carpenters' tools. Until dinner time, at one, he is in the printing-office, where the natives have been composing, printing, and binding for several hours. During the next hour the students dine and read. From two to three the missionary holds private conversation with members of the church, candidates for church fellowship, or inquirers. Four days in the week Bible-classes are held, and at most stations public services take place three days in the week, from five to six. The missionary and his wife generally walk out from six to seven, visiting any who are sick or unable to come to them. For an hour afterwards he is in his study reading, translating, writing sermons, or looking over proof-sheets. The next half hour is occupied in family prayer, and the last in pleasant and instructive conversation with his family and the natives in his household; and thus closes his day of labour. The missionary's wife is as busy with the women and girls as is her husband with the men and boys, and her influence and example are calculated to produce a lasting effect on the rising generation. With this succession of occupations the missionaries have found time to write and to superintend the printing of numerous works in the language of Raratonga,—works which are eagerly sought for and read by all classes of the community,—the elder of whom were once naked cannibal savages. When you write home, mention this with your own experience, and ask whether they do not consider missionaries worthy of support, and the results they have produced an encouragement to perseverance.

"One remark more. You have often heard of the fearful decrease in the population of these islands. Raratonga has been no exception to the general rule, and yet its circumstances are very different from most others. Its climate is perfectly healthy; no foreigners reside on it; and, as it possesses no harbour, the crews of ships can never land on its shores, as they merely call off for supplies and proceed immediately on their voyage. Before the introduction of Christianity, when the islanders had not the slightest intercourse with Europeans,—were, indeed, entirely unknown,—the deaths must have been as six or eight to one in excess of the births. As Christianity spread, the deaths were as four to one, then as two to one, then but slightly in excess; and now I rejoice to say that the births slightly exceed the deaths. It is easy to account for their decrease while they were heathens,—their wars, and famine consequent on it,—disease, produced by immorality, and infanticide destroyed many, and prevented increase. Christianity at once mitigated these evils, but the effects of many of them still existed, and it has taken years before the population could gain that health and strength which is the reward in this world of virtuous and industrious lives.

"I find it stated that a hundred ships touch at the islands of the group annually, and receive produce of native labour for manufactured wares, amounting to not less than three thousand pounds. We have here a notable example of the way in which civilisation, industry, and commerce result from the establishment of Christianity. The commanders of many of those ships must remember the time when they dared not set foot on these shores, from which they now are sure to obtain the supplies on which the health of their crews and the success of their voyage so greatly depends, and will, I trust, be ready to bear witness that thousands on thousands of the once savages of Polynesia have become Christian in name and character, and truly and completely civilised."

CHAPTER FIFTEEN

PASSING ON THE BLESSING

"When describing missionary enterprise, we cannot dwell too much on the value of native agency, and should therefore endeavour to show the importance of establishing training colleges for native youths," continued Mr Bent, who, once having entered on the subject to which he had devoted his life, showed no desire to drop it. "Humanly speaking, not one-third part of the work which has been done could without native help have been accomplished. Mangaia is a notable example. That island is about twenty miles in circumference, and contains about three thousand inhabitants. When Williams visited them in 1822 with a few native married missionaries, who went on shore for the purpose of remaining, the latter were so barbarously treated by the savage people that they were compelled to return on board the mission ship, thankful to escape without loss of life. Two years afterwards, however, he returned with two zealous Tahitians, Davida and Tiere, who swimming on shore through the surf, as did Papehia at Raratonga, with their books and clothes in a cloth on their heads, landed among the fierce natives. God had so ordered it that their reception was very different from what they had expected. An epidemic had attacked the island, carrying off chiefs and people, the old and young alike: and believing that it was a

W. H. G. Kingston

punishment sent by the white man's God in consequence of the way they had treated the former missionaries, the inhabitants hoped to avert the evil by behaving in a more friendly manner to the new comers. The way was thus providentially prepared for Davida, who laboured on alone for fifteen years,—for Tiere was soon afterwards removed by death,—till assistance was sent him from Raratonga, itself lying in darkness when he commenced his ministrations. He received, however, occasional visits from the missionaries at Tahiti. Twenty years passed by before the Reverend William Gill arrived to spend some weeks among them. He found, with but few exceptions, that the whole population had renounced idolatry. Several large churches and schoolrooms had been built. In one school-room from eight hundred to nine hundred children and young persons were present, who, after singing and prayer, were led in classes to attend public worship. The church was very large, and really handsome. The numberless rafters of its roof, coloured with native paint, were supported by twelve or fourteen pillars of the finest wood, carved in cathedral style. It was crowded,—those unable to get in looking through the windows,—not less than two thousand being present. Still many at that time were very ignorant with regard to scriptural knowledge, though many even of the heathens could read.

"A few years have passed by, the heathens have one by one turned to the truth, and sound scriptural knowledge is possessed by the population generally. A European missionary lives among them. They have built a handsome stone church with a gallery, capable of seating two thousand persons. There exist two other large stone chapels and three stone school-houses, each about seventy feet long and thirty-five feet wide. But what is far more important, there are one thousand six hundred children and adults under daily instruction, besides five hundred members in consistent church communion, leaving but one-third of the population who, though educated and nominal Christians, must be looked on as yet not earnest in spiritual matters. Of the former, some seven or more are at the Raratonga training college, and several have gone forth as evangelists to the heathen many thousand miles away; while there are more than one hundred native teachers in the schools, gratuitously employing themselves in instructing the rising generation. The excess of births over the deaths is very considerable, so that the population, which at one time was diminishing, is rapidly on the increase. Davida is dead. He departed just twenty-five years after he commenced his missionary labours. `Is it right,' he asked, in a humble tone, `for me to say, in the language of Saint Paul, "I have fought the good fight, I have finished my course"? These people were wild beasts when I came among them; but the sword of the Spirit subdued them. It was not I, it was God who did it.' Davida and Papehia, and many other dark-skinned sons of these fair isles of the Pacific, themselves born in darkest heathenism, have gained their crowns of glory in the heavens, never to fade away, which the highly educated inhabitants of civilised Europe may have cause to envy.

"People in England are, I hear, astonished at the rapid progress made by Christianity in these islands, and assert that either the accounts are exaggerated, and that the great mass of the people remain heathens as before, or that if they have become nominal Christians, it is because they have been compelled by their chiefs to embrace the new faith. To this last objection I reply, first: You well know how slight is the influence exercised by the chiefs over the people, and in no island with which I am acquainted would a chief be able to compel his followers to abandon idolatry and embrace Christianity. In the greater number of instances by far, a considerable proportion of the people have become Christians before the chief has given up his idols. Pomare was still an idolater when many of his subjects had been

W. H. G. Kingston

converted. There were numerous Christians in Samoa before Malietoa became one; and services had been, held in Tongatabu before any of the chief men turned to the faith; and already numerous churches had been established in Fiji before Thakombau, the most despotic and fierce of the rulers of the isles of the Pacific, bowed his knee in worship to the true God. People who know how utterly savage and barbarous the natives had become will easily understand that numbers among them were pining for a purer faith, for some system which would relieve them from the intolerable burdens, from the utter misery under which they groaned. When Rihoriho overthrew his idols and burned his temples he knew nothing of Christianity; but he had discovered that his idols were no gods, and that the religion of his fathers was utterly abominable and foolish. In many islands, when a chief lotued before his subjects, he did so at the risk of being deposed by them; and in every direction there are instances of rebellions being raised by the heathens against the chiefs who had professed Christianity. For many years the fact, that whole communities of once cannibal savages had become civilised Christians was denied; and now that the fact can no longer be denied, certain so-called philosophers in Europe are at pains to invent explanations to suit their own theories. The natives might answer them as the blind man restored to sight by Jesus did the Pharisees of old: 'Why, herein is a marvellous thing, that ye know not from whence He is, and yet He hath opened mine eyes.' The explanation which should best satisfy Christians is, that God has worked with us. In His infinite compassion and love He has presented instruments exactly fitted for the work to be accomplished; and though He has thought fit in many instances to exercise the faith and patience of His servants, He has at length made the way clear before them.

"If I desired a particular proof that man has fallen from a high estate, and that he came forth pure and bright, and with a mind capable of rapidly acquiring knowledge, from the hands of his Maker, I should point to these savages, among whom, debased as they are, so many have a yearning after a better existence, a consciousness of sin, a desire to propitiate an offended deity, a weariness of their degraded condition, of the state of anarchy, of the bloodshed and immorality amid which they live. If these and other facts were known in England, though people might still wonder at the great change which has taken place in these islands, they would cease to disbelieve the statements which have been made by missionaries and others on the subject.

"But I must go on with my account. I was going to tell you how Christianity was introduced into Samoa,—and here the guiding hand of God can especially be traced.

"When John Williams sailed from Tahiti on his first long voyage in the *Messenger of Peace*, after visiting the Hervey group, and many other islands, he touched at the Tonga, or Friendly Islands, many of the inhabitants of which had already become Christian. The history of the group I will give you presently. At Tonga, a chief of the Navigator Islands, called Fanea, was met with, who had been eleven years away from home. His wife had become a Christian, and he himself was favourable to the new religion. He offered to accompany Mr Williams, and to introduce him to his brother chiefs. His account of himself being found correct, his offer was accepted, and he and his wife embarked. The voyage was prosperous, and Sapapalii, or Savaii, an island two hundred and fifty miles in circumference, was reached. Fanea now showed how especially fitted he was to assist the missionaries in their task. Calling them aside to a private part of the vessel, he requested them to desire the teachers not to commence their labours among their countrymen by condemning their canoe races, their dances, and other amusements, to which they were much

W. H. G. Kingston

attached, lest in the very onset they should conceive a dislike to the religion which imposed such restraints. 'Tell them,' said he, 'to be diligent in teaching the people, to make them wise, and they themselves will put away that which is evil. Let the "word" prevail, and get a firm hold upon them, and then we may with safety adopt measures which at first would prove injurious.' Fanea was related to Malietoa, one of the principal chiefs of the island, and was therefore, by his influence with his relatives, able to render great assistance to the work. He expressed, however, his fears that a powerful and perhaps an insuperable opposition would be offered by a still greater chief, who was besides a sort of pope or high priest, the head of such religious institution as they possessed. His name was Tamafaigna. Fanea asked after him in a trembling voice. 'He is dead,—killed ten days,—clubbed to death, as he deserved,' shouted the people, in evident delight, showing that they dreaded more than respected him. 'The devil is dead,—the devil is dead,' cried Fanea. 'There will now be no opposition to the lotu.' This was found to be the case. Had the event occurred a few days before, there would have been time to elect a successor. This man was supposed to have within him the spirit of one of the principal war-gods. The tithes of the two large islands had been given him, and in pride and profligacy he had become a pest and a proverb. He had, however, his supporters, who took up arms to avenge him, and among them were his relatives Malietoa and his brother Tamalelangi, who, although they rejoiced at his death, were compelled, according to the custom of the country, to endeavour to punish those who had killed him. Tamalelangi from the first showed himself a warm friend of the missionaries, and, while his brother was engaged in fighting, assisted them to land with their effects and stores, and to establish themselves on shore. Malietoa afterwards proved their warm friend, and four teachers were left with him, and four with Tamalelangi. Their people showed the teachers the greatest kindness, and, as a mark of it, each man who could get hold of a child carried it off to his own cottage, killed a pig for its food, and stuffed it to repletion before he carried it back to its anxious parents. Fanea, too, was unwearied in explaining the advantages of Christianity and the wonderful knowledge possessed by the missionaries, which enabled them to communicate their thoughts merely by making marks on a bit of paper. It is possible that he was somewhat influenced by ambitious motives, and the credit the introduction of Christianity would bring to him. His wife, however, appears to have been a sincere believer, and by her example and exhortations greatly to have forwarded the cause of truth. Malietoa, who inherited all Tamafaigna's political influence, exerted it to the end of his life in favour of the Christians. The truth was not, as it might be expected, to be established without opposition; and on one occasion a large heathen party approached the dwellings of the teachers, resolved on their destruction. Their friends turned out completely armed in native fashion, with clubs, and bows, and slings, and spears, for their defence, not unfrequently expressing in their tone and gesture the untamed ferocity of their nature by their appearance and loud shouts, even when kneeling in the attitude of devotion. Thus the night was spent in expectation every moment of an attack; but when the morning came it was discovered that their foes had disappeared. The native teachers, who could preach as well as instruct in school, made rapid progress. The people began to eat the fish and other creatures which they had formerly worshipped as gods, and dreaded to injure or even to touch. Some daringly devoured them, others cautiously put the dreaded morsels in their mouths, while the awestruck spectators waited as did the people of Melita when Saint Paul was bitten by a snake, expecting to see them swell or fall down dead. From this the natives concluded that Jehovah was indeed the true God, and were about to cast their war-god Popo, a block covered with a piece of matting, into the sea, and had tied a stone round it to sink it, when the teachers rescued the image, that they might present him as a trophy of the triumphs of the gospel.

"The Samoans, though not such gross idolaters, and certainly not so inhuman in their practices, as most of the other islanders in the Pacific, were much degraded both in mind and morals. They are perhaps the finest people in a physical point of view of any, yet they had more pharisaical pride and less consciousness of sin; and this, it is possible, prevented them from adopting some of those cruel practices prevalent among their neighbours.

"The teachers left by Williams laboured perseveringly. Still they could not persuade Malietoa to abandon the war. He went on one occasion to Upolu with all his fighting men, and three of the teachers resolved to follow him, hoping thus to influence him the more. He had allowed his son to join them. On their way they preached the word at several villages through which they passed, and the people heard them gladly. Malietoa was unmoved, and they had to return; but their journey had not been so bootless as they supposed. Scarcely had they reached home, than a messenger arrived from the chief of a village they had visited at Apolulu, begging them to return in haste, as he and his people were waiting to hear from their lips the truths of the gospel. Three of them set out for the settlement, where they were warmly welcomed by the chief and a thousand followers. After the usual salutations, the chief turned to the teachers and said, 'Have you brought a fish spear?' Surprised at this strange inquiry, they replied, 'No! why do you ask for that?' 'I want it,' he answered, 'to spear an eel. This is my *etu*—I will kill, cook, and eat it. I have resolved to become *lotu*.' He then added that he would afterwards spear and eat a fowl, as the spirit of his god was supposed to reside in that also. And these bold designs were no sooner formed than executed, though none of his followers supported him, nor was it till they saw that no evil results were the consequence, that they ventured to imitate his example. Numbers then declared that they wished to become Christians, and to be instructed in that faith. Returning from this expedition, they saw the stronghold of the heathen party in flames. Malietoa treated the conquered party with great leniency, and on one of their battle-fields erected a church to the service of the true God, while Popo, the god of war, was banished for ever. Many other chapels were built in different directions, and the new faith made great progress, though at that time, probably, many of the converts were very far from enlightened Christians. While these events were taking place in the larger islands, a large canoe with some Christians on board was driven on Tau, the most eastern island of the group, having embarked at Ravavai, one of the Austral group, two thousand miles distant, intending to proceed to some neighbouring island. Their lives and their health had been providentially preserved, and they received a friendly greeting from the natives, to whom they imparted a knowledge of the faith they professed. Several joined them, and the little congregation thus formed without a teacher, was looking forward to the arrival of a missionary ship, which they had heard would bring one, when Williams himself touched at their settlement. Soon after this three English missionaries visited the group, and one remained till the arrival of a considerable number, who came out direct from England for especial service in Samoa. The first care of this most efficient body of men was to master the language, and when this was done they lost no time in commencing a translation of the Bible. A printing-press was set up in 1839, and in July of that year printing was commenced in Samoa. The natives took a deep interest in it, and called it the fountain whence the word of God flowed to all Samoa. The native youths quickly learned to work it, and surrounded by numbers of their countrymen, standing as if riveted to the spot, and gazing with intense interest, now speechless with wonder, now shouting with

W. H. G. Kingston

delight, they endeavoured to show with what dexterity they could throw off the sheets. Numerous works were printed by them—sermons, catechisms, hymn-books, works on geography, astronomy, arithmetic, Bunyan's Pilgrim's Progress, and a native magazine. Upwards of 2,000 pounds was paid by the purchasers of the Scriptures and these books.

"In 1844, the `Samoan Mission Seminary' was commenced. It was on a far larger scale than that I have described at Raratonga, though conducted on a very similar plan. It was for a group, it must be remembered, of considerable extent, containing not less than 34,000 inhabitants. Special attention is paid in the institution to the instruction of the wives of the students, and so highly are the labours of these female teachers prized in the islands, that inferior men are sometimes chosen on account of the high qualifications of their wives. I believe that nearly a hundred and fifty teachers have gone forth from the institution, some to labour in Samoa, and others in the Loyalty Islands, New Hebrides and Savage Island—many with their devoted wives having died from the effects of climate or fallen by the murderous hands of the savages to whom they carried the gospel. A high school is attached to the institution, as well as one for the children of the students. There are, I find, fifty boarding-schools in the group, having 800 scholars; 210 children's day-schools with 6,000 scholars, and 210 adult sabbath and day-schools with 7,000 scholars. When first Williams landed at Samoa, the natives wore no clothing except the most scanty of leaves or native cloth. Now I find it stated, that apart from all other articles of foreign manufacture, the demand for cotton goods alone amounts to 15,000 pounds per annum, and is every year increasing. [See Note 1.] I mention these facts because they are beyond dispute, and I beg that you will repeat them when you write home, as they may convince some who deny that the Polynesian savage can comprehend the spirit of the gospel, that at all events he has made considerable advances in civilisation, and that his connection is worth cultivating. You and I, and all who take the trouble of observing, know that he is as capable as the most highly educated European of understanding the whole scope of the gospel in all its beauty and holiness, and accepting it in all its fulness. We must never forget the saying of our blessed Lord, who knew what was in man, 'that many are called but few chosen,' and that this is true in Samoa as elsewhere. Of the many thousands who have become nominal Christians, we have every reason to hope that some—I might dare to say many—have accepted Christ to their eternal salvation. And Samoa forms but one group out of the many thousand isles of this ocean.

"Let us take a glance at Tonga, at which Williams called, as I told you, on that first voyage, so peculiarly blessed to Samoa. You have heard how a body of missionaries so far back as 1797 were landed at Tongatabu, from the ship *Duffy* by Captain Wilson. They were all ultimately compelled to leave the island, very much in consequence of the conduct of some white runaway seamen or convicts, who set the natives against them. Several were ultimately murdered, the rest escaped to New South Wales with the exception of one, who, sad to say, apostatised, and lived as a savage among the savages for some years. More than twenty years passed by, and the savage character of the wrongly named Friendly Islanders prevented any further attempt being made to offer them the gospel of peace; when God put it into the heart of the Reverend W Laury, a Wesleyan minister residing in New South Wales, who had been interested in the people by a widow of one of the early missionaries, to attempt their conversion. He sailed from Sydney in June, 1822, on board the *Saint Michael*, a merchant vessel, with his family, accompanied by a carpenter and blacksmith, both pious young men. He reached Tonga in safety, and remained for upwards of a year, gaining the language of the people, and protected by the chiefs, but without making any converts. On his return to Sydney he left the two young mechanics, and they were afterwards joined by the Reverend John Thomas, a young ardent missionary from England. They had indeed need of faith and patience. The chiefs who at first protected them proved themselves fickle and treacherous, robbing them of all they possessed, and it was evident that they valued their presence among them on account of the property they brought, not for the sake of the religious instruction they would afford. Just before Mr Thomas's arrival at Hihifo, on the west side of Tonga, two native teachers from Tahiti, on their way to Fiji, had landed at Nukualofa on the north coast. The preaching of these devoted men had awakened such a spirit of inquiry, that when Mr Thomas preached at Hihifo, numbers came over a distance of twelve miles to hear him. Tubou, the chief of Nukualofa, appeared convinced of the truths of Christianity, had a chapel built, and attended service; but tempted by his brother chiefs, who promised to make him king of the whole group if he would adhere to the old faith, he declined for the present to make a profession of Christianity. The work thus commenced at Nukualofa by the London Society's Tahitian teachers, was carried on in a spirit of brotherly love by the Reverend N Turner and William Cross and their devoted wives, sent out by the Wesleyan Missionary Society in 1828. They began schools there, which were well attended, while Mr Thomas opened one at Hihifo, at which, in spite of the opposition of the chief Ata, some twenty boys attended. In two years Mr Thomas could preach fluently in the language of the people, and congregations for public worship were formed and well attended. Mr Thomas had gone over to Nukualofa to preach, when the king Tubou, who had been absent for six months, attended, with two hundred of his subjects, the chapel which he himself had built, and where he now heard in his own tongue from the lips of an English minister the gospel clearly explained. Other chiefs from the two groups of islands to the north, Vavau and Haabai, in the course of the year sent to petition for teachers, or rather, one sent, being indifferent about the matter; the latter, Tui-Haabai, as he was called, came to Tonga in person. Though he earnestly pressed the point, there was no one to send; and so on his return home, finding an English sailor who could read and write, though sadly ignorant of the truths of religion, he made him his teacher. His perseverance and earnestness were to be rewarded. A sick lad, a step-son of Ata's, was the first convert at Hihifo, but on his death, the chief still more hardening his heart, it was agreed by the missionaries that Mr Thomas should remove from that station to Haabai. They however first sent one Peter, a native convert, to prepare the way, a plan which has been almost universally successful. The missionaries now spent some time together at Nukualofa, where the field appeared so promising. So indeed it proved; often so crowded was the chapel, that the missionaries went out amid the encampments of their visitors on the sea-side, that they might preach to them the words of eternal life under the free vault of heaven. It was at this time that King Tubou was baptised with his family and nearly thirty men and sixty women of his tribe. It was indeed a day to make the hearts of the long persevering and faithful missionaries rejoice."

To many readers of missionary reports these statements may not be new, but it was pleasant to have such testimony amidst the scenes themselves.

* * * * *

Note 1. See Turner's "Nineteen Years in Polynesia."

"Of an evening," says Lieutenant Walpole, RN, writing of Samoa, "when, taking advantage of intervals of fine weather, we went for a ramble in the delightful woods, the quiet of the grove was often disturbed by a ruthless savage, who would rush out upon you, not armed with club or spear, but with slate and pencil, and thrusting them into your hands, make signs for you to finish his difficult exercise or sum."

Dr Coulter, surgeon of HMS *Stratford*, has given this testimony: "The power of religion has completely altered the naturally uncontrolled character of the natives, and effectually subdued barbarism. The former history of these islanders is well known to all readers. They were guilty of every bad and profane act. Infanticide and human sacrifices, in all their horrid shapes, were common occurrences. Utter abandonment and licentiousness prevailed over these islands (the Friendly Islands). What are they now? The query may be answered in a few words: They are far more decided Christians than the chief part of their civilised visitors."

CHAPTER SIXTEEN

HOW THE LIGHT CAME TO FIJI

"Tui-Haabai Tuafaahan, or George, the name he assumed when he became a Christian, the chief or king of the Haabai Islands, was no ordinary man. He possessed great influence over his people; and in this instance there can be no doubt that, in consequence of his embracing Christianity, great numbers of his subjects immediately professed it. So much was this the case, that out of eighteen inhabited islands of which the group consists, the people of all but two called themselves Christians when Mr Thomas arrived in 1830. Of course they were very ignorant of religious truths; but at the same time they were aware of their ignorance, and desired to be taught,—and what more could a missionary pray for? They consequently made great progress, though the work nearly wore out the missionary. A second, however, the Reverend Peter Turner, joined Mr Thomas the next year. Their wish at once was to extend the sphere of their labours.

"In April, 1831, King George, now himself well able to expound the gospel, with twenty-four sail of canoes, visited Finau, chief of Vavau, who had once sent for instruction to the missionaries at Tonga. With the king went the faithful missionary Peter, bearing a letter from Messrs. Thomas and Turner. King George, too, endeavoured to convince Finau of

W. H. G. Kingston

the truth, and at length he promised to join in worshipping the Lord on the next sabbath. This he did accompanied by several chiefs and others; and when Monday came he directed that seven of his principal idols should be placed in a row. He then addressed them: 'Listen to my words, that you may be without excuse. I have brought you here to prove you.' Commencing with the first, he said, 'If you are a god, run away, or you shall be burned in the fire which is ready for you.' The idol made no attempt to escape. In the same manner he addressed the next, and the next, till he came to the last. As none of them ran, he directed that their temples should be set on fire. The order was at once obeyed, and some eighteen or more with their idols were consumed. George and all his people capable of explaining the truths of Christianity, were employed in preaching and speaking night and day during their stay, so eager were the people to be instructed. All ordinary occupation was suspended. The reply to any expostulation was, 'We can labour when you are gone: let us while you stay learn how to worship God.' Afterwards two native teachers were sent to Vavau, till a missionary could be spared for them.

"Finau, who had himself once strongly opposed the Christians, now met with opposition from one of his own chiefs, who had been absent at Fiji. This chief threw himself into a strong fort; but it was surprised by the Christians, and the insurgents being brought out, it was burnt to the ground, without one person being killed. Mr Cross was soon afterwards appointed to Vavau, and on his voyage there from Tonga his canoe was wrecked, and his wife was drowned besides twenty other persons.

"It was about this time that the Reverend William Yate, of the Church Missionary Society, visited Tonga from New Zealand. He had heard much of the great change among the people, and was disposed to regard part at least as too strange and too good to be true. He therefore went much among the people, observing their domestic habits, and their attention to their religious duties, and he assured the missionaries that what he saw exceeded all that he had heard.

"Christianity was making progress in all the three groups, though in Tonga a powerful body of heathens, under Ata of Hihifo, still remained, when Finau, king of Vavau, died, leaving his government to King George of Haabai, who thus became sovereign of both groups. He and his wife gave full evidence soon after this that they were Christians not only in name, but in spirit and in truth. They were made class-leaders," and the king was appointed a local preacher. He did not presume on his high civil dignity, but always conducted himself in the house of God with becoming humility. One who heard him preach his first sermon told me that the great court-house, more than seventy feet long, could not contain the people who thronged to hear their king. Every chief on the island and all the local preachers were present. The king led the singing. He preached with great plainness and simplicity, and in strict accordance with the teaching of God's word; dwelling on the humility and love of the Saviour, the cleansing efficacy of His atoning blood, and the obligations under which we are laid to serve and glorify Him. But a few years before part of this very congregation might have been seen in this same house preparing guns, spears, and clubs, in order to slay their fellow-men, and waiting to be led forth to battle by the great warrior who was now the royal preacher. He proved his Christianity in another way. Hearing that the English had abolished slavery and that it is abhorrent to the character of the gospel, he that very day called all his slaves together and forthwith gave them their liberty. He next employed himself in building a church upwards of a hundred feet long and fifty wide, the largest building that had ever been erected in Tonga. He also exhibited his wisdom by framing a code of laws, by which

W. H. G. Kingston

all chiefs as well as people were to be equally bound. They were most judicious, and admirably fitted for the wants of the people. Not one professed heathen now remained in the two groups governed by King George, and the blessings he had received he was anxious to send to others. A missionary and several native teachers therefore went forth and established churches in Samoa, as well as in some small islands lying between the two groups. The missionaries were afterwards removed, it having been agreed between the Wesleyan and London Missionary Societies that Samoa should be left entirely under the charge of the London Missionary Society,—a wise resolve, the object of which does not appear to have been very clearly comprehended by the Samoan Christians, accustomed to the Wesleyan form, or by King George, who made a voyage to Samoa to consult about the matter. The reason of the arrangement was, that the Wesleyan Society might be able to devote all their means and energies to the promulgation of the gospel in the Fiji Islands, a work which they forthwith commenced and have carried on with unsurpassed vigour and success. I will describe it to you presently.

"Josiah Tubou, the king of Tonga proper, or Tongatabu though a consistent Christian, was a man every way inferior to King George in energy and talent, and the heathen chiefs and other ill-disposed persons set his power at defiance. They even went so far as to take up arms, in the hope of deposing him. In this, however, they were disappointed; for King George, with a large body of warriors, came to his assistance, and they were compelled to take refuge in certain strongly-built forts in their native districts, where they continued to hold out against his power. The war thus commenced and carried on for some years, proved a sad hindrance to religion and the advancement of civilisation. Two Roman Catholic priests were also landed from a French ship of war, and took up their residence with the heathens, whom they undoubtedly supported against their chief.

"It was while endeavouring to negotiate with the rebels in one of these forts that Captain Croker of HMS *Favourite*, who had with him a party of his ship's company, was shot at and killed. Another officer and several men fell on the occasion, while many were badly wounded. Several forts were taken or yielded, and the defenders pardoned; but the rebels were still holding out in the strongest, that of Bea, where the Romish priests resided, when Sir Everard Home, in the *Calliope*, arrived at Tonga. Several times the fort had been summoned to surrender, and Sir Everard Home had now the satisfaction of witnessing the way in which it was captured, and the leniency with which the rebels were treated, while he and King George himself were instrumental in saving the property of the Romish priests from destruction. From that time King George has been employed in consolidating his power, and in advancing the material as well as spiritual interests of his subjects.

"The success which attended the exertions of the missionaries at Tonga encouraged them to commence the work at Fiji, with which extensive group Tonga has for years been intimately connected, although the inhabitants are of a totally different race and character. I must go back again from the time of which I have just been speaking to the year 1835. Utterly debased and savage as were the people of Fiji at that period, the mission was commenced under peculiarly favourable circumstances. It was especially supported by King George of Tonga, who was much respected by the inhabitants of Lakemba, the spot which had been fixed on as the residence of the missionaries. Many Tongans also resided there, who could at once be addressed in their own language, which was also understood by the chief and many of the people of Lakemba. As many Fijians were living at Tonga, the missionaries were able likewise to prepare and print some books in Fijian. King George's introduction insured them a favourable reception from the chief of Lakemba, who at once gave them ground for the missionary premises. House-building is short work in Fiji, and a large body of natives, having prepared posts, spars, reeds, etcetera, assembled at the chosen site, and commenced operations. On the third day all the furniture, articles for barter, books, clothes, doors, windows, and various stores were landed, and carried to the two houses, of which the families took possession that evening. Lakemba is thirty miles in circumference, and contains, besides the king's town, eight other towns and three Tongan settlements. Many of the people inhabiting them, on their visits to head-quarters saw the mission premises, and went home to tell of what had excited their own admiration. Thus the number of visitors increased, and many becoming dissatisfied with their own gods, and tired with the exactions of the priests, came regularly on the sabbath to worship at the chapel. As they had to pass the king's town they were observed, and abused for presuming, though common people, to think for themselves in the matter of religion, and even daring to forsake their own gods for the new God of whom the strangers spoke. Threats were used, and the Christians would immediately have been persecuted, had not a chief from Tonga, who had come over to protect the Christians from the people of Mbau, himself adopted the new faith, letting it be known that he would protect his co-religionists. They did not escape altogether: their houses were pillaged, and many had to fly for their lives. They however went to other islands, carrying, as did the Christians of old, their religion with them, and were the means of spreading it to other parts of the group. Many of the Tongans heard the word gladly, though hitherto known for their evil doings, and returned home changed in heart and manners. The king of Lakemba even pretended that he wished to become a Christian, though his profession was not sincere, as he continued to persecute the converts. He at last said that he would lotu if some other powerful chiefs would do so; and suggested that the missionaries should go to Mbau and see what change they could effect in the rulers of that notorious cannibal island. Mr Cross took the king at his word, and with his wife and family embarked for Mbau. On his arrival there, he found that war had been raging, that two bodies were in the ovens, and that very little attention to his preaching could be expected. Though Thakombau, the king's son, promised him his protection and a spot of ground for a house, he considered it wiser to proceed to Rewa, a town about twelve miles away on the main island, where the chief promised to protect him, and to allow as many of his people to lotu as desired it. At first Mr Cross preached in the open air; but a chief of some rank and his wife becoming Christians, they opened their house for worship, and a hundred hearers would sometimes assemble there to listen.

"Off the island of Great Fiji is another small island, that of Viwa. The chief, Namosi, and his nephew, Verani, had captured a French brig and destroyed the crew. The captain, it was proved, had allowed his vessel to be used in the native wars, and had even suffered the body of an enemy to be cooked and eaten on board. To punish Namosi, two French men-of-war appeared off the coast, and the crews landing, burned down his town and destroyed his crops. This misfortune seems so to have affected him, that he begged a teacher might be sent to instruct him in the new religion; and to show his sincerity, he built a large chapel, where many of his people joined him in worshipping God. Thus were two centres formed in Fiji, where two men single-handed battled with almost incredible difficulties, cheered, however, by no inconsiderable success,—that is to say, Mr Cargill at Lakemba, and Mr Cross at Rewa.

"In 1838 three missionaries arrived from England. One of them was the devoted John Hunt, who at once volunteered to go to the assistance of Mr Cross, who was already breaking down with his labours at Rewa. With them also came a printer, a printing-press, and book-binding materials. Early in 1839 Saint Mark's Gospel and a catechism in Fijian were printed,—an important event in the history of a people who three years before had no written language, and who seemed sunk in the utter depths of darkness and moral degradation. Fiji was indebted for Mr Hunt to the Christian liberality of a lady—Mrs Brackenbury, of Raithbury Hall, Lincolnshire, who offered to pay all the expenses of his outfit and passage, and 50 pounds a year for three years, provided the committee would send another missionary, and thus raise the number to seven.

"The mission establishment at Rewa drew many visitors, especially the people from Mbau, who came to make inquiries about the lotu. To this place the printing-press was moved, and it was made the head-quarters of the Fijian mission. On an island off Vanua Levu, or the Great Land, was situated the town of Somosomo, the chief of which, who had considerable power, begged that missionaries might be sent to him.

"Accordingly Mr Hunt and Mr Lyth, with their families, went there, and took up their quarters in a large house provided by the chief. He showed clearly, however, that he only required their goods; and not only were the families neglected, but the most horrible cannibal practices took place close to them, encouraged by the chief. His son was wrecked on an enemy's shore, when he and his followers were killed and eaten. In consequence a number of women were murdered, in spite of the entreaties of the missionaries that their lives might be spared, while captives were constantly dragged before their windows to be killed and baked. Ultimately the station was abandoned, and the chief was murdered by one of his own sons, who was himself murdered by a brother; and such anarchy and confusion reigned, that Somosomo was laid almost desolate.

"After a time the remaining chiefs and people, brought low by distress, turned to the God of the strangers, and great numbers became Christians,—showing that the seed had been sown and taken root, though when the missionaries left the island they were disposed to fear that no good had been effected.

"The truth spread by a great variety of means. A chief named Wai, of the far-off island of Ono, tributary to Lakemba, came to that island to pay his dues. He there met with Takai, another Fijian chief, who had visited Sydney and Tahiti, and had become a Christian. With such knowledge as he could thus pick up he returned home. He there taught his people; and so great a thirst for further instruction sprang up among them, that a whaler calling at Ono for provisions, they engaged a passage in her for two messengers who were to beg the missionaries at Tonga to send them a teacher. A long time must have elapsed before one could have reached them; but the Lord knew the desire of their hearts, and took His own means for giving them the spiritual food after which they hungered.

"Early in 1836 a canoe, on board which was Josiah, a converted Tongan, with other Christians, sailed from Lakemba for Tonga, but was driven out of her course to Turtle Island, about fifty miles from Ono. Hearing when there that the people of Ono were seeking after religious instruction, Josiah hastened there to tell them all he could of the gospel. In a short time forty persons became worshippers of God, and a chapel was built to hold a hundred. In the meantime their two messengers reached Tonga, where they were told that as missionaries were now stationed at Lakemba they must apply there for the help they sought. A

W. H. G. Kingston

teacher was found, once a wild youth, who had been converted at Lakemba. Here he remained two years preparing for his work, till he had an opportunity of going to Ono. On his arrival he found that one hundred and twenty adults had become Christians. A strong heathen party was, however, formed against them, and they had more than once to fight for their lives. Even the king of Lakemba threatened to destroy them because they would not give up a young Christian girl who had in her infancy been betrothed to him. A gale drove back the king's canoe, and some of those of his followers were lost; so that he was persuaded that the God of the Christians frowned on his design. The island was visited several times by English missionaries, and at last one was appointed to reside there.

"All the people have now become Christians, and probably fifty agents have been raised up there to carry the gospel to other parts of Fiji. Christianity spread among the islands in the neighbourhood of Lakemba subject to Somosomo. This was in spite of the belief in a threat of the king, that he would kill and eat any of his subjects who should lotu. The king arrived, and hearing of the tale indignantly denied it. He ordered, however, that tribute should be paid to him on Sunday. This the Christians refused to do, but the following day they appeared with their offerings. This produced a favourable impression on the king, showing as it did, what was the genuine effect of Christianity when carried out. No one was punished, though unhappily the king seemed to remain as complete a heathen as before till his death.

"In Lakemba the Christians multiplied, and the whole population of one town, that of Yaudrana, lotued in one day. They had been ill-treated, and two of their number had been killed by the king or his people. Suddenly they came to the conclusion that their own gods could no longer protect them, and they resolved to pray to Jehovah the God of the

Christians. They accordingly sent to Mr Calvert, the missionary. The chiefs of the town met him to speak on the matter, in the principal temple in the place, and after singing and prayer they bowed down to worship God. The following Sabbath the whole population, by agreement, openly abandoned idolatry. The king sent to forbid them, but his message arrived after the ceremony had been performed, and they replied that they would pay him lawful tribute, but would not abandon their new faith. After this movement of the larger number of his subjects, the king himself became a Christian.

"I can with difficulty recollect the numerous events connected with missionary work as they occurred in the wide extending group of Fiji. Of the most important I have not yet spoken. It is necessary to remember the names of three important places: Mbau, though a small island, contains the capital of the powerful chief Thakombau, now called the king of all Fiji. Twelve miles off, on the mainland, is Rewa; and on another small island two miles from Mbau, is Viwa, the residence of Namosimalua, who had become nominally Christian, or was at all events favourable to the Christians. Here Mr Cross took up his abode, when Thakombau refused him admission to Mbau. Thakombau was the son of Tanoa, the chief of Mbau. Mbau had obtained the influence it possessed over other parts of Fiji in consequence of its having become the abode of Charles Savage, a runaway seaman, a horrible ruffian, a Swede by birth, who managed to obtain a large supply of firearms and ammunition, and led her armies for many years against her neighbours of the larger islands, compelling them to become tributary to her. At length, being defeated in Viti Levu, by a party of natives against whom, in conjunction with the master of an English trading vessel, the *Hunter*, of Calcutta, he was carrying on a war for the sake of procuring a cargo of sandal-wood for the ship, he was, together with fourteen of the crew, put to death and eaten, his body being treated with every mark of detestation, and his bones converted into sail-needles, and distributed among the people as a remembrance of the victory. Namosimalua was looked upon as the Ulysses of those regions. He in conjunction with other chiefs, weary of the exactions of Tanoa, rebelled against him, and compelled him to fly, also advising that his young son Thakombau, whose talents he had discovered, should be put to death. This not having been done, he resolved to gain the friendship of Tanoa without committing himself. He therefore offered to go in pursuit of the king, but secretly sent a messenger to warn him of his danger. When Thakombau restored his father to his possessions, Tanoa saved Namosi's life, though the former never forgave him his intentions towards him.

"Among the greatest warriors and fiercest cannibals of Fiji was a nephew of Namosi's, called Verani, who was a firm friend of Thakombau's. At Rewa a mission had been established, but its chief Ratu Nggara remained a heathen, and was a powerful rival of Thakombau. Some time after the establishment of the missions at Viwa, Namosi its chief became a Christian; and as visitors from Mbau and other places visited the mission-house, the knowledge of the new faith spread in every direction around. The fierce warrior Verani even listened to what the missionary had to say, and hopes were entertained that he too might lotu; but his friend Thakombau urged him to remain firm to the old faith, and to join him as before in his wars. At first, Verani yielded to evil counsels; but, happily, again and again he visited the missionary, till he declared his conviction that Christianity was true; and from that day he became as resolute and bold in promulgating the truth, as he had before been in supporting the customs of heathenism. For several years he held a consistent Christian course of life, and his example had probably an influence on his friend Thakombau. His good influence was, however, opposed by some of the abandoned white men, resident on neighbouring islands, who dreaded, should the king turn Christian, that a stop would be put to their own evil doings. They even went so far, when they thought this possible, as to join the natives in carrying on war against him; and so successful were they that on every side he found his power decreasing. What force or persuasion could not effect, affliction accomplished. During the time of his greatest distress he received a letter from King George of Tonga, urging him to delay no longer, but to turn to the God of the Christians. This letter seems to have decided him.

"On the 30th April, 1854, at nine o'clock the death-drum was beaten—the signal for assembling in the great 'Strangers' House' for the worshipping of the true God. Ten days before, its sound had called people together to a cannibal feast. Three hundred persons were present in the ample lotu dress, before whom stood Thakombau, the chief, with his children and wives. The missionary, who had so long watched for this event, was deeply moved, and could scarcely proceed with the service. It was indeed a day to be remembered in the annals of Fiji. After worship, the people crowded round the missionaries, to ask for alphabets, and gathered in groups to learn forthwith to read. The king, after this, caused the Sabbath to be observed. His deportment was serious, and his own attendance at preaching and prayer-meetings was regular. His little boy, about seven years old, had already learnt to read, and he now became the instructor of his parents, who were both so eager to acquire knowledge, that their young teacher would often fall asleep in the midst of his lesson.

"Among the most implacable enemies of Thakombau was the king of Rewa. Elijah Verani undertook a mission to that chief, in the hopes of bringing about peace, when he and most of his companions were traitorously murdered and

W. H. G. Kingston

eaten. Not long after this the king of Rewa himself died, and his people sued for peace.

"Thakombau, the once cannibal and homicide, was not allowed to remain quiet. He had enemies on every side; some of them he conquered in war, but often his life was in danger from his own former associates and relations. The effect, however, was good, as it made him turn more and more to God for pardon through Jesus Christ and to the consolations of religion. At length he triumphed, and his enemies were subdued under him. He had from the first prohibited cannibalism; murder was now declared to be against the law. The first two murderers guilty of the crime before the law was promulgated were pardoned, but the next, though a chief, was tried, and being found guilty of the murder of his wife, was publicly executed by his countrymen at Mbau, the missionary wisely absenting himself at the time. In the same year three chiefs of rank were publicly married, each to one wife, a step afterwards taken by the king himself. Churches were now built in every direction, and thousands of the people of Fiji abandoned their horrible customs, put away their idols, and turned to the true God."

CHAPTER SEVENTEEN

THE COURAGE OF KAPIOLANI

"Although the change in Fiji is very great, much remains to be done. It is not more than we may justly say, that cannibalism and the more abominable crimes once common have ceased to exist wherever English missionaries reside, and in most places where native teachers have gained a footing. The kingdom of peace is making daily progress. The gospel has firmly established itself in the heart of Fiji. Thakombau remains firm and consistent in his profession of Christianity, and though certain chiefs rebelled against him, he has dealt as leniently with them as the maintenance of authority and order will allow, and has striven as far as possible to avoid bloodshed.

"It is satisfactory to see the way Captain Erskine, of HMS *Havannah*, speaks of those who have contributed to bring about this state of things. I cannot refrain from touching on a circumstance which he mentions, redounding as it does so greatly to the honour of the wives of two of the missionaries, Mrs Lyth and Mrs Calvert. It occurred while old Tanoa was still alive, and of course long before Thakombau became a Christian.

"A powerful tribe had sent a deputation to Mbau with tribute,

W. H. G. Kingston

and it was necessary to provide them with a banquet, a portion of which must, according to custom, be human flesh. The chief whose business it was to provide for the occasion, not having any enemies, set forth by night and captured a number of women belonging to a village along the coast, who had come down to pick shell-fish for food. Immediately Namosimalua, the Christian chief, heard of it, he hastened to the missionary station; but the missionaries' wives alone were at home. These heroic women, however, resolved to go themselves, and to endeavour at all risks to save the lives of the captives. Accompanied by the faithful Christian chief they embarked in a canoe for Mbau. Each carried a whale's tooth decorated with ribbons, a necessary offering on preferring a petition to a chief. As they landed near old Tanoa's house, the shrieks of two women then being slaughtered for the day's entertainment chilled their blood, but did not daunt their resolution. Ten had been killed; one had died of her wounds; the life of one girl had been begged by Thakombau's principal wife, to whom she was delivered as a slave, and three only remained. Regardless of the sanctity of the place, it being tabooed to women, they forced themselves into old Tanoa's chamber, who demanded, with astonishment at their temerity, what those women did there? The Christian chief, presenting the two whales' teeth, answered that they came to solicit the lives of the remaining prisoners.

"Tanoa, still full of wonder, took up one of these teeth, and turning to an attendant, desired him to carry it immediately to Navindi—the chief who had captured the prisoners—and ask, `If it were good?'

"A few minutes were passed in anxious suspense. The messenger returned. Navindi's answer was, `It is good.' The women's cause was gained, and old Tanoa thus pronounced his judgment: `Those who are dead, are dead; those who are alive shall live.' The heroic ladies retired with their three rescued fellow-creatures, and had the satisfaction besides of discovering that their daring efforts had produced a more than hoped-for effect. A year or two ago, no voice but that of derision would have been raised towards them, but now returning to their canoe, they were followed by numbers of their own sex blessing them for their exertions, and urging them to persevere.

"Captain Erskine, who heard this account from the ladies themselves, and gives it much as I have done, adds, 'If anything could have increased our admiration of their heroism, it was the unaffected manner in which when pressed by us to relate the circumstances of their awful visit, they spoke of it as the simple performance of an ordinary duty.' He continues: 'I could not fail to admire the tolerant tone of the missionaries when speaking of these enormities. Accustomed for years to witness scenes such as few believe are to be seen on the face of the earth, and to combat the wildest errors step by step, with slow but almost certain success, these good men know well that a constant expression of indignation, such as must naturally arise in the mind of a stranger, would not produce the desired effect on the unhappy beings to whose loftiest interests they have with much self-sacrifice devoted themselves. Navindi, the cannibal chief of the fishermen, whose natural disposition they describe as kindly and confiding, was received quite on the footing of a friend, and Thakombau was also spoken of as a man of great energy and good intentions, by whose instrumentality much good might yet be effected among his numerous subjects or dependants. The wisdom of their conduct has been proved. These men have been won over to the truth. When our blessed Lord walked on earth He reproved in strongest language the scribes and Pharisees who knew the law, but not the publicans and sinners who knew it not. Captain Erskine describes the missionaries as engaged in the translation of the Scriptures and other religious works to be completed before a given time—a labour to be carried on in the midst of constant interruptions, to which the members of this mission and their families are liable at all hours of the day. Besides being referred to in cases of quarrels and disputes, the care of the sick and the distribution of medicines are duties which they have undertaken, and carry out with unremitting attention.'

"I wish that people in England knew of the efforts made by the priests of Rome to impede the progress of the pure gospel. Their mode of proceeding is very clearly described in a few words by Captain Erskine. He says, 'There are two French Roman Catholic missionaries stationed at Lakemba, but, as at Tongatabu, it is to be feared that their presence will tend rather to retard than advance the improvement of the natives. The practice of this (Roman Catholic) mission, in availing themselves of the pioneer-ship of men of a different sect, for the purpose of undermining their exertions, cannot be too severely reprobated. Being very irregularly furnished with supplies from their own country, these two are sometimes dependent for the common necessaries of life on the Wesleyans, for whom they entertain the strongest dislike, and who cannot be expected to treat them otherwise than as mischievous intruders; nor are their privations in any way compensated by success in their objects.' He describes a visit to the fortress of Bea, in Tonga, where two Roman Catholic priests reside, and which is inhabited partly by Roman Catholics and partly by heathens. 'The appearance of the people in this fortress was not such as to impress one favourably, compared with the others of their countrymen we had seen. They were more scantily clothed, and apparently less cleanly in their persons and houses, a natural conse-quence of living in a more confined space; and the absence of that cordiality which we everywhere met with from persons connected with the Protestant missions was very apparent. I heard also among the younger officers of pockets picked and handkerchiefs stolen, showing a more lawless state of life, and a retention of their old habits, which were so obnoxious to their early European visitors.' The priests complained to Captain Erskine of the way the missionaries spoke of them, on which he says, 'It is perhaps sufficient to remark that, even if the Wesleyans were guilty (which I do not believe) of all the improper conduct attributed to them by M Calinon, it has been occasioned entirely by the obtrusion of the Society to which he belongs into ground previously occupied by others, who would undoubtedly, had their efforts remained unopposed or unassisted, soon have numbered the whole of the population among their fellow-worshippers.'

"The priest also wrote to Captain Erskine, repeating his accusations of intolerance against the Wesleyans, and expressing his fears that their efforts to disparage him would be renewed on their departure, and the flight of the pope from Rome, of which they had heard, represented as the downfall of the Catholic Church.

"The captain says, 'I thought it right to answer his letter, as I could exonerate the missionaries from any charge of having attempted to prejudice us against the Roman Catholic priests, nor did I believe that they would make use of any unfair argument against their faith, founded on the political position of the pope.' I must also express my conviction that the charge against the Wesleyans made by the priests of adopting as proselytes all who offer without examination is quite unfounded. The putting away of all but one wife—no small sacrifice on the part of a people who have practised polygamy for ages—is always insisted on as a first step, and regular attendance on religious worship is also expected. Among the older Christians I saw every evidence of their having adopted the new faith from conscientious conviction,

W. H. G. Kingston

and the chiefs of the highest distinction are probably better read in the New Testament than any of the English met with among the islands.

"Captain Erskine also bears testimony to the character of other missionaries. Describing the work at Samoa, he says: `The first circumstance which must strike a stranger on his arrival, and one which will come hourly under his notice during his stay, is the influence which all white men, but in particular the missionaries, exercise over the minds of the natives.

"`No unprejudiced person will fail to see that had this people acquired their knowledge of a more powerful and civilised race than their own, either from the abandoned and reckless characters who still continue to infest most of the islands of the Pacific, or even from a higher class engaged in purely mercantile pursuits, they must have fallen into a state of vice and degradation to which their old condition would have been infinitely superior. That they have been at least rescued from this state, is entirely owing to the missionaries; and should the few points of asceticism which these worthy men, conscientiously believing them necessary to the eradication of the old superstitions, have introduced among their converts, become softened by time and the absence of opposition, it is not easy to imagine a greater moral improvement than will then have taken place among a (once) savage people.

"`With respect to those gentlemen of the London Mission, whose acquaintance I had the satisfaction of making in Samoa, I will venture, at the risk of being considered presumptuous, to express my opinion, that in acquirements, general ability, and active energy, they would hold no undistinguished place among their Christian brethren at home. The impossibility of accumulating private property,

both from the regulations of the Society and the circumstances surrounding them, ought to convince the most
sceptical of their worldly disinterestedness, nor can the
greatest scoffers at their exertions deny to them the
possession of a virtue which every class of Englishman
esteems above all others, the highest order of personal
courage.' [See Note.]

"But I need not quote further from Captain Erskine, nor from
other unprejudiced writers, to convince you, and through you
your friends, of what has been accomplished through the
instrumentality of missionaries. You will have many oppor-
tunities of judging for yourself. There is, however, another
subject to which I would urge you to draw attention, that is,
the attempts made by French priests of the Church of Rome
to counteract the efforts of the missionaries. You know what
has been done at Tahiti. You hear from Captain Erskine what
is doing at Tonga and Fiji. The same attempts are being
made at Samoa and elsewhere, wherever English missionaries have pioneered the way, and there are good harbours,
but not otherwise. This almost looks as if their designs are
political as well as religious, and that the object of those who
send them is to establish French posts across the Pacific, so
that in time of war they may have coaling stations and
harbours of refuge in every direction. As they have by means
of these priests a party in each group, they will never want an
excuse for interfering in the affairs of the islands whenever
they may have occasion to do so.

"But I must tell you more of many other islands brought
under Christian instruction. Savage Island offers a notable
example of what can be done in a short time. Captain Cook
gave it that name, on account of the savage appearance of the
inhabitants. When Williams first visited them in 1830, they
appeared to be in no way improved. Several at length were
induced to visit Samoa, where at the training college they

gained so sound a knowledge of Christianity, that in 1846 two of them were well fitted to impart it to their long-benighted countrymen. They narrowly, however, escaped with their lives, and some time elapsed before they could gain the confidence of those they came to instruct. When visited by the Reverend A Murray in 1852, about two hundred converts had been made, and many others had learned to look at the teachers with affection. Unhappily that very year several of the natives were killed by the crew of a man-of-war which had called off the island, because one of them had stolen a carpenter's tool, and among them was the chief who had protected the missionaries on first landing. Still they were already too well instructed to wish to return evil for evil, and with simplicity complained that the punishment was rather severe, especially as the innocent suffered, though not altogether undeserved. From this time forward, under their native teachers, the people made great progress in their knowledge of religious truth, and so rapidly were numbers added to the Church, that in a few years not a heathen remained on the island. It was not indeed till quite lately that an English missionary was placed on the island, and he found five large churches built, one of which was capable of holding more than a thousand people; and many young men were anxious to be trained, that they might carry the gospel to other lands. I might give you a similar account of the way Christianity has been introduced into many other islands, and small groups of islands in this part of the Pacific; but I have a very different one to give of the western part, or of those islands which form what is called Melanesia. They consist of five groups, and not only do the inhabitants of each group speak different languages, but frequently those of neighbouring islands.

"We will begin with the large island of New Caledonia, on which the French have lately formed a convict establishment. To the south of it is the Isle of Pines, and to the east the three islands of Mare, Livu, and Uea, forming the Loyalty group. At Mare and Livu chiefly, Christianity has made progress, and Protestant missionaries have for some years been residing on them, while the people of Uea have gladly received the word; but the Isle of Pines has been stained with the blood of several native missionaries; and not only did the savage people reject the offer themselves, but they impeded its progress on New Caledonia, by threatening all who became Christians, till the French arrived and put a stop to the promulgation of Protestant truth among the people. Altogether, the influence of Romanism has been most pernicious in these islands.

"To the north-east of them are the New Hebrides, the most southern of which is Aneiteum; next Tanna, Eromanga, Fate, Malicolo, Espiritu Santo, and many others. The next group is that of Banks' Island, with Santa Maria, and many small isles. The Santa Cruz group is the fourth in the list; and to the north-west of them the Solomon Isles, consisting of many large islands, make the fifth group. The London Missionary Society have made every effort to carry the gospel to the inhabitants of the two first named groups, and in some instances successfully.

"It was at Eromanga that the devoted missionary John Williams fell, with his young companion Mr Harris, struck down by the club of a chief. This sad murder did not prevent the Society from making further efforts to send the gospel to the benighted inhabitants. Those efforts have been blessed, and among the converts was the chief who committed the deed, and who gave up to a missionary the very weapon with which the fatal blow was struck. On Aneiteum, English missionaries are located, Christian Churches have been established, and, with few exceptions, the whole of the population have in name become Christian.

"These five groups are now called Melanesia. They have for some years past been regularly visited by the energetic Bishop of New Zealand, who has induced young men from most of them to accompany him in his mission vessel to New Zealand, where at the Auckland training college they are prepared to carry back the gospel to their savage country-men. A missionary bishop has lately been appointed to superintend the work, which, if carried on in the spirit with which it has been commenced, must with God's blessing prosper.

"These islands were long noted for the deeds of blood committed on their shores, for the number of vessels cut off, and both white and native missionaries murdered, and the natives have been looked on in consequence as of the most fierce and sanguinary character. That they deserved it in a degree there is no doubt; but at the same time it is very certain that their conduct towards foreigners was caused by the unjust, cruel way in which they were treated by the crews of vessels which came to procure sandal-wood on their shores. These men shot them down, cheated them, and ill-treated them in every possible way, sometimes carrying off chiefs and people from one place to exchange them as slaves for sandal-wood in another. Over and over again natives have been shot both on board vessels and on shore by the traders. Such was the cause of the death of the lamented John Williams and young Harris. A trading vessel had touched at Eromanga a short time before their arrival, her crew having shot several natives, among whom was the son of a chief, who afterwards confessed that it was in retaliation he had instigated his countrymen to the attack, and had himself struck the fatal blow.

"But time will not allow me to give a further description of this portion of the Pacific. I have as yet told you nothing of the Sandwich Islands, or, as they are now called, the

Hawaiian Islands, with their capital Honolulu, in the isle of Oahu, and their late sovereign, King Kamehameha the Fourth. They consist of several large and beautiful islands: that of Hawaii (Owhyee), containing two mountains, Mouna Kea and Mouna Roa, said to be eighteen thousand feet in height, and by far the most lofty in the whole Pacific. The inhabitants are a fine and handsome race. Their religion was one of gross superstition, and so overloaded with restrictions, constantly increasing, and curtailing the liberty of all classes except the priests, that the chiefs and people at length became utterly weary of it. Even when visited by Captain Vancouver in 1793, some of the chiefs requested him to send them instructors in the Christian faith,—a prayer to which little attention appears to have been paid.

"It was not till the year 1820 that the young King Rihoriho, who had ascended the throne established by his victorious father, no longer believing in the power of his idols, and weary of the restraints of the old religion, at one stroke broke through the hitherto sacred taboo and the entire system of priestcraft.

"Just before this eventful time it had been put into the hearts of Christian men in the United States, who formed the American Board of Missions, to send missionaries to the long-known savage murderers of Captain Cook. A band of devoted men, admirably selected, arrived on the 30th March, 1820, in sight of Mouna Roa. They were received in a friendly way by the king and many of the chiefs, and three stations were soon occupied by them and their families.

"Two years afterwards, Mr Ellis, of the London Missionary Society, was invited to come from Tahiti to aid in the work, which he was happily enabled to do. He came accompanied by some native Tahitian teachers, who were of the greatest assistance to the missionaries. He remained until the

W. H. G. Kingston

ill-health of Mrs Ellis compelled him to return to England. The king of the Sandwich Islands and his excellent queen, after they had become Christians, paid a visit to England, where they soon died from the measles, which they caught on landing. King Rihoriho, who had assumed the title of Kamehameha the Second, was succeeded by his younger brother, the islands being well governed in the mean time by his mother and one of his chiefs.

"The missionary stations were increased in number, many schools were established, and the natives began to understand the truths of the gospel, and to accept its offers, when there came a rude interruption from an outbreak of heathen chiefs, set on by their priests. After some severe fighting the rebels were defeated, and the insurrection completely put down. Christianity and civilisation once more again made progress; but the missionaries had to contend with opposition not only from the heathen natives, but from so-called Christian strangers, who were furious at finding that they could no longer indulge in the gross licence in which in former days they had been accustomed to revel. Not only were they insulted by masters of whalers, but the American missionaries complain that they were ill-treated by the commander of one of their own men-of-war, and by all his subordinates. From such sources have arisen the numerous calumnies current against the missionaries in the South-Sea."

[See Note 2.]

"In about ten years from the landing of the first missionaries one-third of the population were under instruction, and there were no less than nine hundred native teachers; but even at that time, and much later, there were many heathens, and vice and immorality were very prevalent among professing Christians. Still among all classes there were notable examples of true piety, and ardent zeal for the propagation of the truth. The excellent queen-mother, Kaahumanu, by her precept and example did much to advance the cause of religion. I must tell you of another native lady, Kapiolani, the wife of Naike, the public orator of the kingdom, by whose courage and faith one of the most terrible of the old superstitions of Hawaii was overthrown. The old religion was coloured by the awful volcanic phenomena of which these islands are the theatre. The most fearful of all their deities was Pele, a goddess supposed to reside in the famous volcano of Kilauea. Here, with her attendant spirits, she revelled amid the fiery billows as they dashed against the sides of the crater. To the base of this volcano the old heathenism, driven from the rest of Hawaii, slowly retreated, though the priestesses of Pele several times ventured even into the presence of the king, to endeavour by threats of the vengeance of the goddess to induce him to support the faith of his fathers. These impostors still exercised considerable influence over the uneducated masses.

"Kapiolani, bold in the Christian faith, resolved practically to show how utterly powerless were these supposed fiery gods. After a journey of a hundred miles, as she neared the side of the mountain, a prophetess of the supposed goddess met her with warnings and denunciations of vengeance. But undauntedly she persevered, and as she stood on the black edge of the seething caldron she addressed, in words of perfect faith, the anxious bystanders watching for the effects of Pele's wrath: 'Jehovah is my God: He kindled these fires. I fear not Pele. If I perish, then you may believe that she exists, and dread her power. But if Jehovah saves me, then you must fear and serve Him.' As she spoke, she cast with untrembling hand the sacred berries into the burning crater, quietly waiting till the spectators should be convinced that no result was to follow. Thus she succeeded in breaking through the last lingering remnant of the long-dreaded taboo; and while the priests and priestesses were compelled to support

W. H. G. Kingston

themselves by honest labour, their votaries abandoned their heathen practices, and in many instances sought instruction in the new faith.

"The examples I have given will show you the mode in which Christianity has spread over the isles of the Pacific. But there are still numberless dark spots to which the gospel has not been carried, and in all, the Churches still require the support, strengthening, and instruction which in general white men can alone afford."

* * * * *

Note 1. "Journal of a Cruise among the Islands of the Pacific," by Captain J Elphinstone Erskine, RN, page 100.

* * * * *

Note 2. The *Quarterly Review*, 1853, in noticing accounts of voyages in the Pacific, after quoting the favourable testimonies of some writers, thus refers to others: "There is one circumstance which produces a very painful impression: it is the extreme unfairness which has been brought to bear against the missionaries and their proceedings, even by reporters whose substantial good intentions we have no right to controvert. Surely their work was one which, whatever exception we may take against particular views or interests, ought to have excited the sympathies, not only of those who belong to the religious party, as it is commonly called, but of all who do not take a perverse pleasure in contemplating human degradation as a kind of moral necessity. The object of these devoted men was to redeem the natives from no mere speculative unbelief, but from superstitions the most sanguinary and licentious. Even those who were careless as to the great truths which the Polynesians had to learn, must feel, upon reflection, that merely to unteach the brutal and defiling lesson of ages of darkness was to confer a priceless blessing. Every prejudice should surely be in favour of the men who have by general confession accomplished the first and apparently most laborious part of this task; instead of which a large class of writers find a species of satisfaction in thinking nothing but evil."

W. H. G. Kingston

CHAPTER EIGHTEEN

A HAZARDOUS EXPLOIT

Mr Bent had been waiting for my recovery to restore Alea to her father, and to revisit the newly-established Christian community in her native island. It was important to lose no time in doing this. Mary Bent would have accompanied us; but as her father proposed being absent only a short time, and as the inconveniences of voyaging in a native canoe were very great, he wished her to remain at home. She was, however, not alone; for the widow of a missionary resided with her, and shared her onerous duties in instructing the native girls, an occupation in which both ladies took the greatest delight. All the inhabitants of the island now, it must be understood, professed Christianity, and might justly be called thoroughly civilised. Many also were true and sincere believers; so that these two English ladies, left alone on a small island of the Pacific, felt as secure as they would have done in the centre of civilised England.

As we drew near her father's island, Alea showed considerable trepidation and anxiety as to the way in which she would be received. She could not persuade herself that one from whom she had fled so short a time before, and left a fierce, ignorant heathen, would be willing to forgive her, and treat her with kindness. Might he not also, after all, compel her to become the wife of the cannibal chief to whom she had been betrothed? That was the most dreadful thought. Mr Bent used every possible argument to calm her apprehensions. Although the poor girl had felt the influence of grace in her own soul, she scarcely as yet comprehended its power to change the heart of men. I had entertained a sincere interest in the fate of the young princess from the day we had found her and her perishing companions on board the canoe. I was now able to exchange a few words with her, and there was one subject on which she was never tired of dwelling,— the praise of Mary Bent,—in which I could always join.

Believing that my future lot would be cast among the people of these islands, I had begun seriously to study their language, and I took every opportunity of practising myself in speaking it. We had two native teachers on board, who were to be left among the new converts, and all day long I was talking to them, so that I found myself making rapid progress in their somewhat difficult language.

With a fair wind, the missionary flag flying from the mast-head, we entered the harbour. The shore was crowded, and more and more people came rushing down from all quarters. It was evident that they would not receive us with indifference. Mr Bent had wished to prepare the king for his daughter's return; but she was recognised before we reached the beach, and several people hurried off to inform her father of her arrival. As the vessel's keel touched the strand we saw the people separating on either side, and between them appeared the old chief hurrying down towards us. We instantly landed with Alea, and no sooner did her father reach her than, contrary to all native customs, he folded her in his arms, and kissing her brow, burst into tears?—but they were tears of joy.

"Forgive you, daughter!" he answered to her petition. "It is I have to be thankful that I could not succeed in ruining your soul and body as I proposed. What agony should I now be feeling had I cast you into the power of the child of Satan, to the destruction of your soul and body alike!"

These words made Alea truly happy, and still more so when her father gave her free permission to become the wife of Vihala. During their first interview we stood aside; but now the king came forward, and invited us to come up to his abode. He had evidently some reason for wishing us to come at once. What was our surprise to see on the summit of a hill a building beyond all comparison larger than had ever been erected in the island. The king pointed it out to us with no slight pride. It was a church built entirely by the natives, according to the descriptions given them by Vihala, and the assistance of two or three of them who had seen Christian places of worship during their visits to other islands, though they were at the time themselves heathen. Often have I since seen heathens sitting at the porch of a place of worship, or standing outside the circle of eager listeners; and I have hoped, not without reason, that those men were imbibing some portion of the seed thus scattered, to bring forth fruit in due time. This fact alone is encouraging; indeed there is every encouragement to persevere in missionary labour throughout the Pacific. Where, indeed, is it not to be found, if waited for with patience? The missionary, too, feels that he goes not forth in his own strength,—that a far higher influence is at work, and on that he places his confidence of success.

Nothing could be more satisfactory than the reception afforded us by the chief; but I need not describe the number of hogs and fowls, of bread-fruit, of taro, of the sweet potato, and of numerous other articles of food which were collected to make a feast in honour of our arrival. Mr Bent lost no time in carrying out the object of our visit, in addressing the people, and in installing the teachers in their office. One of our first works was to plan a school-room and houses for the teachers, and to suggest certain alterations in the church to make it more suitable for public worship. It had been arranged that we should return before the next Sabbath; but as it was possible to complete the building by that day, Mr Bent resolved to remain and open it in due form, the natives redoubling their efforts, and working almost day and night to effect that object. I lent a hand, and in sailor fashion erected a pulpit, which, as there was no time to carve, I covered with matting and native cloth, which had a novel, though not unpleasing, appearance.

I did not before speak of my ship: I scarcely expected to find her here on my arrival. Indeed the captain, I understood, thought that all on board the boat had been lost. He had waited, however, day after day, till losing all patience, he had sailed at length the very day we had reached the missionary station. I was most concerned to hear that my boat had not reached the island, though I had a hope that she had fallen in with the *Golden Crown*, and been picked up. If, on the contrary, she had been lost or captured by savages, I felt how grateful I should be for having escaped destruction. Captain Buxton, fully believing that I was lost, had left no message for me, so that I could not tell where the ship had gone, nor what were his intentions.

I must now return to the subject of the church. The opening was one of the most interesting sights I ever beheld. It was crowded at an early hour with people, old and young, all clothed in native cloth, and with their hair cut short,—signs that they had lotued, or become Christians; while numbers were seen approaching from all directions, many of whom, being unable to obtain seats inside, crowded round the doors and windows. Mr Bent's address was most fervent, and, though I could understand but little of it, yet, judging from the way in which the attention of every one present was absorbed, it must have been deeply interesting. Of course but comparatively a small number of those present were really Christians, or understood even the great principles of Christianity. They now required the instruction which man can give, and the work of the Holy Spirit to change their hearts. I may here remark, that I have often heard missionaries accused of over eagerness to increase the number of their flocks; but I should say that Protestant missionaries are never willing to consider those converted who are not really so, and that no ministers of the gospel are more strict in the tests they apply to ascertain the fitness of converts for baptism. Mr Bent well knew the character of his congregation, and addressed them accordingly; but surely it was glorious progress to have some hundreds of persons, not long ago untamed savages, listening attentively to the truths of the gospel. No work of man could thus have progressed,—no mere civilising influence would have produced such an effect. When the morning service was over, the people assembled on the hill-side and in open spaces in the neighbourhood of the church, and there, while eating the provisions they had brought with them, they eagerly discussed the subject of the discourse they had just heard. The teachers I observed went about among them, now sitting down with one group, now with another, and were thus able to answer questions, to give information, and to correct the erroneous notions which were likely to be entertained. Alea scarcely ever left her father's side, and was continually engaged in imparting to him the instruction which she had received from Mr Bent and Mary; and it was interesting to observe the avidity with which the old man received the truth from the lips of the young girl.

I heard reports, however, that the heathen party, still numerous, were mustering strongly in another part of the island. It had been ascertained also that a canoe manned by heathens had left the island some time back, but where they had gone was not known. These circumstances I thought suspicious, and I feared foreboded evil. The meeting at the service in the afternoon, of the natives professing Christianity, was fully equal to that in the morning, but there were fewer heathens. The service continued with prayer and songs of praise, and an address full of instruction and exhortation from Mr Bent. It was almost concluded, when a heathen chief, an old friend of the king, I found, rushed breathless into the building, announcing that a large fleet of double canoes was approaching the island,—that it was that of the cannibal chief to whom Alea was betrothed, coming undoubtedly with hostile intent.

"How far off are the canoes?" asked the king.

"Some distance as yet," was the answer.

"Then we will pray for protection from One mighty to save," exclaimed the king. "We shall now judge which is the most powerful,—Jehovah, whom we have lately learned to worship, or the false gods whom we have cast away."

None of the people moved from their places. The missionary concluded his discourse, and then offered up an earnest prayer for protection from all dangers, to which every one present repeated a loud Amen. They then moved in an orderly manner out of the church, when the greater number hurried up the hill, whence they could see the approaching canoes. Of these there were some fifteen or twenty of different sizes, but most of them large enough to contain a hundred men at least. They were making for a sandy point some way from the town or settlement, where we concluded the enemy would land. I could see with my glass the warriors dancing, and shaking their spears, and gesticulating violently, in a way intended to insult those they had come to attack, and to strike terror into their hearts. A council of war was now held. It was believed that the enemy would not attempt to make an attack that night, but would wait till the morning; still it was necessary to be prepared. The warriors accordingly armed themselves, and assembled in strong bodies under their different leaders. It was a difficult position for Mr Bent and me. He, however, at once stated that he could not assist our friends except by his advice and prayers, but he told me that I might act as I thought fit. Should I fight, or should I not? There was a sore conflict within me. My inclinations prompted me to fight, but my new-born principles taught me to pray rather than to fight, where not called on positively by duty to do so. In either case, my example might be of service. I prayed (as all men in a difficulty should pray) to be guided aright. I decided to remain with the missionary, and use every means to stay the fight, or to mitigate its horrors should it take place.

"I am glad, my son, that you have so resolved," remarked Mr Bent, when I told him of my determination. "Surely the prayers of a believing man are of more avail than the strong arm of the bravest of warriors. It is a trial of your faith, certainly; but oh, pray that your faith may not waver."

While I had been consulting with Mr Bent, I found that a herald from the enemy had arrived with a demand that the Princess Alea should be forthwith delivered up to his master, and threatening the king and all his adherents with utter destruction if he refused compliance.

"Tell your chief that once I was in the dark as he is. Then I thought it no sin to give him my daughter; now I have light, and see my wickedness and folly. When he has light, he likewise will see as I do. My daughter cannot be his wife." This bold speech seemed to astonish the herald, who, having repeated his threats, took his departure.

Active preparations were now commenced for the defence of the settlement, and such fortifications as the natives use were thrown up on all sides. Slight as they may appear, they are capable of offering a considerable resistance, and on one occasion, in the island of Tongatabu, a brave English naval officer and several of his men lost their lives in an attack on one of them held by a rebel and heathen chief who had set at defiance the authority of King George.

As evening drew on we could see the enemy on the sand-bank, dancing round large fires which they had kindled, the sound of their war-shrieks and shouts, and the blowing of their conch-shells reaching us through the calm night air. Meantime the missionary repaired to the church, which during the night was visited at intervals by the whole Christian population. The king also sat frequently in council with his chiefs. One of the youngest, who had, however, greatly distinguished himself, arose and proposed leading a band of chosen warriors to attack the enemy before they commenced their march in the morning.

"While they are singing and dancing, they will not keep a good watch, and thus we may approach them without being discovered. Jehovah will aid us. It is Satan fights for them. We will prove which is the strongest."

All approved the words of the young chief, and he had no lack of volunteers. About two hundred men were chosen and well armed; they at once set out on their hazardous exploit. They had resolved to conquer and save their brethren or die, and yet, perhaps, there was not one who did not expect to be victorious. I had not seen Alea for some time. While I was with the king, who was surrounded by several of his chiefs, she unexpectedly made her appearance among us. She was weeping bitterly.

"Father," she said, "I am the cause of all the bloodshed which is about to occur. Let my life be sacrificed rather than that of so many of your friends. Give me up to the chief. He can then have no cause to complain. I will never be his wife. I may make my escape or I may die, but the lives of you and your friends will be preserved."

On hearing this noble resolve, the chiefs to a man exclaimed that nothing should induce them to abandon the princess. Prayers from all sides were in the mean time offered up for the success of the band of warriors who had gone forth to attack the enemy. No one, however, slackened in their efforts to fortify the town, and all, from the king, when not engaged in council, down to the slave taken in battle, carried baskets of earth or posts for stockades, during the greater part of the night, to those parts of the fortifications which required strengthening. As the hours drew on we waited anxiously for the result of the expedition. I could not help feeling how critical was our position. I was not anxious, however, on my own account, but I could not help reflecting on the sad condition to which Mary would be reduced should her father and I be cut off, as we might too probably be if the heathens gained the victory. Then came the blessed and consoling thought that God cares for the orphans, especially of those who serve Him; what strength and courage does it give those who rest on His sure promises—a comfort which people of the world can never enjoy.

I went the rounds of the fortifications a short time before dawn, and found all the warriors at their posts. I then rejoined Mr Bent, and was conversing with him, when a loud shout from a distance reached our ears, followed by a confused sound of shrieks and cries mingled with the shouts, which continued without cessation for many minutes. Scouts were sent out to ascertain the cause, but no one returned before day broke. The light then revealed to us the fleet of the enemy shoving off from the land. Some of the canoes had already got away, others were hoisting their sails, while a body of the enemy were defending themselves on the beach, hard pressed by our friends. On seeing this the warriors in the town rushed from their trenches, but before they could reach the scene of action not an enemy remained on their strand, with the exception of three or four slain and some thirty or more taken prisoners. The rest sailed away in hot haste, seized with an unusual, if not an unaccountable panic. As their sails had become mere dots on the horizon, the victors entered the town singing, not as before songs of triumph in honour of their idols, but praises to Jehovah, to whom they ascribed their victory. Mr Bent and I, with the women and children and aged men who had not gone forth to the fight, met them, when the king, in set form, recounted what had occurred. The first band had remained concealed till near daylight, when the enemy appeared to be getting drowsy after all their feasting and dancing. At a signal from their leader they dashed forth on the foe, who, totally unprepared for them, were seized with a sudden panic, and the greater number, leaving even their arms, fled towards their canoes. The few who were killed had refused to receive quarter, and as many as could be seized were taken prisoners. These latter fully expected to be slaughtered immediately, and to be offered up to idols, if not to be eaten. They had been somewhat surprised in the first instance to see that their friends who had been killed in the fight were decently interred where they fell, instead of being dragged ignominiously by the heels to the town. They only concluded that this was one of the new customs of the lotu people, and had no expectation in consequence of escaping the common doom of captives. Several of them were chiefs who had attempted to defend the rear while their countrymen were embarking. They stood with downcast, sullen looks, prepared for torture and death. The king now approached them. "Why, O chiefs, did you come to attack my island and my people?" he asked calmly. "We are now among those who wish to live at peace with all men, to have enmity towards no one. Why did you desire to do us harm?"

"We came against you because our king and master ordered us," answered one of the prisoners, looking up with a fierce scowl of defiance on his countenance. "Our object was to carry off your daughter to become our king's wife; the rest of you we should have killed and eaten."

"And I, O chiefs, let you go free because my King and Master orders me to be merciful, that I may obtain mercy," answered the king. "You, O chiefs and people, are free to return to your own island, but before you go you must learn something of the new religion which we have been taught, that you may go back and speak of it to your people, or wherever you may go."

The astonished captives could scarcely believe their senses, the treatment was so unlike anything those they had known taken in war had experienced. They consulted together and expressed their willingness to accept the offer. They were completely overcome when the king promised them a large canoe and ample provisions for their return. The people having taken some refreshment, assembled at the church, where hearty thanksgivings were offered up for the deliverance they had experienced. The captives attended. I watched their countenances. They seemed lost in amazement. All the sentiments were so new and strange. The reign of the Prince of Peace was spoken of. They soon after came to the missionary desiring that they might be allowed to serve so good a Master. They never seemed tired of receiving instruction in the new doctrine, and I was struck with its wonderful adaptability to unsophisticated man, and its power of satisfying his heart yearnings, from the avidity with which they seized each point as presented to them.

It was now time to return to the mission station. We bade an affectionate farewell to Alea, promising to send her intended husband back to the island as soon as possible. The now liberated captives agreed to embark on the same day. Their chief entreaty was that a missionary or a teacher might be sent them to instruct them in the way of eternal life, that way which, by a wonderful combination of circumstances, they were now anxious to follow. Thus the Almighty works often, and thus He has thought fit in an especial manner to work throughout the Pacific.

The difficulty was to obtain a teacher. Mr Bent had several under training at the station, and he told the captives that if they would accompany us he would endeavour to find one who would return with them to their island. They were delighted with the proposal, and exhibited an extraordinary eagerness to set forth. Their hurry was at the time unaccountable, as they were evidently sincere in their expressions. Anxious to please them, we accordingly had our canoe launched, taking several of them on board, the remainder going in the canoe given by the king. The wind being fair, we had a quick run till more than half way across. Just then, through our glasses, we caught sight of a canoe, which, on discovering us, as it seemed, paddled off at right angles to avoid us—her people evidently mistrusting our character. We instantly altered our course to cut her off, and approached her with our missionary flag flying. No sooner was this discovered than the canoe turned again towards us. She soon drew near, when we recognised the people in her as belonging to the station. By their gestures and countenances we had too much reason to believe that they brought us evil tidings. "Haste! haste! haste!" they exclaimed, leaping on board. "A heathen fleet has arrived at the island, and the chief threatens to attack the station. Even now he may have begun the onslaught, for his fury was great. Haste! haste! haste!"

CHAPTER NINETEEN

THE LAUNCH OF THE OLIVE BRANCH

We now understood more of the dangers to which the families of missionaries have often been exposed in all parts of the world. I must own that in my fears for Mary Bent's safety, my own faith and fortitude were well nigh giving way. Mr Bent retained his calmness in a wonderful manner. "All things are in God's hands," he observed. "He will guide them as He knows to be best. We have to go on labouring to the utmost of our power, leaving the rest to Him." I felt that I must be in action, and hauling the canoe on board with the aid of her crew, we got out the paddles and urged our craft ahead somewhat faster than the wind was doing. Every moment might be of consequence. As the cannibal chief, exasperated at having been deprived of Alea, might attempt to carry off Mary, the very thought drove me almost distracted. I had had few or no trials in life, and was not prepared for this one.

Mr Bent wished to ascertain whether, if required, we could depend on the assistance of our new friends. They had heard what had occurred, and at once volunteered to use every means in their power to prevent their chief from doing harm, even to turning against him.

"He will live perhaps to thank us," one of them, a young and intelligent chief, observed. "At all events you have bound us to serve you."

All now seemed to depend on our arriving before the attack had begun. We trusted that if not begun we should be able to prevent it. Meantime all we could do was to offer up constant, earnest prayer for the protection of one so dear to us, and for all those at the settlement. The wind, hitherto blowing a strong breeze, now fell light, and our progress was slower than before.

"All is for the best, depend on that, my son," repeated the missionary several times, when he observed my look of anxiety. "God's loving mercy endureth for ever. Pray against doubt—pray against doubt. Put on the armour of faith. In that you will find strength to quench all the fiery darts of the evil one."

My venerable friend spoke the truth, and already my fears began to subside, although I could in no way see the mode of deliverance. I expressed the same to Mr Bent.

"Nor did we the other day, but God clearly fought for us as He did in days of old for the children of Israel, by putting fear into the hearts of their enemies, and so can He now find some means for the protection of those who serve Him."

On we glided over the calm blue water. Now the breeze freshened, and as the surface became rippled over, it sparkled brightly in the sunbeams. As the island came in sight my heart beat quicker and quicker, and with difficulty I could restrain my impatience. I stood at the bows with my glass at my eye directed constantly at the spot where the station was to be found. As the sun then was, objects close in under the land were not distinctly discernible, but as my glass every now and then swept the horizon on either side, the sails of a fleet of canoes came into view. The instrument almost dropped from my hand. We were too late. The attack had been made and the victors were sailing away with their captives. My first impulse was to give chase, and to attempt their recovery. I did not consider how powerless we were even should our new allies remain faithful. For some time I could not bring myself to tell my fears to Mr Bent; but it was necessary to alter our course if we were to pursue the enemy. At length, therefore, it became necessary for me to tell him what I had seen. He took the telescope, and after a severe scrutiny of the horizon in every direction, and especially of the island, he asked, in a more cheerful voice than might have been expected:

"Can you not assign some other cause for the flight of the foe? Look again."

I did so; and now, the sun having come round a little, I saw close in with the missionary station a large ship at anchor. She might be the *Golden Crown*, come to take me away. I hoped not. My heart again sunk. As we drew nearer I saw that she was much larger—a man-of-war. The station was safe. Otherwise she would have been sailing in pursuit of the canoes. With one voice we burst forth in the native tongue with songs of praise and thanksgiving; and now the canoe seemed to glide more swiftly over the glad blue sea. We entered the harbour, where lay a fine English frigate. As we passed her I hailed and inquired if the station was safe.

"Yes, yes, all right," was the answer. "We came in just in time to prevent mischief."

Our eagerness to reach home prevented us from stopping to make further inquiries. No sooner did our boat's keel touch the strand than we leaped on shore. Even then before leaving the beach the missionary knelt down and offered up a few words of thanksgiving for the mercies vouchsafed us. We reached the house. Mary and her companion did not come out to welcome us. Voices reached our ears from within. One I thought I recognised. We looked in. Mary was doing the honours of the tea-table with some other ladies. There were three naval officers and two gentlemen in black coats. One of the latter turned his face. It was that of my brother John. I had time to greet him while Mary was receiving her father and introducing her guests. Then came my turn to be received by her. I need not describe that. I was very happy. The whole scene was so different from what I had but a short time before expected, that I was perfectly bewildered. I felt deeply grateful that Mary had escaped all the dangers I apprehended, and which had really threatened her.

The frigate had appeared off the station just at the very moment that the cannibal chief and his followers were about to land. She brought up with her guns commanding the approach to the town. The captain, suspecting mischief, instantly despatched an armed boat to warn the chief that he would allow no warlike demonstration to be made in his presence, and that if he attempted to land he would blow his canoes to pieces. The warning had had at first very little effect, and the chief, in defiance, leaping on shore with his followers from the largest canoe, left her deserted. The officer in charge of the boat immediately fired the gun in the bows right into her, and almost knocked her to pieces. The interpreter then shouted out, "If the small gun of this little boat will do all this mischief, what would all the great guns of the big ship do?"

The argument was irresistible. The chief, leaping on board another canoe, begged that no more damage might be done, and offered to sail away immediately, promising never again to come near the settlement. This he was allowed to do on

W. H. G. Kingston

condition of his returning directly home without committing further damage on the way, and he was compelled to leave two hostages as a guarantee that he would perform his promise. All this was told in a few words, and John now introduced me to his devoted wife; and as I heard of some of the many trials and dangers they had gone through, and how calmly she had endured them, I felt how admirably she was fitted to be the helpmate of a missionary. The captain of the frigate was, I discovered, an old family friend—one who, convinced of the importance of missionary labour, was zealous in aiding and supporting missionaries of the gospel wherever he met them engaged in their Master's work. He had found John suffering from hard work and anxiety, and had persuaded him and his wife to take a trip among several of the Polynesian groups, to visit as many of the missionary stations as could be reached, in the hopes that he might return home with renewed strength for his work. One of the ladies was his wife's sister, who had come out to assist her in her labours—not the only example of self-devotion to a glorious and thrice blessed cause. The other gentleman in plain clothes was the chaplain of the ship. While conversing with him an idea occurred to me which I took an early opportunity of communicating to John, who highly approved of it, and undertook to broach the subject to Mr Bent while I mentioned it to Mary. It was one which concerned us both very nearly, for it was a proposal to take the opportunity of marrying while a legally authorised person was present to perform the ceremony, with my own brother and our naval friend as witnesses. Mary had no objections to offer, and we soon overcame those Mr Bent suggested.

The benefit of the visit of the ship-of-war to the different missionary stations was very great, besides having preserved ours from almost certain destruction. The admirable discipline of the crew had a great influence on the minds of the heathen natives, so different from what they had been accustomed to witness on board many whalers; the perfect order of everything on board the ship, and the mighty power of her guns, awed them still more, and showed them the folly of offending people who had in their possession such instruments of punishment. I will not say that the appearance of any ship of war would do good. Unless discipline is strict and no licence is allowed, they might do, as some have done, a great deal of harm.

One of the worst of this kind, was that of Captain Kotzebue, commanding a Russian exploring expedition. Wherever he went he outraged decency by the licence he allowed his crew, and on his return home malignantly abused the English missionaries whom he found nobly struggling, against innumerable difficulties, to reclaim the hapless natives from the sin and corruption which he had done his utmost to encourage. Others, from ignorance or from vicious dispositions, followed his line of abuse, though happily the greater number of their publications have sunk into deserved oblivion, while the glorious result of missionary labour, evident to all who will inquire, proclaims the falsehood of their accusations. To the honour of the British navy be it said that by far the greater number of captains who have visited the isles of the Pacific have rendered essential service to the missionary cause while on the spot, and have spoken and written heartily in its praise on their return home.

We had very little time to prepare for the wedding as the frigate could not remain long. I employed the interval in getting assistance from the ship's carpenters in building a vessel, and instruction, with the necessary plans for continuing the work after the frigate had gone. I had some knowledge of the art to begin with, so that I knew exactly what information I required. My ambition was to have a fine, serviceable little vessel, and I had every hope of succeeding. I was thoroughly up to rigging and fitting her.

The time passed very rapidly, and my wedding-day arrived, and Mary became my most loving and devoted wife,—a bright example to those among whom our lot was cast. I have not dwelt on the visit of my brother John, or the enjoyment and benefit I derived from his society. Our station was healthy, but the surgeon of the ship recommended his continuing the voyage, and with reluctance I parted from him, hoping, however, to visit him when my schooner should be completed. Once more the missionary station was left in its usual quiet state; but, though quiet, no one was idle. There were schools both for adults as well as children,—the males, under the superintendence of Mr Bent, with native teachers; the women and girls under Mary and her friend. Classes also assembled during most days in the week for religious instruction. Mr Bent was also frequently engaged in teaching the young men and boys various mechanical arts: house-building in its various departments, agriculture and gardening, and last, though not least, printing and book-binding. It is wonderful with what rapidity many acquired the art of printing, and many learned to bind books with great neatness and strongly. I meantime, aided by my wife, was making fail progress in the language, so that I was able to talk without difficulty to the men who assisted me in building the vessel. She was at length ready for launching. I proposed calling her the *Mary*, but to this my wife would not consent. We had a discussion on the subject round our tea-table during that pleasantest of all meals in most missionary, indeed in most quiet families. The *Ark* was proposed, and then the *Olive Branch*. The latter was the name decided on.

It was made a day of rejoicing and prayer and praise on the occasion of launching the little *Olive Branch*. Formerly one, or perhaps several, human victims would have been offered up to their idols by the then benighted inhabitants. The vessel herself was decked with flags and garlands, and surrounded by high poles, from which gay-coloured banners were flying.

A feast was prepared also, at which the chief, who came in state, presided. We had limited the quantity of provisions, or else, according to custom, far more than could have been consumed would have been collected. A large bower or tent of boughs and flowers had been erected for the chief and his principal attendants,—a very elegant, though a rapidly created structure. Mary named the vessel as she glided down the ways, and a hymn of thankfulness, combined with a prayer for the safety of all who might ever sail in her, was sung by the children of the school at the same time, the effect being admirable. I was somewhat anxious till I saw the little craft floating safely in the water.

We had purposely avoided anything savouring of heathenism, such as breaking a bottle of wine on her bows, taken evidently from the Greek custom of pouring out a libation to Neptune; nor would we make a mockery of the rite of baptism, by pretending to christen her. Living among heathens, it was our duty to be especially circumspect in all our proceedings. The natives are very acute, and are accustomed to make enquiries as to the meaning and origin of everything they see. How unsatisfactory would have been the answer we should have had to give, had we, without consideration or thought, adopted the practice generally followed in England.

The missionaries have endeavoured as much as possible to abolish all heathen customs, so that the evil-disposed may have no temptation to return to them. In this they show wisdom. Even the sports and pastimes of heathenism, though they may by some be considered harmless in themselves, are generally adverse to the spiritual life of a Christian, and therefore they have been discouraged. The missionaries have in consequence been accused of being morose and narrow-minded. Far, far different is their real character. As a class, they are zealous, earnest, devoted men, full of life, activity,

W. H. G. Kingston

and energy,—courageous and persevering,—gifted with high and varied attainments, which would enable them to shine among civilised communities, but they have joyfully abandoned home and country, and, in obedience to their Lord and Master, have gone forth to teach the heathen the unsearchable riches of Christ. Let those who may fancy that I overpraise these men, read their memoirs, and they will be convinced of the truth of my statements.

The native carpenters worked admirably. I had spars, rigging, and a suit of sails ready, supplied me by the frigate, with a compass and such nautical instruments as I required, so the *Olive Branch* was soon ready for sea. I proposed in my first experimental trip to pay a visit to Vihala, to leave two more native teachers on the island, and then, on my return, to see Alea, and to ascertain the progress made by her father and fellow-islanders in religion. Mary begged that she might accompany me, and, as her father made no objections, I was too glad of her company to refuse. For several days, however, I first made frequent trips out of the harbour, to exercise my native crew, who, although they had never before been on board a vessel, became efficient hands in a wonderfully short space of time. The reason of this was that they gave their minds thoroughly to their work, and were anxious to learn everything I could teach them.

The *Olive Branch* was completed to my satisfaction and to that of all who saw her. I was indeed very proud of her, as chiefly the work of my own hands; and yet when I compared the slight difficulties I had had to overcome with the great ones conquered by Mr Williams at Raratonga, when building the *Messenger of Peace*, I felt sensibly how little cause I had to boast.

As Mr Bent had promised to relieve Vihala of his charge as soon as possible, two teachers had been trained for the purpose, and these we now took on board. We had with us a number of axes and knives, and other articles most prized by the natives, both to pay for provisions or whatever we might require, as also to bestow on Vihala, hoping that, if he were thus richly endowed, the old king would not refuse longer to give him his daughter.

Two of the men who had come as heathen enemies now remained as friends, and earnest searchers after truth. The remainder, deeply imbued with the spirit of Christianity, had returned to their own island, we hoped to pave the way for a missionary among its still heathen and cannibal inhabitants.

Thus during the few months since I had left my ship I had seen a way made for the entrance of the gospel into these thickly-inhabited islands. Thus it has pleased God to work through human agency among a large proportion of the isles of the Pacific; nor has He ever failed to afford, after a time, superabundant encouragement to His faithful labourers. Oh that some of the many thousands and thousands of young men and women who read this would consider the noble, the glorious nature of missionary work, and esteem it as a high privilege to be allowed to employ their energies in the cause!

How different was our voyage from that which Mary, Mr Bent, and I before took in the same direction! But where were our companions? Were we the only ones alive out of the whole party? At all events, we had ample reason to be grateful. The wind was fair, and our passage promised to be as calm and pleasant as we could desire.

On getting near enough to the island to distinguish objects on shore, we saw a number of people hurrying down to the beach, from among the trees, while some launched their canoes and paddled off through the opening in the reef towards us. Their object was to welcome us, and to pilot the schooner into their harbour. They knew that the schooner was a missionary vessel from her flag, but they had not guessed who was on board. Their delight, when they recognised Mr Bent and Mary, was excessive; and so completely did they forget all about the vessel, that had I not kept a good look-out she would have run right on to the reef. On our enquiring for Vihala, the answer was, "He is well, and we all Christian."

The glorious news we found on landing to be true. Vihala received us with joy unfeigned, and it was some little time before we could proceed, from the number of people who crowded round us to express their satisfaction at our arrival. Great also was ours when, at length moving on, we saw before us a handsome structure, a church erected entirely by the natives, under Vihala's superintendence, capable of holding seven or eight hundred persons, and near it a school-house and two neat residences for teachers.

"Your church is indeed large," observed Mr Bent, after expressing his admiration of it to Vihala.

"Yes," was the quiet answer; "but all desire to hear the word, and why should any be excluded? The kingdom of heaven is wide enough for all."

Alas! that any should so mistake the gospel message as to think differently, and to act as if all should be thrust out who do not conform to certain rules and regulations of man's invention, although they with deep repentance trust in the blood of Christ alone for salvation. Many a once heathen savage will rise up in the day of judgment to condemn those men. Would that, for their own sakes, they could even now voyage amid the isles of the Pacific, and behold the glorious work wrought by the instrumentality of true Christian men of various branches of the one Church, and I believe that they would be compelled to acknowledge that an unction from on high is of more avail in saving souls alive than any mere official and external qualification, such as the Romish priesthood with its pretended apostolic succession claims. The means are best judged of by the result, and that can be known of all men. "By their works ye shall know them." It was remarkable that, except for the few days Mr Bent had preached on the islands, none of the inhabitants had heard the truth from a white missionary, and yet the majority of them had cast away their idols, and become nominal Christians,—while many of them were really converted.

We had a most delightful time on the island. The two new teachers we brought somewhat reconciled the people to the loss of Vihala, though their grief was most unmistakable when they were told that he must leave them for a time at all events.

Again we were on the ocean, and approaching the island where Vihala expected to meet his promised bride. He had long been separated from her. He acknowledged that it had been for his good, and he hoped that, with the spiritual benefits he had received while engaged as a teacher, they should the better be able to walk together on their heavenward way, and lead others on to the same happy goal.

W. H. G. Kingston

CHAPTER TWENTY

A FEARFUL HURRICANE

But a few years ago, before the power of God's word was felt among the inhabitants of the fair islands of the Pacific, to the numerous dangers usually encountered by mariners, that of being attacked and cut off by cannibal savages was to be added throughout its whole extent. Now, throughout the eastern portion, the greater number of the islands may be visited, not only without fear, but with the certainty of a friendly reception. There are still some,—like the Marquesas and parts of the Pomautau group, or Low Archipelago,— which still remain in the darkness of heathenism; but on the western portion of that mighty ocean, the bright spots on which the gospel shines are the exception to the general rule, and over the widest parts the spirit of evil reigns supreme. It was here that true soldier of Christ, the energetic Williams, fell; and here, too, Mr Gordon and his wife and family were lately murdered by the savage inhabitants.

It was towards a group of islands in the eastern Pacific that the *Olive Branch* was now holding its course. We had seen Vihala happily united to Alea, with the full consent of the old king, and they had devoted themselves for missionary labour wherever they might be required. This was surprising to many, and to the heathen perfectly incomprehensible. It was as astonishing to them as it would be to people in England, if a young noble of high rank were to declare his resolution of going forth as a missionary of the gospel to these heathen lands. Yet what undertaking more glorious, what work more pleasing to the Lord and Master, whom Christians of all ranks, rich and poor, profess to serve. We had likewise visited the island of the once cannibal chief, who had heard of the new religion from his countrymen, had confessed its vast superiority to his own, cast away his idols, and gladly received the two teachers we had brought with us. All this had been most cheering and encouraging.

We had landed Mr Bent at the station, and now we hoped shortly again to meet my brother John and his wife, and to convey them, and some other missionaries and their wives, to a general meeting to be held shortly at the central station. We had received on board a variety of stores, and books, and numerous articles to distribute among the various stations at which we were to touch. Indeed, it was highly satisfactory to me to find how useful my little *Olive Branch* could be made.

Hitherto the little vessel had not encountered a single storm. It was like the rest we might suppose the ocean enjoyed after the subsidence of the waters when the ark rested on Ararat,—not a calm, though; for gentle breezes filled our sails, and rippled over the blue surface of the sea with glittering wavelets, laughing joyously in the sunbeams. A lovely island hove in sight, with blue mountains, and rocks, and sparkling waterfalls, and green shrubs, and pastures, and graceful palm-trees, and yellow sands; and we sailed in through an opening in the never absent reef, and dropped our anchor in a sheltered and beautiful harbour, and numbers of canoes surrounded us. But we had no boarding nettings up, no guns loaded, no pistols in our belts, no cutlasses and pikes ready at hand; for the gospel ruled here. The canoes were filled with well-clothed, intelligent natives. Not an oath was heard, not a man showed an angry temper, and not one who could not read the word of God, and understood it too, and could give a clear reason for the hope that was in him, and who was not probably, even in secular matters, far better educated than the larger portion of the watermen of any port in England, or other long-civilised country in the world.

Provisions of various sorts had been brought in the canoes; but when I enquired for John Harvey, and announced that I was his brother, and that my wife was the daughter of Mr Bent, not an approach to payment would any one receive. When we landed they lifted us up in their arms, and carried us thus to the mission house, where our appearance was a pleasant surprise to our sister-in-law, who had not been made aware of our arrival. My brother was away, but every hour expected back.

I had looked upon Mr Bent's station as a model of neatness; this was larger, and superior in many respects; nor was it inferior in respect to spiritual things. The church, built entirely of stone, was a large and handsome building, and the most conspicuous object from the sea. Running parallel with the shore were two rows, facing each other, of neat cottages, many of stone, with verandahs round them, and gardens both in front and in the rear. Between them was a broad hard road, with two rows of trees, and a stream of sparkling water led through the centre, fed by a waterfall which came foaming down the side of a rocky hill at a little distance inland. Several streets of equal width had been commenced at right angles with the main street, and on the same plan, and new houses were in course of erection in several directions. Here it was evident, indeed, was the commencement of a large town. The cottages were all very fair copies of the mission-house, though on a smaller scale. Those of some of the chiefs, however, were of good size, and were arranged so that they could enjoy all the privacy of domestic life.

And why, it may be asked, was this congregation of natives in one place? What could be the attraction? My love and admiration of John suggested the answer, and I was right: the power of God's word put forth through His faithful servant. The inhabitants of this town had been collected by concern for their soul's welfare, and the belief that the nearer they were to the preacher the more that welfare would be cared for. They displayed a wisdom which is foolishness to the world, and is, alas! too often neglected by those at home, by those who profess to be seeking after the food which perisheth not. I write this, as well as other comparisons I have made, not to find fault with my countrymen at home, but that (should my journal ever be read by any of them) I may excite in them a holy emulation with these so late savage heathens, that they may examine themselves, and ascertain whether they are using all the means in their power to attain to holiness of life and conversation, and without which their spiritual life will too probably languish.

I found my sister-in-law actively engaged from morning till night in her household duties, and in affording instruction of every description to native women of all ages. She declared with perfect sincerity her belief that she was one of the happiest of her sex. She retained the most perfect health, though her figure was slight and delicate, and she had been most gently and tenderly nurtured. Not only that, but she had been what is called highly educated, and was not a stranger to the gay and brilliant assemblies of "civilised" life. It was not that she knew no other lot, and therefore esteemed her present one the best; but she had weighed it with many others she did know, and found it immeasurably superior. She knew from experience that worldly rank hides many a heavy or vacant heart where God is not acknowledged, that wealth cannot give peace of mind, and that gaiety and dissipation most assuredly quench spiritual life. She had found, too, that even a decent church-attending style of existence may be unprofitable to the soul, and as certain to lead to spiritual death. My sister-in-law was not entirely alone. There were two other stations on the island, which was large, and the missionaries and their wives enjoyed frequent intercourse, thus encouraging and supporting each other.

Indeed, I have as a rule found the stations the most prosperous both spiritually and physically where two missionary families have been living together, or where they are near enough to meet frequently. A missionary's wife has to attend to her household duties, often not slightly onerous when she has children requiring instruction. Then she has the female schools to look after, adult classes to receive at her own house, to afford advice to all who ask it, to call on the sick and to administer medicine, and to visit often from house to house. She must correspond with friends at home; she has her private devotions, and must take time for reading and self-examination, or she will find that she can ill perform her other duties. I do not believe that I have overstated the amount of work I have known my sister-in-law and other missionaries' wives perform. Indeed, my own wife was in the habit of getting through not less daily, for weeks together.

Although the greater number of the inhabitants of the island had become Christians in name, there was still a large district the powerful chief of which remained a stubborn heathen. He seemed to hate the gospel with a deadly hatred, and threatened to club any of his subjects who should venture to lotu. Notwithstanding this, several who had heard the truth, either directly or through their friends, had secretly escaped to Christian villages. Many of these persons had become really converted, and were of course longing to induce their relatives and friends to become Christians likewise.

Such was the state of things when the *Olive Branch* arrived at the island. A more beautiful picture could scarcely be found than that presented by the calm bay on which our little vessel floated, with her mission-flag flying,—the glittering sand, the tall cocoa-nut and bread-fruit trees, the wild rocks and fantastic-shaped hills, the green fields, the foaming waterfalls and shining streams, and the rows of neat habitations, the church and school-houses,—all showing that the gospel had indeed here found an entrance, and made it doubly beautiful in our sight.

We had been some hours on shore when we saw the natives hurrying out of their cottages and assembling in the chief street, and the cry arose that the missionary was coming. I was scarcely prepared for the warm and affectionate greeting with which they welcomed him. There was no adulation and nothing cringing in their manner; but it was evident that they knew him from experience as a sincere and loving friend.

Great as was our mutual satisfaction at again meeting, so multifarious were his duties that we had but little time for private conversation. I was able, however, to ascertain that John's heart was in his work, and that he infinitely preferred being a missionary in the South-Seas to holding the highest secular office at home. The Sabbath came. It was a day of toil to the preachers and teachers, and yet a day of refreshing to them as it was to hundreds of others, who collected from all quarters to worship the true God, and to hear His word expounded. Many came with their wives and little ones, bringing their provisions, to spend the day of rest in obtaining spiritual food for their souls' welfare. The service over, numbers collected round my brother and the native teachers, and almost the whole interval between the services was devoted to affording advice and consolation to these seekers after life eternal.

But the faith of the young Christian community in the

especial providence of God was sorely to be tried. All things were prepared for our departure, and we were about going on board the *Olive Branch*, when the somewhat threatening appearance of the weather made me resolve not to sail before the following morning. I was convinced shortly that a gale of more or less strength was coming on, and leaving Mary at the mission house, I went on board to secure the vessel and make all things snug. Scarcely had I got out a second anchor and two fresh warps than dark clouds were seen rushing across the sky, the wind howled among the hills and trees, lightning flashed brightly, and the thunder roared and rattled fearfully. I was in hopes, however, that the vessel would, notwithstanding, ride in safety, when it struck me that the sea outside was roaring louder than usual, and in an instant a huge roller appeared rushing with fearful violence into the harbour, while before I could look round I found the vessel lifted up, cables and anchors dragging, and warps giving way, and on we drove helplessly towards the shore. My crew held on to the bulwarks with affrighted looks, for we could expect nothing else than that our little vessel would be dashed to pieces, and if so, that we ourselves should be swept out of the harbour by the receding wave. Another dread seized me, that the roller might sweep up to the mission house and overwhelm those so dear to me. This feeling made me forget all fear for my own life, or for those with me. As I gazed landward, I saw the devastation the hurricane was already committing. Several cottages were in view. Now the wind lifted the roof of one and bore it in shattered fragments to a distance. Now the walls of another trembled and fell; tall trees were bending and breaking, or being torn up by the roots and laid prostrate; house after house was thus destroyed; whole groves of trees, as it seemed to me, fell to the ground; darkness appeared to be coming down like a thick mantle to add to the horrors of the scene.

On drove our little vessel; the rocks against which I expected to be dashed appeared; these were covered, and over them we were carried by the raging tide, above even the sands, and lifted high up on to a soft bank amid brushwood stern first, where she hung while the waters rushed back leaving her uninjured on the shore. We were mercifully preserved from the sudden death we expected, and were grateful; but yet, though not cast down, knowing all would be for the best, I felt most anxious to assure myself of the safety of my dear wife and her companions.

We had come on shore, as far as I could judge, half a mile or more from the mission house, a distance which it would be not only difficult but extremely dangerous to traverse while the storm was raging and tall trees were being hurled about like straws. One of my crew—a true Christian man— volunteered to accompany me. The *Olive Branch* had already been made snug aloft, so when I had seen her securely shored up, trusting and believing that no second roller would come to move her, I set off, leaving the rest of the people on board to attend to her. My companion and I provided ourselves each with a stout pole. I led the way, he to help me should I fall, and I promising to turn back should he cry out.

The noise of the tempest prevented our having anything like conversation with each other, indeed it was only when we shouted at the very top of our voices that they could be heard. The darkness had increased, and as I began to move on I felt that the attempt was almost beyond my power; still the incentive was so great that I resolved to persevere. I prayed for strength and protection. In my own arm I knew that I could not trust. There were no stars to guide me, and the flashes of lightning sadly confused and dazzled my eyes, so that it was only by keeping as near as possible to the shore that I could hope to keep in the proper direction. This way was longer, however, and very rough where rocks covered

W. H. G. Kingston

the ground, and I dreaded a return of the roller, when we might have been swept helplessly away. The dangers to be encountered by keeping inland were equally great. We might be struck by lightning, crushed by falling trees, or losing our way, fall into some gully or chasm.

Feeling the ground before us with our poles, my companion and I began our hazardous march, I desired him to keep as close behind me as he could, and to shout frequently to assure me that he was following. The tempest increased in fury, the rain came down in torrents, causing such floods as in some places almost to sweep us off our feet.

We had made good some five or six hundred yards, when I thought that we might make faster progress on the higher ground, where the water would not be so great an impediment to our progress. I knew also that we should be able to steer our course more or less directly by feeling the direction the water was flowing, so that we might always regain the sea by following down the streams. Accordingly we attempted gradually to gain the higher ground, but as we ascended, we felt the wind blowing with greater force, and were again nearly carried off our legs by it. I had to exert all the energies of my mind not to become totally bewildered. Over rough rocks we climbed, and fallen trunks of trees, and through the beds of streams, down which the fierce waters now rushed foaming and roaring with fearful force, and across swamps and marshes, till at last we reached a grove of tall trees. We could discover no way round it, so I resolved to push through it by a path in which we found ourselves. The trees were bending and writhing, and the loud crashes we heard told us that every instant some were hurled to the ground. Now one fell directly before me, and impeded my progress. I climbed over it, my companion followed, and we continued our course, guided as before by the way the rain beat on our heads and the waters flowed past our feet. Again the thunder rolled loudly and the lightning flashed with startling vividness, casting a horrid glare over the whole scene, now darting amid the lofty boughs, and then snake-like running with loud hisses along the ground. How utterly helpless and insignificant I felt amid the war of the elements.

Still onward we must advance. How much farther I could not tell. My companion's frequent shout cheered me. Perhaps trusting to the aid of another made me more careless, for neglecting for an instant to keep my stick feeling the ground before me, I stumbled forward, and found myself floundering in a foaming stream. My cry prevented my companion from falling likewise. Descending more cautiously he rushed into the flood after me, and seizing me by the jacket just as I was being borne down, assisted me to regain my feet, and helped me across, the water being scarcely up to our middles. In another instant I should have been carried helplessly down the stream beyond my depth. We struggled out, I scarcely know how, and pushed on.

Again, I took the lead. We were passing through a second grove of bread-fruit trees. Another tall tree fell directly before me. I climbed over it. Crash succeeded crash. I prayed for preservation from the fate which might any moment overtake me. I began to hope that we were approaching the station. Still we were not out of the wood. I was working my way on when it occurred to me that my companion had not sung out to me for a longer time than usual. I called to him. There was no answer. Eager as I was to push on, I could not desert him. I turned back. Again and again I called. There was no answer. I reached a fallen tree. Was it the one I had climbed over, or was it one which had fallen after I had passed? I felt along it. My foot struck against a soft substance. I stooped down. There lay a human form—quite still though—the hand I lifted fell powerless. My companion was dead. "One shall be taken and the other left." God in His

W. H. G. Kingston

good providence had thought fit to spare me. My companion was trusting wholly in Christ's blood. I could not mourn him as one without hope.

It was no time to delay. Once again I was straining all my energies to find and follow the right way. It appeared to me that far more than double the time had passed which I had believed would suffice to reach the station. I almost ran against the gable end of a house the greater part of which was in ruins. I heard a loud moan. It was repeated. I hunted about till I came on a native crouching down and endeavouring to find shelter under part of the building yet standing. I asked him if he would guide me to the mission house. My voice roused him, and he said he would gladly do so. He sprang to his feet, and led me on by the hand. "Here it is!" he exclaimed; but, alas, it was roofless and deserted.

* * * * *

Note 1. In the course of this volume the author, it will be observed, has transcribed much from the actual reports of missionaries, and from the journals of naval officers who have visited the South-Seas. Even in the connecting thread of narrative, and in descriptive scenes such as this of the storm, the writer has stated nothing for which he has not ample authority in published works. In a most interesting book, "Gems from the Coral Islands," by the Reverend William Gill, volume two, chapter 9, an account is given of the fearful hurricane of 1846, which devastated the island of Raratonga. Dr Bourne, son of the Reverend R Bourne, one of the founders of the Tahitian mission, the friend and associate of Williams, thus writes concerning the illustrations which accompany our letterpress, proofs of which he had seen: "The engravings represent the tropical aspect of the vegetation with great correctness. Many are not aware of the grandeur of the mountain scenery in some of the islands. Dr

Darwin, who was with Captain Fitzroy's expedition, says of Tahiti: `Until I actually visited this island, and tried to penetrate its mountain fastnesses, I could never understand the statement made by Ellis, in his "Polynesian Researches," that after the great battles of former times the defeated party took refuge in the mountains, where it was impossible to follow them.' Mr Darwin then describes the rugged ravines and forest-clad precipices, wilder than anything he had witnessed in the South American Andes or Cordilleras." Raiatea, Eimeo, and others in the Society group, are composed of vast and abrupt mountain ranges, rising almost abruptly from the sea, and having very little habitable ground, but all covered with the densest vegetation. The most stupendous volcanoes in the world are those of the Sandwich Islands, compared with which Etna and Vesuvius are mere hillocks.

W. H. G. Kingston

CHAPTER TWENTY ONE

THE RUINED VILLAGE

For an instant the horror of finding the house in ruins, and being unable to discover my wife and the dear ones with her, almost overcame me. I should have sunk to the ground exhausted, had not the native supported me.

"Trust in Jehovah, friend," he remarked, quietly. "He knows what is best for us all: your wife and our good missionary are in His hands."

"How long have you been a Christian?" I could not help asking.

"Two years," was the answer. "Before that I was a gross idolater and cannibal; there was no wickedness I did not do. But, praised be the Lord Jesus Christ, I was, through the teaching of the Holy Spirit, brought out of darkness into the light of His glorious truth."

I felt rebuked, and grasping my staff once more, braced myself up to continue my search. The native accompanied me.

"They may have escaped to the mountains," he observed.

"We will go there. I can find the path even in the dark, and there is a cavern not far up, where they may have taken shelter. Once, when we were devil's people, we dreaded to enter it, thinking it the abode of evil spirits; now that we are God's people, we know that God is everywhere, and have no fear."

Again I felt how the remark of this babe in Christ, this late savage heathen, would rebuke many of those in our own dear England who, even in this professedly enlightened nineteenth century, yet tremble at the thoughts of ghosts, witches, and other similar phantoms of their foolish imaginations.

It appeared to me that the hurricane was subsiding; but still our progress was slow and painful. It was, however, an advantage having a beaten path, though that in many places was cut up by the water, and in others, trees and roofs of cottages had been blown across it. I found that we were ascending,—higher and higher up the mountain we got. Lofty rocks appeared on every side,—the lightning seemed to be more vivid,—the crash of the thunder, as it reverberated in rattling peals amid the cliffs, was even louder than before. I remembered my companion's remark, and felt no fear.

"There is the cavern," he said, at length.

I hurried in through a narrow opening, following closely at his heels. A light was shining at the farther end: it was from a fire, round which a number of persons were collected. On the opposite side, with the light shining full on his countenance, stood my brother John. A book was in his hand,—the book of books undoubtedly. His eyes were turned toward heaven: he was praying for the safety of all those exposed to the fury of the tempest. My own name was mentioned. I advanced, and knelt down by the side of my own Mary. "God hears prayer," I whispered. "He has preserved me."

She soon lay in my arms, weeping tears of joy. I now learned that no sooner had the signs of the coming tempest appeared than several of the principal natives came to the mission-house, and advised John to remove his family, with his books, and such articles as the water might spoil, to a place of safety, offering to assist him. Of this kindness he gladly availed himself; but the journey was not performed without great danger and difficulty, as the tempest broke before they had proceeded far, and the wind and floods impeded their progress. Mary suffered most, from her anxiety for me. Now we praised God together joyfully for the preservation he had awarded us.

It was daylight before we were able again to set forward to return to my brother's now desolate home. Still we could rejoice, and be thankful that none of those most dear to us had been lost. We hoped that the poor natives might have escaped as well; but we had not descended far through the lower ground before we found one crushed by a fallen tree, and another drowned in a water-hole, into which he had apparently stumbled. The lightning had struck a third whose blackened corpse we found beneath a tall tree stripped of its branches. These were beyond human help.

"Grant that they died in the Lord," observed the missionary, as we noted the spots where they lay, that we might send and bury them.

The numbers wandering houseless and without food most claimed our sympathy. Our worst apprehensions were realised. In the late neat and pretty village not a cottage retained its roof, and by far the greater number lay levelled with the ground, some mere heaps of ruin, while of others not a remnant was to be seen, the whole building having been carried off by the floods or wind. Of the church only part of the walls remained standing; and even the heavier timbers of the roof lay scattered about in every direction. This destruction naturally deeply affected the missionary. "Still I pray that the faith and trust of the people will not be found wanting under this trial," he murmured as we passed on.

The school-houses were much in the same condition; but happily the printing-office, a strong stone building, had escaped any serious damage, as had its valuable contents. Here not only was printing carried on, but the Bibles and other books were stored, as were the machines for binding, a work performed very neatly by the natives. This circumstance again raised my brother's spirits: "While the Book of God remains, we have nought to fear."

It was sad to see the natives collecting from all points to which they had fled to escape the flood and storm, as they first caught sight of their ruined habitations.

"The village must be rebuilt on Christian principles," said my brother with a smile; and going among the people, he called them around him, and advised them to lose no time in collecting food and rebuilding their houses, urging those without young children or unmarried to assist those with families, or the sick and aged, before attending to their own wants. The reply was most satisfactory, and all agreed to follow his advice.

We now repaired to the mission-house, and, clearing out the rubbish from within the angle formed by two walls, were soon able to obtain some shelter and privacy for the ladies and children. It was melancholy work hunting about for the furniture, crockery, and other articles, among the ruins. However, we obtained a sufficient number of things to furnish our make-shift abode, though it was long before we could get the bedding sufficiently dry to be of any use. The flour and many other articles of food, were spoilt, or had disappeared; but we raked up sufficient for the present wants of the household; and as we assembled round a table once more together, we returned our grateful thanks to Heaven that we were still preserved to each other.

Among the ruins a chest of axes, and some saws, and other carpenters' tools was found, and these my brother distributed among the chiefs and other principal people, that they might the better be able to rebuild their abodes. When assembled to receive these valuable gifts, their answer was: "We accept them with thanks, on one condition,—that we may first be allowed to rebuild our missionary's abode." They would take no denial; and forthwith forming themselves into gangs, some set to work to clear away the ruins, while others went off to cut fresh uprights and rafters to replace those that were broken. It was gratifying, as being so purely spontaneous, and showing the high estimation in which they held their missionary for his work's sake. Thus, aided by zealous friends, the work proceeded rapidly.

I meantime hastened back to my vessel, taking with me some natives to aid in launching her. On our way we came unexpectedly on the spot where lay the body of my poor companion who had been crushed to death. We buried the remains not far off on the hill-side, while I offered some prayers and a short exhortation for the benefit of those present. As I went over the ground again I was more than ever surprised that I had been able to accomplish the journey on such a night, and deeply thankful that I had been preserved from the numberless dangers I had encountered.

On reaching the *Olive Branch*, I found that my mate had been making most judicious preparations for getting her off.

He had formed a strong cradle, with rollers under her keel and posts ahead, to which to secure some strong tackles. By hauling on these tackles he hoped to get her off several feet every day. "Slow and steady wins the race, you know, sir," he observed. His hopes of success were not without foundation.

Day after day we toiled on, aided by the indefatigable natives, who gave every evidence that they were working from pure Christian love.

"You have brought us the blessings of the gospel,—ought not we, who highly estimate its blessings, labour to enable you in your ship to carry it to others?" said the chief of the party, when I was one day thanking him for the energetic way in which he and his people were working. Their satisfaction when the *Olive Branch* at length floated securely in the harbour was nearly equal to mine.

Little time as there was to spare before the meeting would take place, at which my brother wished to be present, he was anxious to see the people housed before he would leave them. They meantime were working most heroically, and I was surprised to see the rapid way in which they put up their houses, and set to work to replant the fields of taro and other roots, which had been destroyed by the flood.

At length we were ready to continue our voyage. It had been intended that our wives should accompany us; but as, in consequence of the delay, John's absence would be shorter than had been expected, it was thought better that they should remain and restore order to the establishment. As we were about to go the chief men of the island sent to beg that we would receive certain gifts which they had stored up to increase the funds devoted to sending missionaries to the other islands of the Pacific yet lying in heathen darkness.

W. H. G. Kingston

"Had it not been for the storm, they would have been far greater," they observed; "but, though we are feeling a want just now of this world's goods, we are rich in gospel blessings; nor can we make our present condition an excuse for denying those blessed privileges to brethren in other lands, for whom our Lord died as well as for us."

Surely, I thought, these remarks, were they known at home, would put to shame too many who are ready to make any slight decrease of income an excuse for not assisting the cause of the gospel either among the ignorant around them or in other countries. Since I went among these so late heathen savages, I have often had to think with grief and shame of the very low standard of Christian excellence considered requisite by many at home who profess, and probably have a wish, to be religious. Often and often I have wished that I could paint to them in their true and vivid colours the self-denying, laborious lives of the devoted missionaries, and the humble, zealous, faithful, truth-searching behaviour of the converts.

With a fair wind we sailed, praying that God would protect our dear ones, and bring us back to them in safety. We took up several missionaries who were going to the conference, and who had been waiting for the *Olive Branch*, and also some native teachers, who were destined to act as pioneers in islands where the light of the gospel had not yet penetrated.

Without any adventure especially worthy of notice we reached the head station, where a considerable number of missionaries were collected awaiting our arrival. All had more or less felt the storm at their respective stations, but few with the violence that we had. The discussions which took place at the meeting were most important and interesting, and encouraging to all to persevere in the work; but I must not now report them. Although only in a certain sense a looker-on, I felt greatly refreshed, and my spiritual life renewed by the exhortations delivered and the prayers engaged in. I had the privilege of attending all the meetings. Several had taken place, when the subject of the new stations to be occupied was brought forward. John was named to fill one of them. The inhabitants were looked upon as among the fiercest of the savages of the Pacific; the climate was far from salubrious. But John did not hesitate a moment; on the contrary, his countenance was radiant with satisfaction. It was an important post, and it was believed that a large accession might be made to the kingdom of Christ by the establishment of a mission there. "Wherever my overseer and brethren consider our holy cause can most be advantaged by my presence, there I am ready to go," answered my brother, after the offer had been made him.

The ground had already been broken by native teachers, who had earnestly petitioned for an English missionary. Our passage to my brother's station was somewhat circuitous, as we had to leave several missionaries at their posts, to carry stores and books to old stations, and to leave native teachers at new ones. We had brought with us the missionary who was to succeed John, whom I was directed to carry on to his new station.

We were received on our return to my brother's home with unmistakable signs of pleasure by the natives, who collected to welcome him. I expected, however, that when he came to announce to his wife the proposed change, that it would be a sad damper to her happiness; but she simply observed: "Wherever you are called to go, dear husband, it will be my joy to go also. How much better am I off than the wife of a soldier serving in the army of some earthly monarch. She may not accompany him to the war; if he falls wounded, she may not be near to tend him; if he is slain, no reward is of value to him. Where, too, is her assurance that they will be reunited? Where my husband goes I may go,—if he is ill, I may watch over him,—if spirits and strength fail, I may support him. When death separates us, I know that we shall be reunited; and I know, too, that a glorious crown, the prize of his high calling, will assuredly be his, and that that crown I shall share with him, and full draughts of joy unspeakable for ever and ever."

These words were spoken in so low and gentle a voice by my dear sister-in-law, that a stranger would scarcely have understood the firm faith and high resolve they indicated. The packing up occupied but little time. John's household goods were few, nor did his library fill many boxes.

"But you will sell your cattle and poultry?" I observed.

"I do not consider them mine," he answered. "I look upon them as belonging to the Society, and as necessary to my successor. A missionary should have as few worldly incumbrances as possible to draw him away from his work. He should labour solely for the Lord, and to the Lord leave the care of his wife and little ones. A missionary sent out by a Society should feel secure that they would provide for his worldly wants while he can work, would support him in his old age, and care at his death for his widow and children."

Thus with perfect faith my noble brother went forth in the gospel's glorious cause to conquer souls for Christ's kingdom.

The grief of the people among whom he had ministered since his arrival in the Pacific, when they heard that he was to leave them, was excessive. At first they threatened to put a restraint upon him, and not to let him go.

"Would you then selfishly deprive others of the blessings

you enjoy?" he asked. "Would you, who know the gospel, keep back the instrument which brought it to you from presenting it to others? No, no; surely you, dear friends, have not thus learned Christ."

"Go, go; our prayers will ever be lifted up for your safety and success."

CHAPTER TWENTY TWO

MARTYRED FOR THE TRUTH

Scarcely a native in the settlement who was not present to bid farewell to their beloved missionary, and amid tears and prayers, he embarked on board the *Olive Branch*. My wife accompanied me, and though the little vessel was much crowded, we had a very happy party.

The weather was fine, and as we had numerous places to touch at, we were not more than twelve days without obtaining fresh provisions. Formerly, when the islands of the Pacific were little known, crews starving or suffering from scurvy must often have passed just out of sight of land, where they might have obtained an ample supply of fresh provisions; but now, very much through the instrumentality of the missionaries of the gospel, scarcely an island remains unknown, and entirely through their instrumentality the greater number may now be visited, not only without fear, but the voyager is certain to receive a Christian welcome on their shores.

An instance came under my notice where the natives did not only return good for good, but good for evil. The master and crew of a large English ship had grossly misbehaved themselves and ill-treated the people of an island. Scarcely had they sailed when a gale sprung up, and their ship was driven on shore and lost. The cargo and other property in the ship was taken possession of by the natives, who considered that they had a right to it. On the captain, however, claiming it through the missionary, the chiefs met and decided that it should be given up, which it was forthwith without a word of complaint. Here the brown Christian set an example to the white man, virtually a heathen.

The new post to which my brother was appointed was on a lovely island, fertile in the extreme, and thickly populated. Indeed it might have been said of it, "that only man was vile." No natives appeared on the shore to welcome him, but after a time the teachers came off in their canoe, and gave us accounts which were far from cheering. Chiefs who had appeared friendly had turned against them, and some had prohibited their people from listening to the Word of God, or attending school or chapel. I suggested to my brother that under the circumstances it might be wiser not to land.

"What, because the enemy begins the fight shall the soldier desert his standard?" he asked, with a look of surprise. "No, David, you would not counsel such conduct."

I could say nothing. The teachers were of opinion that he would be treated with indifference rather than actual hostility, at first, by the great mass of the people, and that his life at all events would be perfectly safe. They mentioned one chief who appeared to be more friendly disposed towards Christianity than the rest, and to him accordingly, we at once went to pay our court. The chief looked like a perfect savage, with his hair long and frizzed out, his eyes rolling wildly, and with scarcely any clothing on his dusky body. Still he received us politely, and not without a certain dignity, and promised if the missionary now remained he would be answerable to me for him, should I again visit the island.

W. H. G. Kingston

The man was still a heathen, and I felt very unwilling to put any confidence in his promises. It was too evident to me that he wished for a missionary for the sake of axes and saws, and other articles he expected to obtain, rather than for any spiritual benefit he hoped to derive from his presence. I had, however, no alternative, than to land my dear brother with his wife and little ones, and household goods. My only consolation was that I was able with my crew to assist in putting up a house for him, many of the parts of which we had brought with us.

The teachers were good carpenters, and had already, with the aid of some natives whom they had instructed, prepared some stout uprights and beams and planks. Notwithstanding this, the rapidity with which we got up the house, dug up a garden and fenced it round, caused great astonishment among the people. Before we left, my brother had already begun a school-room, to serve also as a chapel till a larger edifice could be erected, while he received inquirers at his own house. My sister-in-law had also two female classes of adults and children, to whom she imparted such religious instruction as they would receive, and some of the arts of civilised life, while round the station resembled a busy hive, all the natives who had professed Christianity being actively employed as sawyers or in some other mechanical work. His aim at this early stage of the mission was to show the natives the advantages the Christians possessed over the heathens, and thus to make them look with favour on Christianity. He never failed while they were thus engaged to impart so much religious instruction as they could receive. Everything appeared now to be going on favourably. When I remarked that I now had reasonable hopes that he would succeed—

"Who can doubt it?" was his answer. "If I do not my successor will. The gospel will most assuredly cover the earth as the waters cover the sea. God has said it."

One of the saddest moments of my life was that when I parted from my devoted brother as he stood on the beach while I returned for the last time to my vessel. Yet I asked myself more than once, Why should I grieve? why should I be anxious? He is engaged in the noblest cause in which the energies of a human being can be employed—gaining subjects for the Redeemer's kingdom.

Still I was his brother, and as such I could not contemplate without fear the dangers to which he was exposed. I was now to return direct to Mr Bent's station, where I proposed refitting the *Olive Branch* to be ready for any work she might be called on to perform. We found that great progress had been made at the station, both spiritual and material. There were many new converts, and several excellent little houses built, surrounded by neat gardens and fields. It had not been done without cost, and it was too evident to Mary and me that her father's health and strength were failing. She spoke to him, and suggested a change of scene.

"Here I have been planted by the Lord of the vineyard, and here let me, if He so wills it, wither and fall, dear one," he answered.

It was too evident to us that his body was withering, but not so his spirit—that was expanding more and more, ripening for heaven. It seemed to burn with a deep and unextinguishable love for the conversion of all the islanders among whom he had so long laboured—not those of his own group only, but for the inhabitants of all the isles of the Pacific, "ay," he would finish, as if there had been a shortcoming of his love for the souls of his fellow-men, "of the whole heathen world. May they all come to know Thee, O Lord, and accept Thy great salvation." Still his more constant prayers were for his own people. Gradually he sunk— evidently entering into the rest prepared for those who love

Christ—his joy increased, his end was peace. Thus has many a missionary died, and who would not change all the world can give to be assured of such a death. Mary felt her father's death severely, but yet as one who mourned with assured hope of a joyous resurrection.

My brother had earnestly petitioned to have another missionary or a native teacher of superior attainments sent him, and while I was debating what course to pursue, I received directions to carry the teacher Vihala and his wife to him, and to visit many other stations on my way. Vihala and Alea were delighted to see us again, but when they heard of Mr Bent's death they shed tears of unfeigned sorrow at the thought that they should see his face no more. They both had advanced greatly in Christian knowledge, and Vihala appeared to me equal to the taking entire charge of a station, however large. He was delighted to hear that he was to join my brother, and made all his preparations with alacrity.

As I was preparing to sail, a ship hove in sight. She was from England direct, and brought letters for me and John.

I opened mine with trembling hands. All were well at home; but they contained news and of importance too. A distant relative had died and left a considerable fortune to my father's second son, but in the case of his death it was to belong to the next, and so on. It could only descend to the children of the brother who had possessed it for five years. Thus John was to be the first possessor. It at once occurred to me, would it prove a snare to him? Would it induce him to abandon his high and holy calling? Would the man of property be unwilling to remain the humble missionary? Still I thought I knew what John would do. I felt that I was wronging him by having any doubts on the subject.

The delay was providential, for a gale sprung up as we were

weighing anchor, and again dropping it, we remained safely in port till the storm had subsided. We had several places to call at, and baffling winds still more prolonged our voyage. At last we anchored in the beautiful bay opposite my brother's station.

I looked out anxiously expecting him to come off to us. I was then about to land with Mary, thinking to take him and his family by surprise, when a canoe appeared with one of the native teachers on board. His first words were, "I am the only one left alive." My heart sunk within me.

I put Mary again on board and went on shore. On the way the teacher told me the sad tale. At first the natives in the district had been friendly, but instigated by the heathen chiefs, they had, after a time, refused provisions or assistance. Even some who had professed Christianity were afraid to come openly to receive instruction. A little band was faithful, and many came at night to hear the word of God, and brought food, or the mission family might have been starved. Still my brother persevered, and not without effect. Fresh converts were made. Children were allowed to come to the girls' school, and when it was discovered what useful arts they learned there in addition to reading and writing, even some chiefs became desirous of sending their daughters for instruction. This unexpected progress, made, in spite of opposition, by the missionaries, exasperated the heathen chiefs still further, and a plot was formed to cut off all the Christian teachers. Their safety was, however, watched over by their converts, and all attempts defeated. Treachery was next attempted, and one of the most savage of the heathen chiefs pretended to be desirous of hearing the truth. He sent to my brother, begging him to come to him. He was urged not to go.

"What, and run the risk of allowing a soul to be left in

W. H. G. Kingston

Satan's power which may be rescued!" was his answer. He went, accompanied by a teacher and two Christian natives. They were unarmed. Day after day passed, and no tidings came of them. At last the bodies of all four were found. They had been barbarously murdered; but whether or not they had reached the old chiefs residence could not be ascertained. He sent a message expressing his regret that the missionary had not come to him. My sister-in-law was supported in a way the Holy Spirit can alone support a person in distress. Her longing desire was to meet him in heaven, and to prepare their two boys to follow in his footsteps.

Notwithstanding all that had occurred, Vihala undauntedly resolved to remain.

"If I fall, it is in God's cause, and to advance His glory," was his only remark.

Having done all I could, with a heavy heart I quitted the station with my sister-in-law and her children, and returned to head-quarters, where I had the satisfaction of presenting the *Olive Branch* for the service of the mission. I persuaded my sister-in-law to accompany Mary and me to England, where I have devoted a certain portion of the fortune of which I so painfully became possessed to her support and the education of her children, and at Mary's urgent request, another, what the world would consider a no inconsiderable portion, to the support of missions. We live in a humble way, but are far more happy than we should be did we spend our wealth on ourselves. Our nephews, too, are amply rewarding us, and will, I trust, prove efficient soldiers in that glorious army which goes forth under the banner of the cross to fight against idolatry, ignorance, vice, and all the foes Satan can array against the truth as it is in Christ Jesus.

ABOUT THE AUTHOR

William Henry Giles Kingston (1814 - 1880), writer of tales for boys, born in London, but spent much of his youth in Oporto, where his father was a merchant.

His first book, The Circassian Chief, appeared in 1844. His first book for boys, Peter the Whaler, was published in 1851, and had such success that he retired from business and devoted himself entirely to the production of this kind of literature, in which his popularity was deservedly great; and during 30 years he wrote upwards of 130 tales, including The Three Midshipmen (1862), The Three Lieutenants (1874), The Three Commanders (1875), The Three Admirals (1877), Digby Heathcote, etc.

He also conducted various papers, including The Colonist, and Colonial Magazine and East India Review. He was also interested in emigration, volunteering, and various philanthropic schemes. For services in negotiating a commercial treaty with Portugal he received a Portuguese knighthood, and for his literary labours a Government pension.

W. H. G. Kingston

Choose from Thousands of 1stWorldLibrary Classics By

A. M. Barnard
Ada Leverson
Adolphus William Ward
Aesop
Agatha Christie
Alexander Aaronsohn
Alexander Kielland
Alexandre Dumas
Alfred Gatty
Alfred Ollivant
Alice Duer Miller
Alice Turner Curtis
Alice Dunbar
Allen Chapman
Alleyne Ireland
Ambrose Bierce
Amelia E. Barr
Amory H. Bradford
Andrew Lang
Andrew McFarland Davis
Andy Adams
Angela Brazil
Anna Alice Chapin
Anna Sewell
Annie Besant
Annie Hamilton Donnell
Annie Payson Call
Annie Roe Carr
Annonaymous
Anton Chekhov
Archibald Lee Fletcher
Arnold Bennett
Arthur C. Benson
Arthur Conan Doyle
Arthur M. Winfield
Arthur Ransome
Arthur Schnitzler
Arthur Train
Atticus
B.H. Baden-Powell
B. M. Bower
B. C. Chatterjee
Baroness Emmuska Orczy
Baroness Orczy
Basil King
Bayard Taylor
Ben Macomber
Bertha Muzzy Bower
Bjornstjerne Bjornson

Booth Tarkington
Boyd Cable
Bram Stoker
C. Collodi
C. E. Orr
C. M. Ingleby
Carolyn Wells
Catherine Parr Traill
Charles A. Eastman
Charles Amory Beach
Charles Dickens
Charles Dudley Warner
Charles Farrar Browne
Charles Ives
Charles Kingsley
Charles Klein
Charles Hanson Towne
Charles Lathrop Pack
Charles Romyn Dake
Charles Whibley
Charles Willing Beale
Charlotte M. Braeme
Charlotte M. Yonge
Charlotte Perkins Stetson
Clair W. Hayes
Clarence Day Jr.
Clarence E. Mulford
Clemence Housman
Confucius
Coningsby Dawson
Cornelis DeWitt Wilcox
Cyril Burleigh
D. H. Lawrence
Daniel Defoe
David Garnett
Dinah Craik
Don Carlos Janes
Donald Keyhoe
Dorothy Kilner
Dougan Clark
Douglas Fairbanks
E. Nesbit
E. P. Roe
E. Phillips Oppenheim
E. S. Brooks
Earl Barnes
Edgar Rice Burroughs
Edith Van Dyne
Edith Wharton

Edward Everett Hale
Edward J. O'Biren
Edward S. Ellis
Edwin L. Arnold
Eleanor Atkins
Eleanor Hallowell Abbott
Eliot Gregory
Elizabeth Gaskell
Elizabeth McCracken
Elizabeth Von Arnim
Ellem Key
Emerson Hough
Emilie F. Carlen
Emily Bronte
Emily Dickinson
Enid Bagnold
Enilor Macartney Lane
Erasmus W. Jones
Ernie Howard Pie
Ethel May Dell
Ethel Turner
Ethel Watts Mumford
Eugene Sue
Eugenie Foa
Eugene Wood
Eustace Hale Ball
Evelyn Everett-green
Everard Cotes
F. H. Cheley
F. J. Cross
F. Marion Crawford
Fannie E. Newberry
Federick Austin Ogg
Ferdinand Ossendowski
Fergus Hume
Florence A. Kilpatrick
Fremont B. Deering
Francis Bacon
Francis Darwin
Frances Hodgson Burnett
Frances Parkinson Keyes
Frank Gee Patchin
Frank Harris
Frank Jewett Mather
Frank L. Packard
Frank V. Webster
Frederic Stewart Isham
Frederick Trevor Hill
Frederick Winslow Taylor

Friedrich Kerst
Friedrich Nietzsche
Fyodor Dostoyevsky
G.A. Henty
G.K. Chesterton
Gabrielle E. Jackson
Garrett P. Serviss
Gaston Leroux
George A. Warren
George Ade
Geroge Bernard Shaw
George Cary Eggleston
George Durston
George Ebers
George Eliot
George Gissing
George MacDonald
George Meredith
George Orwell
George Sylvester Viereck
George Tucker
George W. Cable
George Wharton James
Gertrude Atherton
Gordon Casserly
Grace E. King
Grace Gallatin
Grace Greenwood
Grant Allen
Guillermo A. Sherwell
Gulielma Zollinger
Gustav Flaubert
H. A. Cody
H. B. Irving
H.C. Bailey
H. G. Wells
H. H. Munro
H. Irving Hancock
H. R. Naylor
H. Rider Haggard
H. W. C. Davis
Haldeman Julius
Hall Caine
Hamilton Wright Mabie
Hans Christian Andersen
Harold Avery
Harold McGrath
Harriet Beecher Stowe
Harry Castlemon
Harry Coghill
Harry Houidini

Hayden Carruth
Helent Hunt Jackson
Helen Nicolay
Hendrik Conscience
Hendy David Thoreau
Henri Barbusse
Henrik Ibsen
Henry Adams
Henry Ford
Henry Frost
Henry James
Henry Jones Ford
Henry Seton Merriman
Henry W Longfellow
Herbert A. Giles
Herbert Carter
Herbert N. Casson
Herman Hesse
Hildegard G. Frey
Homer
Honore De Balzac
Horace B. Day
Horace Walpole
Horatio Alger Jr.
Howard Pyle
Howard R. Garis
Hugh Lofting
Hugh Walpole
Humphry Ward
Ian Maclaren
Inez Haynes Gillmore
Irving Bacheller
Isabel Cecilia Williams
Isabel Hornibrook
Israel Abrahams
Ivan Turgenev
J.G.Austin
J. Henri Fabre
J. M. Barrie
J. M. Walsh
J. Macdonald Oxley
J. R. Miller
J. S. Fletcher
J. S. Knowles
J. Storer Clouston
J. W. Duffield
Jack London
Jacob Abbott
James Allen
James Andrews
James Baldwin

James Branch Cabell
James DeMille
James Joyce
James Lane Allen
James Lane Allen
James Oliver Curwood
James Oppenheim
James Otis
James R. Driscoll
Jane Abbott
Jane Austen
Jane L. Stewart
Janet Aldridge
Jens Peter Jacobsen
Jerome K. Jerome
Jessie Graham Flower
John Buchan
John Burroughs
John Cournos
John F. Kennedy
John Gay
John Glasworthy
John Habberton
John Joy Bell
John Kendrick Bangs
John Milton
John Philip Sousa
John Taintor Foote
Jonas Lauritz Idemil Lie
Jonathan Swift
Joseph A. Altsheler
Joseph Carey
Joseph Conrad
Joseph E. Badger Jr
Joseph Hergesheimer
Joseph Jacobs
Jules Vernes
Julian Hawthrone
Julie A Lippmann
Justin Huntly McCarthy
Kakuzo Okakura
Karle Wilson Baker
Kate Chopin
Kenneth Grahame
Kenneth McGaffey
Kate Langley Bosher
Kate Langley Bosher
Katherine Cecil Thurston
Katherine Stokes
L. A. Abbot
L. T. Meade

L. Frank Baum
Latta Griswold
Laura Dent Crane
Laura Lee Hope
Laurence Housman
Lawrence Beasley
Leo Tolstoy
Leonid Andreyev
Lewis Carroll
Lewis Sperry Chafer
Lilian Bell
Lloyd Osbourne
Louis Hughes
Louis Joseph Vance
Louis Tracy
Louisa May Alcott
Lucy Fitch Perkins
Lucy Maud Montgomery
Luther Benson
Lydia Miller Middleton
Lyndon Orr
M. Corvus
M. H. Adams
Margaret E. Sangster
Margret Howth
Margaret Vandercook
Margaret W. Hungerford
Margret Penrose
Maria Edgeworth
Maria Thompson Daviess
Mariano Azuela
Marion Polk Angellotti
Mark Overton
Mark Twain
Mary Austin
Mary Catherine Crowley
Mary Cole
Mary Hastings Bradley
Mary Roberts Rinehart
Mary Rowlandson
M. Wollstonecraft Shelley
Maud Lindsay
Max Beerbohm
Myra Kelly
Nathaniel Hawthrone
Nicolo Machiavelli
O. F. Walton
Oscar Wilde

Owen Johnson
P.G. Wodehouse
Paul and Mabel Thorne
Paul G. Tomlinson
Paul Severing
Percy Brebner
Percy Keese Fitzhugh
Peter B. Kyne
Plato
Quincy Allen
R. Derby Holmes
R. L. Stevenson
R. S. Ball
Rabindranath Tagore
Rahul Alvares
Ralph Bonehill
Ralph Henry Barbour
Ralph Victor
Ralph Waldo Emmerson
Rene Descartes
Ray Cummings
Rex Beach
Rex E. Beach
Richard Harding Davis
Richard Jefferies
Richard Le Gallienne
Robert Barr
Robert Frost
Robert Gordon Anderson
Robert L. Drake
Robert Lansing
Robert Lynd
Robert Michael Ballantyne
Robert W. Chambers
Rosa Nouchette Carey
Rudyard Kipling
Saint Augustine
Samuel B. Allison
Samuel Hopkins Adams
Sarah Bernhardt
Sarah C. Hallowell
Selma Lagerlof
Sherwood Anderson
Sigmund Freud
Standish O'Grady
Stanley Weyman
Stella Benson
Stella M. Francis

Stephen Crane
Stewart Edward White
Stijn Streuvels
Swami Abhedananda
Swami Parmananda
T. S. Ackland
T. S. Arthur
The Princess Der Ling
Thomas A. Janvier
Thomas A Kempis
Thomas Anderton
Thomas Bailey Aldrich
Thomas Bulfinch
Thomas De Quincey
Thomas Dixon
Thomas H. Huxley
Thomas Hardy
Thomas More
Thornton W. Burgess
U. S. Grant
Upton Sinclair
Valentine Williams
Various Authors
Vaughan Kester
Victor Appleton
Victor G. Durham
Victoria Cross
Virginia Woolf
Wadsworth Camp
Walter Camp
Walter Scott
Washington Irving
Wilbur Lawton
Wilkie Collins
Willa Cather
Willard F. Baker
William Dean Howells
William le Queux
W. Makepeace Thackeray
William W. Walter
William Shakespeare
Winston Churchill
Yei Theodora Ozaki
Yogi Ramacharaka
Young E. Allison
Zane Grey